Erich W. Streissler
Gunther Tichy

How to Forecast Economic Developments During and After Crises

ÖSTERREICHISCHE AKADEMIE DER WISSENSCHAFTEN
PHILOSOPHISCH-HISTORISCHE KLASSE
DENKSCHRIFTEN, 429. BAND

Erich W. Streissler
Gunther Tichy

How to Forecast Economic Developments During and After Crises

Verlag der
Österreichischen Akademie
der Wissenschaften

Wien 2012

ÖAW

Vorgelegt von w.M. ERICH W. STREISSLER in der Sitzung am 17. Juni 2011

Die verwendete Papiersorte ist aus chlorfrei gebleichtem Zellstoff hergestellt,
frei von säurebildenden Bestandteilen und alterungsbeständig.

ISBN 978-3-7001-7089-1

Satz und Layout: Druckerei Berger, 3580 Horn
Druck: Prime Rate Kft., Budapest
Printed and bound in the EU

http://hw.oeaw.ac.at/7089-1
http://verlag.oeaw.ac.at

Contents

Preface

The series of ten essays presented here is concerned with long-run macroeconomic diagnosis and with forecasting, with forecasts of global developments during the first and second decades of the 21st century. Erich W. Streissler first started in 2002 to warn in lectures and newspaper articles of an imminent global financial crash, and repeated those warnings again and again. His warnings – or rather an installment thereof – were presented to the Austrian Academy of Sciences in a lecture in January 2009 ("The Financial Market Crisis") and have been finalized in this book, which contains altogether seven of his essays written over the two years consequent upon that first presentation. Between Streissler and Gunther Tichy, both already for many years full members of the Austrian Academy of Sciences, there exists a close affinity in thought. Appropriately, the essays by Streissler are therefore placed in a framework of Tichy's meticulous analyses of the initial situation and the preconditions of forecasting the crisis.

The book starts out with three essays by Gunther Tichy on the difficulty of foreseeing crises. Tichy asks "Could We Have Foreseen the Financial Crisis?" and "Why Did Policy Ignore the Harbingers of Crisis?". One of the main features of the recent crisis was the unusually irresponsible behaviour of banking institutions in large parts of the world. Therefore Tichy's last essay considers the question of "Regulation of the Banking Sector". The essays by Streissler on forecasting experiences follow.

"Saving and Investment in the Long Run" explains that above all saving and not so much investment is the root cause of the secular process of economic growth. "Using Economic Theory for Forecasting" reviews some of Streissler's past forecasting successes, while the essay titled "i.i.d." deals with basic misjudgements of macroeconomic developments in the most prominent American literature, i.e. with analyses some of which were crowned with Nobel Memorial Prizes in economics, but later proved to be faulty. The essays on "The Financial Market Crisis" and "Waiting for Financial Consolidation" are complementary, dealing with the financial crash of 2008 from slightly different viewpoints or, in other words, with different audiences in mind. The essay on "Rare Events" is a technical analysis of the most appropriate probability distribution for analysing times of occurrence and magnitudes of crises. With pertinent figures dating from April 2011, a summary forecasting exercise of future world economic development is presented in the last essay. It is the most daring endeavour of all.

The authors thank Monika Streissler for her translations and painstaking editorial work.

Previous Publications

"Could we have foreseen the financial crisis?" is an English translation by Monika Streissler of an article published in German "War die Finanzkrise vorhersehbar?" by Gunther Tichy in *Perspektiven der Wirtschaftspolitik,* 11(4), pp. 356–382 (2010).

"Why did policy ignore the harbingers of the crisis?" by Gunther Tichy had originally been published in *Empirica,* 38 (1), pp. 107–130 (2011).

"Regulation of the Banking Sector" is an English translation by Monika Streissler of an article originally published in German, "Reicht Bankregulierung zur Vermeidung schwerer Finanzkrisen?" by Gunther Tichy in Kubon-Gilke, Gisela, Held, Martin, and Sturn, Richard (eds.), *Jahrbuch Normative und Institutionelle Grundfragen der Ökonomik,* Vol. 10, *Ökonomik in der Krise,* pp. 65–91 (2011).

"Forecasting World Trends During the 2010s" by Erich W. Streissler will also appear in a Festschrift for a surprise recipient, edited by Karl Hardach, Kleinmachnow/Germany.

The Austrian Academy of Sciences gratefully acknowledges the assistance of the respective copyright-holders and their permission to reprint these essays.

Gunther Tichy*

Could we have foreseen the financial crisis?

"Why did no one see it coming?" were the words in which Her Britannic Majesty politely reproached the economic profession for its forecasting inabilities, while the media, less polite, were turning economist bashing into one of their favourite sports. To be reproached and made fun of is one of the risks of a profession that deals – *inter alia* – with the future. Of greater consequence is the increasing self-criticism on the part of economists: They blame their failure to predict the crisis on inappropriate models, the neglect of financial elements, undue concentration on equilibrium problems, naive assumptions about the genesis of expectations, wrong training etc.[1] Even if all of those insider strictures were correct, they would not go to the core of the problem: for, assuming all those flaws could have been remedied, would economists have foreseen the extent of the recent financial crisis and its very real consequences and global repercussions? Hardly. The destabilising effects of many of the factors that both caused and deepened the crisis were certainly recognized by the analysts – as will be shown below; indeed, quite a number of people were aware that every single one of those factors might dampen growth or even trigger a recession. But there were two remarkable aspects to this: Firstly, those analyses were mostly ignored – by policy makers and regulators as well as by academic economists. Secondly, no one realized how the various critical factors would interact, to say nothing of the surprise effect of what was *novel* in this crisis, unheard of in earlier crises. Recent analyses have shown that even in the past those financial crises that involved the real economy and more than one country had always been caused by innovations, something new, as yet unknown, whose effects would surprise everyone. This time it was the *financial* innovations whose impact, extent and (side) effects were to surprise both theorists and practical economists. But if surprise effects and the panic they spread should be ascertained as the final and crucial causes of major crises, then economists must accept that although they will (hopefully) be able to predict "ordinary" crises, they cannot predict really big ones. No imaginable improvement of econometric and statistical methods and instruments could alter that fact. From this, it follows (1) that economists must state quite clearly what kind of forecasts may (or must not) be expected from them, (2) that major crises – *ex ante* indistinguishable from ordinary ones – cannot be prevented by economic policy measures implemented while they are already building up.

Much rather, economic policy must be targeted at the economic system as a whole with the purpose of increasing its crisis-resistance.

In what follows, the most important explanations of the recent crisis are summarized in section 1 in order to prepare the reader for section 2, an analysis of those elements whose destabilizing effects

---

* The author gratefully acknowledges valuable comments and suggestions by his colleague F. Hahn and the two referees.

[1] See Kirchgässner (2009) or Spaventa (2009), both referring to the pertinent arguments by Acemoglu, Buiter, De Grauwe, Eichengreen, Johnson, Krugman, Perotti, Reichlin, Visco and Wyplosz.

had already been realized before the crisis broke out. Section 3 will deal with those causes of the crisis that had not been diagnosed *ex ante*. Section 4 will present a summary and pertinent conclusions.

1. Explanations of the recent crisis

Analysing the financial crises of the last 120 years, Bordo et al (2001) found that although such crises have become more frequent, they have neither become longer nor deeper, while Reinhart and Rogoff (2008) discovered that systemic banking crises have always followed upon asset price bubbles, massive capital imports and a fast expansion of the volume of credits. Borio (2005) attributed the increasing frequency of crises and the macroeconomic fluctuations due to financial factors and excessive asset price fluctuations to changes in the financial and monetary regime, particularly to liberalization, globalization and increased trust in central bank policies that keep such asset-price excesses from turning into general inflation. In all of these respects, the recent financial crisis and the brief time-span separating it from the last one would have fitted in nicely with the historical patterns. But the empirical evidence and the latest analyses paint a different picture: Both as to its causes and its effects the recent crisis seems considerably more wide-spread than former ones, and its impact might have been even deeper had it not been counteracted by policy measures both on national and international levels. In view of the budgetary consequences of such counteraction, however, any predictions as to the duration of the crisis are inadvisable. As befits the obviously diverse causes of the crisis, any number of (mutually non-exclusive) explanations have been attempted.

1.1 Subprime bubble, monetary policy and deregulation

Without any doubt the crisis originated in the *subprime segment of the US mortgage market.* There, a bubble had developed: a self-enforcing dynamic of rising real estate prices and credit-financed speculation. Although in the long run house prices are constant and mean-reverting, in the short run they show noticeable autonomous fluctuations and may depart considerably from their equilibrium values (Sørensen 2006). While there is general agreement as to the auto-dynamism of the bubble, this is not true of its causes.

According to Franke and Krahnen (2009) increasing intermediatization tends to make for bubbles. Haldane (2009), on the other hand, attributes them to the homogenization of financial institutions. Others hold the expansionary monetary policy of the USA and their low interest rates responsible for the recent bubble: Low (short-run) interest rates increase the banks' risk-propensity (Maddaloni et al, forthcoming) and together with ample liquidity make for high asset prices (Borio and Lowe 2002; Mussa 2004); Buiter (2008) suggests that liquidity-assistance could be obtained far too easily, actually intensified the crisis, and resulted in adverse selection. Others stress the influence of global disequilibria, especially of a "savings glut" (Bernanke 2005) or an "investment draught" (Cova et al 2009) – at any rate an oversupply of money looking for investment chances on the US financial market. The American balance of payments deficits "have flooded the US asset markets with funds seeking placement outlets" (Arestis and Singh 2010). Still another explanation of this oversupply points to a structural problem: as emerging economies lack developed capital markets, private capital accumulated there is "exported" to be invested in the USA or Europe (Abiad et al 2009);[2] it also points to the increasingly unequal income distribution and the growing significance of a "generation of

[2] The surplus savings of emerging economies have drastically changed the situation on financial markets world-wide: from debtors they have turned into creditors; contrary to the simple or rather: simplified, logic of economics capital flows "upstream" – from the emerging economies to the industrialized countries. The surplus of savings is built up from profits from oil and other natural resources accruing to a wealthy class in those economies, which is forced to save because the social order there has broken down.

heirs" who invest their wealth mostly in financial instruments (Finanzgruppe 2007). In combination with the very low interest rates the oversupply caused a rush into speculative real estate.

Another strand of explanations refers to *changes in the US financial system* as the underlying cause of the crisis: "The mortgage market turbulence is as much about the breakdown of the structure of U.S. financial markets as it is about bad debt" (Dodd 2007, p. 15). Globalization and deregulation were the crucial forces. Globalization has enormously extended the networks within which financial operators act. Network theory has taught us that too-closely knit networks may prove unstable; in addition they have become too complex: "Each market participant and policymaker knows their own local world, but understanding all the possible linkages across these different worlds (...) is too complex. This change in paradigm, from irrelevant to critical linkages, triggers massive uncertainty" (Caballero and Kurlat 2009, p.2).

In the literature, *deregulation* features prominently (Barth et al 2009). First of all, the traditional US system of keeping the various types of banks separate was abandoned. The concentration – typical of post-deregulation-periods – on expansion and stiff competition for market shares (Reid 1982; Englund 1999) caused the share of subprime credits to rise quickly while the risk premium went down (Sapir 2008). The 1996 Amendment to Basel I permitted risk evaluation of assets in a bank's trading book on the basis of bank-internal models – thus considerably reducing equity requirements. Furthermore, in 2004 the rule specifying minimum equity requirements for US investment banks was abandoned altogether, which caused equity to decline from 8.25 % to slightly above 3 %. Such a precarious capital set-up is generally assumed to be a serious crisis-amplifier (Flannery 1994). "Leverage magnifies risks of any kind, so it is reasonable to be concerned about excessive leverage. However, this concern is amplified many times when the aggregate exposure comes through new financial instruments which have not been tested through crises, since they are susceptible to severe panic-driven runs" (Caballero and Kurlat 2009, p. 15). Buiter (2008) interprets US deregulation as an instance of regulatory capture of the respective authorities by the banking lobbies. According to Kaminsky and Reinhart (1999) liberalization and deregulation of the financial sector have frequently preceded a financial crisis, while Borio and Drehmann (2009) have shown that large increases in credit- and asset prices usually foreshadow a crisis. As though deregulation were not enough, the remaining rules were circumvented (Tichy 2009): US investment banks invented and established hedge funds, while banks in EU-countries founded so-called conduits,[3] both these novelties operating on just the tiniest bit of equity, while excessively doctoring credit terms (borrowing short – lending long) and avoiding regulation. Thus, non-bank financial intermediaries became ever more important in the financial markets; creditors and debtors moved ever farther apart; incentive problems appeared (Petersen and Raja 2002), and new possibilities of systemic risk opened up (Chan et al 2005). "Moreover, if new, unregulated firms emerge to fund bank-type loans with short-term liabilities, the economy might be no more stable, because new firms that move in to fill the vacuum left by banks may inherit the problem of runs' (Diamond and Dybvig 1986, p.57)" (Flannery 1994, p.329).

The pressure on credit terms – and thus the subprime bubble – did not come from the traditional mortgage banks, but from the (deregulated) big banks and their non-bank daughters that – for lack of other investment opportunities – rushed into this new market, offering rather aggressive terms

[3] Conduits are non-profit companies, often seated in Ireland. Their returns accrued to the respective mother firms that were liable for them – at least theoretically –, but the transactions of such a company need not be registered in the mother's balance sheets; thus, the mother firm did not have to meet any equity requirements with respect to those transactions.

(Dell'Ariccia et al 2008);[4] by bundling[5] and often completely reselling those credits they were able to minimize their own risk from those credits, but they (more than) compensated this by giving out far riskier credits (Cebenoyan and Strahan 2004; Franke and Krahnen 2009). The crucial element in all those misdirected deregulation measures turned out to be the virtual exclusion of liability on the part of borrowers and/or the sellers of derivatives: Because of the negligible amount of equity, in the last resort the risk was shouldered by the investors and/or their financiers, more or less on their own.[6]

Regulators as well as bank managers and a number of economists ignored the (published!) finding that credit risks are not independent from each other and are not normally distributed, but much rather have fat tails; in consequence, they underestimated the danger of systemic crises (Wyplosz 2009). The regulation reform of Basel II had been designed from a purely technical and microeconomic perspective; its effects are pro-cyclical, and it over-stresses short-term risk at the expense of medium- and long-term risks and builds on summing over individual risks instead of evaluating entire portfolios (Hahn 2000); to assume that risk, volatility, and liquidity are not determined by the system, but are exogenous, is fatal in a crisis, especially if everyone is using the same risk model (Danielson et al 2001).

According to Spaventa (2009) the system had gone off its sustainable course even before the shocks of the summer of 2007; a year earlier Spaventa (2008) had pointed out that control of non-bank intermediaries was lacking – a lack that had caused an "unregulated shadow financial system". Even before the shocks came *The Economist* (2006) had already spoken of the "dark side of the debt": credit transactions were no longer made publicly, in markets, but obscurely over-the-counter: "In a panic, incomplete paperwork could cause the whole system to collapse".

1.2 Financial innovations and the dynamics of the system

Other authors consider financial innovations and the dynamics of the financial system, as driven by those innovations and by deregulation, to be the final cause of the crisis. Among those innovations particular stress is laid upon the standardization of credit contracts, their bundling and their being sold in bunches with different risks: a junior (equity-)tranche that will have to stand in first, in case of failure, a mezzanine and a senior tranche, the last-named considered to be safe because it could only be resorted to after both of the other tranches had been used up in case of losses. Innovations have been explained by deregulation and the stronger competition by the new kinds of financial institutions (non-bank intermediaries): the concomitant expectations of high returns had forced the banks to concentrate on more complex transactions. Already in 1987, Drexel Burnham Lambert had invented bundling of CDOs, collateralized debt obligations (Dodd 2007), but only in the latter half of the 90s when they were introduced to the mortgage market, did these gain ground. This had three immediate and important consequences with respect to the subsequent crisis.

Firstly, with increasing securitization of mortgages, i.e. relatively small transactions, mortgage *contracts had to be increasingly standardized and their liquidation automated.* Instead of being de-

[4] The MBS [mortgage-backed securities] share of the established mortgage banks Fanny Mae and Freddy Mac dropped from 76% in 2003 to 43% in 2006.

[5] In 2006 three fourths of all subprime credits were "collateralized", i.e. bundled and sold (Ashcraft and Schuerman 2007).

[6] In the US mortgage market, borrowers' liability is usually restricted to their piece of real estate; personal liability is almost always excluded. Speculation with a view to rising housing prices represents a very small risk, therefore; if prices should go down, borrowers could simply return their piece of real estate to the bank, thus ridding themselves of any and all obligations. That this was not an unexpected development of the market, but deliberate policy, is shown by the OECD, which in 2004 still recommended deregulation of housing credits in Europe, too, with a view to boosting the market (Catte et al 2004).

termined by individual screening of prospective borrowers, contract terms were increasingly defined by "hard facts", above all by FICO scores, a mechanical projection of the credit risk based on a customer's previous record of payments and indebtedness.[7] With respect to the crisis it was important that the statistical FICO credit failure model considerably underestimated the risks – because it was based upon data from a period characterized by careful individual screening, by greater stability, and by the absence of systemic risks (Rajan et al 2008).

Secondly, bundling and selling off credits caused a questionable *change of incentives:* Not only did the financial institutions that gave out the credits refrain from individual screening of borrowers,[8] they even relaxed their selection criteria: increasingly they gave credits to borrowers who barely managed to reach the critical FICO-limit of 620. Thus, the probability that a portfolio intended for bundling would fail was increased by 10–25 % (Keys et al 2010). Banks highly active in the OTD market (= "originate to distribute") typically dealt in credits of glaringly poor quality (Purnanandam 2009). The borrowers were aware of this adverse selection, which also showed in the price, so that they were not particularly keen on debtor-specific (soft) information. Inevitably the quality of borrowers deteriorated (Rajan et al 2008).

Thirdly, neither borrowers nor regulating authorities nor the majority of economists were aware of the risk of the new CDO product, and indeed the risk could only be guessed at. "For structured products for credit risk, the basic paradigm of derivative pricing – perfect replication – is not applicable so that one has to rely on a kind of rough-and-ready evaluation of these contracts on the base of historical data. Unfortunately, historical data were hardly available in most cases which meant that one had to rely on simulations with relatively arbitrary assumptions on correlations between risks and default probabilities" (Colander et al 2009, p.5). Simulations in the form of mathematical models suggested exactness, but that was a wrong cue, on two counts: firstly, because the time series used were much too short and pertained to a period without serious disorders; secondly, and even more problematic, because correlations may change over night (Chan et al 2005) – and in systemic crises they actually do. Add to this that the time dimension of risks, especially in periods of disorder subsequent to deregulation or innovations (Borio 2005), is much more difficult to estimate than the cross-section risk that banks have more experience with (Flannery 1998).

The *indirect consequences of deregulation and financial innovations* are even more important than the direct ones. A lot of business shifted from banks proper to non-bank financial intermediaries, to the "shadow finance system"; transactions based on margins (deposits, credits) were replaced by transactions based on premiums, intermediatization spread even farther; the system would behave in a new way. More recent models stress that these developments made the economy more efficient, less volatile and less vulnerable, making liquidity more easily accessible and markets thicker (Gai et al 2008). Thus, the probability of crises would decrease, but if a crisis should occur, it must be deeper because its inflationary effects would show up later (Borio 2005) and because innovations would increase indebtedness and the leverage of agents (Gai et al 2008). The financial institutions, particularly

---

[7] The Fair Isaac Corporation (FICO) designed the system in 1970 for the credit-card of American Bank and Trust. The score runs from 1 to 100 and is composed as follows:
– 35 % Payment History: paying back of credits
– 30 % Credit Utilization: utilization of the line of revolving credits
– 15 % Length of Credit History: decreasing weight of previous events
– 10 % Types of Credit Used: positive if and when there are various types of credit
– 10 % Recent search for credit and/or amount of credit obtained recently: negative if and when simultaneous credit applications are filed with different potential lenders.

[8] There must be incentives for credit screening (Holmstrom and Tirole 1997); they are tantamount to the risks that those credits entail for the company's own balance sheet (Diamond and Rajan 2003).

the less risk-averse hedge funds, have less liquidity than macroeconomically optimal. In case of shocks they are therefore forced to throw assets on the market ("fire sales"), thereby pushing down their price, reducing equity shares and damaging good-will, thus necessitating further sales: a recessionary spiral is formed (Gai et al 2008; Korinek 2008). The process may be likened to a competitive market in which the transactions of single individual agents cannot affect the market price. The cumulative slump of asset prices is the bigger the worse the shock, the more complex the intermediation (Korinek 2008), and the more pessimistic the expectations (Gai et al 2008).

1.3 Behaviour of the finance industry

On the one hand, those financial innovations necessarily caused the quality of credits to deteriorate while making it increasingly difficult to recognize and assess risks, and on the other hand they increased the susceptibility of the system to major crises. The behaviour of the finance industry served only to increase and intensify those problems. Spaventa (2008, p.1) sees "deep flaws inherent in the new business models of banks". Financial institutions made full use of the opportunities seemingly opened up by the new risk assessment models – without fully understanding the models and without realizing the questionable character of the underlying data: "Apparently, a lot of models used for structured products were pretty good, but the inputs were awful" (Scholes, quoted in *The Economist* 2009). Well, they *had to be* awful because of the structural breaks caused by the innovations. Even if and when financial institutions shifted risks by selling junior tranches, their risk position deteriorated in most cases, for they gave out ever riskier credits (Franke and Krahnen 2005) and operated on ever less equity. "[T]hese results suggest that banks that improve their ability to manage credit risk may operate with greater leverage and may lend more of their assets to risky borrowers" (Cebenoyan and Strahan 2001, p.4).

The situation worsened when the financial institutions – crassly contrary to the theoretical ideas underlying the "innovation" of bundling – kept the senior tranches and sold the junior (first-loss) tranches (Franke and Krahnen 2009); thus, the incentives for a careful screening of borrowers were lost. The risk of a bundled product was very difficult to assess; this fostered adverse selection on the part of lenders and made buyers more vulnerable. Mian and Sufi (2008) found out that, while the bubble lasted, mortgage credits expanded most of all in those regions where the rates of refusal had been highest earlier on; those were also the regions with the highest disintermediation. These authors took it to be a strong indication of moral hazard that in those very regions the failures of credit bundles were above average, with the exception of the bundles sold as "affiliated entities". There is also evidence of fraud perpetrated by overvaluing real estate and by cash-back-transactions (Ben-David 2008).

"Underestimation of risk contained in newly issued assets, the opacity of the derived securities on the balance sheets of financial institutions, the connectedness between financial institutions both within and across countries, and finally, the high leverage of the financial system as a whole" (Blanchard 2009, p.4) are counted among the major causes of the crisis. Still another element should not be ignored: a certain amount of arrogance on the part of the managers. The generation that had grown up in the settled and well-to-do period of Great Moderation was self-assured, strongly performance-oriented (Giuliano and Spilimbergo 2009)[9] and relied on its experience that had carried it fairly well through several (minor) financial crises ever since 1987 (Wyplosz 2009). Therefore its surprise and the loss of mutual trust were only that much bigger when the crisis broke out.

[9] Generations that grew up during a recession tend to explain success by luck rather than good performance.

1.4 Lack of information and surprise effect

The bundling of credits and their sale in tranches with different risks was meant to transfer the risk to those best able to bear it, and it was thought that this had actually been achieved: "the new instruments of risk dispersal have enabled the largest and most sophisticated banks, in their credit granting role, to divest themselves of much credit risk by passing it to institutions with far less leverage" (Greenspan 2005). For Franke and Krahnen (2009), the broad consent in this matter, hardly ever questioned, is a case of "intellectual capture", as reality was totally different: Since contracts were not traded on an open market but in direct transactions (over-the-counter, OTC), neither prices nor volumes were known to anyone but the immediate parties to the transaction, to say nothing of the distribution of tranches among the buyers. This "limited disclosure on who holds what in the OTD-chain" (Blinder 2007; Stiglitz 2007) had a purpose: "... people who were issuing these derivatives had big incentives to keep what they were doing secret. ... If the banks put on their books all the risky loans they were carrying, all the risky loans they were making, the Federal Reserve would step in" (Levy 2009). That is exactly what *The Economist* (2006) referred to as the "dark side of the debt".

Spaventa (2008, p.2) pointed to the "deep information gap, affecting supervisors no less than market participants, as to the extent and location of risks: it came as a surprise that at least half of the credit risk that had been ostensibly transferred had directly or indirectly flown back to the banking system through conduits, SIVs [special investment vehicles], asset management entities, proprietary trading desks. ... It is a fact, in any case, that the extent of leverage and risk exposure of banks, hedge funds, and other investment vehicles that came to light during the crisis was far larger than anybody – market participants as well as regulators – had realized. ... [T]he financial consequences of bursting this bubble in the brave new world of securitisation were never considered. There was a literature on financial innovations in the field of structured credit product, but the nature of the new business model known as 'originate to distribute' (OTD) and its macro- and microeconomic implications were never properly explored if not to provide an unqualified praise of its benefits." When the volume of transactions, of asymmetric information, and the number and variety of those concerned became known,[10] it came as a shock ("surprise") and *by necessity* caused a breakdown of the inter-bank market (Heider et al 2009); Knightian uncertainty spread (Caballero and Krishnamurthy 2008) and caused a panic among bank managers – a panic that would shape subsequent developments.

The most important cause of the size and amplitude of the recent crisis thus appears to be the shock brought on by the breakdown of a system of information and trust, so that quite suddenly financial innovations and their effects could not but appear in a totally different light, "... nobody thought that this might happen. ... But the number of things that have gone wrong and the ferocity, with which they have gone wrong, I think, was beyond the imagination of almost everyone" (Blinder 2009). In this sense, too, Louis Garicano, Dean of the LSE, answered Her Majesty's question: "At every stage, someone was relying on somebody else and everyone thought they were doing the right thing" (Beattie 2008).

Caballero and Kurlat (2009) define three core elements of big financial crises in developed markets: firstly, a significant negative surprise, something novel, rare and confusing, a change of paradigms (not merely unfavourable tendencies or outcomes in a familiar probabilistic environment), a complex development, not easy to grasp: "Surely there are common patterns across the preludes of crises, but these cannot be at the core of the problem or we would have solved it a long time ago"

[10] To illustrate the magnitudes let me quote the IMF (2010) data on write-downs and additional allowances (in bill. $)

	US	UK	EURO	Others
Realized write-downs or loss provisions Q2 2007–Q4 2009	650	350	400	100
Expected additional Q2 2010–Q4 2010	200	100	250	250

(Caballero and Kurlat 2009, p.6). A second component of a major crisis is the excessive concentration of aggregated risks[11] in system-relevant financial institutions with little equity (a long lever); a third element, according to these authors, is the slow reaction of economic policymakers.

2. Which indications of a crisis were perceived?

Kirchgässner (2009) shows very clearly that the character, scope, and consequences of the recent financial crisis were not understood: neither by the German Council of Experts nor by the Joint Forecast nor by the OECD. Arnold (2009, p.4) quotes the IMF Global Financial Stability Report of October 2007, which estimated required loss provisions at 200 billion $ – a figure that turned out to be a mere fraction of the actual losses incurred (see note 10). As to institutions concerned with economic policy, the prevailing impression is that – apart from the Bank for International Settlements and its staff, and partly the IMF – they actively suppressed any intimations of impending problems: Even in the summer of 2007, after the New Century Financial Corporation had had to stop granting credits, after the IMF had warned of the risks that US mortgage problems posed for the global financial market and after two Bear Sterns hedge funds had gone into a spin, President Bush refused to interfere in the mortgage market – he wanted the market to operate on its own. In this, he certainly was not alone: Geithner (2007), then President of the Federal Reserve Bank of New York, stressed even in 2007 that "there are few signs that the disruptions in the credit market will have a lasting impact on credit markets as a whole" – not even on credit markets, to say nothing of the US-economy or the world economy. The Federal Reserve Bank of Kansas City – host to the Jackson Hole Symposium every August – showed at least some awareness of the problem: In 2007 the topic was "Housing, Housing Finance, and Monetary Policy"; so the topic was discussed before the crisis broke out. Speakers Shiller (2007), Leamer (2007), Mishkin (2007) and Feldstein (2007) made it quite clear that there existed an asset bubble; they realized the need for counteracting policy measures, although they saw the danger of a *US recession* only, not of a global financial crisis. Nearly all co-speakers and discussants, however, found but calming words: Mayer (2007) did not think the fall of housing prices was any worse or more problematical than in the 1990s; Smets (2007) opposed Leamer's (2007) request for stabilization of house prices by the FED; Gramlich (2007) pointed out the positive aspects of the building boom; Ludvigson (2007) suggested that even a substantial drop in house prices would but inconsiderably affect private consumption; Hamilton (2007) advocated regulation of the mortgage market, but saw no need for monetary measures. Only by the time of the 2008 Symposium, "Maintaining Stability in a Changing Financial System", all speakers and discussants had become aware of the danger of a major crisis, the possible causes of which were then discussed – after all, in the meantime several banks had run into serious difficulties, the IMF had predicted losses in the magnitude of trillions, and Congress had approved a program running into billions to fight the crisis. For a long time, policy makers would not accept that there were any serious problems exceeding those of a "normal" recession, and nobody realized the depth and the global dimensions of the crisis; yet there were economists, both academic and practical, who were aware that at least certain segments of the market were headed in the direction of danger. Survey 1 (p. 25), listing about eight dozens of pertinent analyses, is far from complete and perhaps not even representative, but it does provide substantial evidence of such awareness. This survey was assembled from a critical (though by necessity incomplete) perusal of the literature (including the Internet); it is an attempt to register those theoretical and empirical papers that pointed out the vulnerability of the financial system and/or the risks of its being left unchanged. Survey 1 indicates the date of the respective contribution, the name of the author (not only

[11] Aggregated risks were especially high this time because when the system broke down senior tranches, too, were found to be at risk.

economists but also individual financial analysts[12]), his/her classification of the problems diagnosed and one typical quote each. Fitting in with the analysis in section 1, the following classes of problems have been defined: asset-bubbles (A), monetary policy (M), regulation (R), financial innovations (I), lack of information and behaviour of financial institutions (B), surprises (S) and macro-imbalances (U). Survey 2 shows the time distribution and the types of causes adduced.

Survey 2: Distribution of recognized instabilities

	90s	2000	2001	2002	2003	2004	2005	2006	2007	2008	Σ
asset bubbles (A)	1	3	2	1	1	7	1	13	8	1	38
monetary policy (M)	–	–	1	–	–	1	–	–	–	–	2
regulation (R)	2	2	2	–	–	1	1	3	1	4	16
financial Innovation (I)	–	1	2	1	1	1	2	1	1	6	16
behaviour (B)	–	1	–	–	–	–	–	2	4	11	16
surprises (S)	–	–	1	–	–	–	1	–	–	1	3
macro-imbalances (U)	–	–	–	–	–	2	–	2	1	–	5
Σ	3	7	8	2	2	12	5	19	15	23	96

Source: Survey 1 in the Appendix; multiple attributions

Unsurprisingly, two fifths of the authors noted a problematic and unsustainable development in the problem zone of *asset markets*. As early as 1997 Shleifer and Vishny had shown that arbitrage cannot always keep prices from deviating from their fundamental values, and the less so the more pronounced the deviation. Three years later Shiller (2000) studied the stock bubble and its effects, while Godley and Wray (2000) diagnosed the rising prices of housing as a mortgage bubble; Richebacher (2001) and Baker (2002) analysed this bubble and warned that it might burst. Bordo and Jeanne (2000, p. 18) showed that "[a]sset price reversals can be very costly in terms of declining output". From 2005, warnings became more frequent and more dramatic, but a full five years after the first warnings had been sounded in 2007, President Bush still wished markets to be left alone, and many of the participants at the Jackson-Hole-Symposium could not detect anything out of the ordinary.

Up to 2008, there were at least 38 contributions available that recognized both the existence and the precarious character of asset bubbles; thus, it can hardly be doubted that an economic diagnosis of bubbles and a forecast of their effects is possible in principle: It remains to be seen why the respective warnings were systematically ignored – a question to be dealt with in the next section. Before that the other instabilities remarked on by various authors must be sketched. Note, however, that the attribution is only a rough and ready one as several papers cite more than one cause of instability.

Well over one fifth of the studies included in Survey 1 considered *insufficient regulation* to have caused the instability. From the early 1990s onward, various features of financial markets were criticized: the increasingly insufficient equity base of financial institutions – an effect of their deregulation – was pointed out (Calomiris and Kahn 1992; Flannery 1994) as well as the need for regulation of imperfect markets (Allen and Gale 2004); others took exception to the pro-cyclical character of most regulatory measures (Hahn 2000, Danielson et al 2001, Adrian and Shin 2007). As early as 2003, Diamond and Rajan (2003) warned of the effects of bank crashes on macroeconomic liquidity and urged appropriate counter-measures. According to Borio (2005) and Gai et al (2008) changes in the financial and monetary regimes, especially increased price variability, foster the formation of asset price bubbles and make for cyclical fluctuations.

[12] The contributions of finance experts are for the most part cited according to Bezemer (2009) or Internet-entries.

Interestingly enough, financial innovations rank only third among the causes of instability of the system. An early example are Cebenoyan and Strahan (2000), who were the first to show that financial innovations do not reduce the risks of banks because banks tend to compensate them by taking other, higher risks. A year later, Caballero and Krishnamurthy (2001) pointed out that the system had become so complex that it generated Knightian uncertainty and was susceptible to panic.[13] Stein (2002) criticized that bundling acted as a disincentive for careful screening of credits. Getmansky et al (2204) noted the high correlation among the risks of hedge funds, while Chan et al (2005) underlined that the risks of hedge funds involved banks in various ways, thus increasing their vulnerability. Thus, at least individual authors called attention to the problems of financial innovations and their implementation quite early, long before the first banks crashed; the majority of observers, however, saw virtually nothing but the advantages, textbook-style, of an improved distribution of risks.

On a par with the financial innovations, the *behaviour of the finance industry* is considered to have been an important cause of instability. Apart from Cebenoyan and Strahan (2000), who noted the innovation-induced tendency among banks to make riskier investments, the earliest pertinent analyses appeared only in 2007 – rather late. Among the developments criticized were the tendency of independent lenders (i. e. non-banks) to sell off the junior tranches (Gramlich 2007), their careless credit investigations (Keys et al 2008), and above all the deliberate opacity of transactions (Blinder 2007). Here is one of the main reasons why such an important cause of the crisis hardly figured in the literature: Academic economists certainly analysed the advantages of bundling and the respective risk transfers; what they did not and could not realize was that the finance industry did not behave according to the model and that the risks eventually fell upon those who had little equity to show and were very busy borrowing short and lending long (Arnold 2009). When this was finally realized, it came as a *surprise* not only for the academy, but even more so for insiders. Accordingly, only three contributions deal explicitly with surprises, i. e. unexpected important events: one of them is the early paper (already mentioned in connection with financial innovations) by Caballero and Krishnamurthy (2001), the others are two articles in *The Economist* (2005; 2006) that pointed out the sudden and unexpected liquidity loss of Triple A bonds even before the crisis broke. In a certain sense the revision of the EU forecast of November 2008, too, may be regarded as surprise-driven.

Other possible causes of instabilities are of minor importance. The small number of "mentions" of *macro-imbalances* and *monetary policy* is mainly due to the specific selection criteria of the present paper, which concentrates on analyses of the financial crisis; therefore only contributions dealing directly and explicitly with the financial crisis have been included. From the vast literature on the US twin deficits and on US monetary policy only those papers have been included here that see these factors as immediate causes of the *financial* crisis.

Thus, three points should be remembered: Firstly and positively: Many economists, both academic and practical, did indeed realize and publish on the instabilities in important areas, above all on the problems of asset markets, on deficiencies of regulation and on questionable financial innovations. There are two negative points, however: There was not a single paper to be found that had predicted the depth of the crisis and its global spread. Thirdly, those causes that today are considered to have been decisive, viz. the element of surprise and the interaction of the various contributing causes, were hardly noticed or remarked upon.

[13] The specific problem is that in a panic "economic agents behave as if the likelihood of a catastrophe were much higher than it actually is (at least in the absence of the panic itself)" (Caballero and Kurlat 2009).

3. Why did no one realize the extent of the crisis?

The principal reason for the non-predictability of the depth and scope of the financial crisis seems to have been the *unexpected combination of several elements,* all of which had definitely been recognized as critical: the burst of an asset bubble and the changes in the system including innovation-driven reactions combined with the realization of the opacity of the system and the consequent serious loss of mutual trust in as well as within the finance industry. Not only academic economists and regulating authorities found the innovations on the financial markets to be quite opaque, those with practical experience of those markets did, too. Thus, the "surprise" – the shocking realization that those concerned and therefore the entire system behaved in novel ways, that the rules of the game (which had evolved with the system) were changed – turned out to be *the* distinctive feature of this crisis. In their answer to HM the Queen, Besley and Hennessy (2009) spoke of the "failure of collective imagination"; this was what had made the crisis unforeseeable. As mentioned above, Caballero and Kurlat (2009) showed that major financial crises are always triggered by innovations whose consequences come as a surprise, for they *cannot* be assessed beforehand, but appear in combination with the aggregated risks of central financial institutions; this time, both factors were especially momentous.

The collective unwillingness to accept the diagnosis of the fragility of the system was underpinned by the influence of "Great Moderation" (Stock and Watson 2002). Over the past two or even three decades *everyone in the social order,* not just economists and bankers, had got used to decreasing and eventually rather low volatility; policy makers and bankers were under the illusion of being in complete control of the situation: after all, ever since 1987 they had weathered several (minor) crises (Kirchgässner 2009). A generation of self-assured and ambitious bankers, eager for yields, knowingly accepted risks that they thought had been made secure by sophisticated risk models. The *authors of the risk models* relied on the efficiency of their models, with no regard to their implementation (Scholes, as quoted by *The Economist* 2009): They ignored that available time series were too short and restricted to a period of little volatility, that there were "fat tails" to a skewed distribution, and independent shocks, and they ignored the fact that the correlation depended on the system. Many of the *policy makers* (in the widest sense) believed in oversimplified market models – markets clearing in no time, stabilizing speculation and quick-working tendencies to regain macroeconomic equilibria (Acemoglu 2009) – and considered interventions in the market to be rather counterproductive. With very few exceptions, economists must stand accused of having concentrated on specific partial instabilities, while neglecting the interaction of the diverse causes of the crisis.

Nevertheless, it must be stressed once more that even if all the deficiencies of economic theory and its models had been repaired (which is hard to imagine), the nature and the extent of the crisis still could not have been foreseen: the central feature was the *surprise and the unexpected combination of several, only partly recognized and/or recognizable causes.* All along, those concerned had been and were still thinking in the categories of Great Moderation. What really aggravated the crisis was the shock from the surprise that the framework of their thinking, their conception of the world and their strategies had become obsolete overnight.

4. What can we learn from this experience?

The fact that economists cannot hope to predict the next major crisis in time does not mean that theorists, regulating authorities and policy makers cannot learn anything from the experience of the recent crisis. Probably the most urgent matter to be investigated in this connection must be the question why those analyses that pointed out the possible dangers of rising asset prices, wrong incentive structures, lack of equity or insufficient and mistaken regulation were totally ignored. Many of those critical papers had been presented to monetary authorities and regulating agencies – even before publication, in other words: quite in time. With the single exception of the Bank of International Settlements and, partly, the IMF, everybody ignored those warnings.[14] Business interests and lobbying may have something to do with it, but can at best explain part of the problem; problems of communication among the – certainly not unimportant – research departments and the managers of central banks and regulating agencies probably had more to do with it. The social sciences urgently need to analyse the reasons why policymakers would consider recent economic findings and insights to be irrelevant to their work; but economists will be able to contribute but little to such analyses.

On the other hand, economists will have to work hard in order to adapt their models to the new reality. We need not go into any details here, as this is generally understood by now. There is also a growing literature on this topic, which stresses, however (in contrast to a number of flippant remarks), that we should adapt models we already have rather than try a completely novel approach. Examples are Acemoglu (2009), Kirchgässner (2009), Lechner (2009), or Schneider and Kirchgässner (2009). Proposals range from the analysis of the actual efficiency of financial markets, their instability and the inclusion of the financial sector in "real" models to increased consideration of risks and institutions and to improvements in the training of economists: more realism, less specialization (Besley and Hennessy 2009). As to comparative systems analysis, the advantages and disadvantages of alternative systems should be investigated, e. g. by comparing the capital-market-dominated US system with the European bank-credit-centred system or the system of functionally separate banks with the universal banking system – although one would always have to keep in mind that in real life those systems virtually never are as clear-cut as in text-books.

The *necessity of stricter regulation* has been widely discussed; there is no need to go into any details here. There is widespread agreement that unregulated financial markets cannot avoid excessive developments and that reputation-driven self-restraint of agents does not suffice (Acemoglu 2009). Usually, discussions focus on the regulation of individual financial institutions and of forms of transactions that frequently tend to enforce the cycle inherent in the financial sector, while proposals for "macroprudential regulation" of the financial system as a whole have met with little interest.

Another point not yet touched upon either in public discussions or in the academy, is the question of what *type of forecasts* may (or must not) be expected from economists. If it is correct that major (financial) crises always have an element of surprise in them that makes for a widespread and deep shock and perhaps even panic, then economists must accept and will have to explain to the public that no improvement of their tools will suffice: even in the future it will not be possible to forecast major (financial) crises. For: "Theoretically we may well expect an increasing convergence of forecasts and future reality, provided the matter on which we want to be informed changes more slowly than our knowledge of it" (Borchardt 1979, p.7); but that is exactly what does *not* happen in major crises – because of the surprise element typical of them. That is to be regretted, for those are the very situations when forecasts are most in demand. "It has always been the case that in times of increased need for forecasts the conditions for making correct predictions were comparatively bad. From historical experience one can conclude that there is a fundamental forecasting dilemma: In times of relatively stable development patterns, when forecasting conditions are favourable, there is little demand for scientific forecasts. If and when demand for them increases, the chances of deducing conjectures about the future from observations of the past as a rule have already considerably worsened" (Borchardt 1979, p.22).

The insight that even in the future we shall not be able to avoid or to forecast serious financial crises, must have consequences for theoretical as well as applied *economic policy*. The point is not to use

---

[14] It would be interesting to find out whether that has anything to do with better and quicker accessibility of data, less involvement with lobbies or with more efficient methods of analysis.

up material and immaterial resources in – vain – attempts at developing indicators and models that might yet be able to predict serious crises. Instead, we must accept that there will be crises and that they will be unexpected; that means we have to take care to contain their negative effects. We must identify those elements of the system that are less or least susceptible to surprises, less or least crisis-prone. Such elements may range from figuring out maximum bank size (i. e. not "too big too fail") and from bookkeeping and evaluation rules and equity requirements to pension financing and the architecture of the system (financing via the capital market vs. credit financing, duties of the central bank). To sum up: Instead of stressing short-term efficiency, survival in times of crisis must be secured.

References[15]

Abiad, A. et al, [2007 IMF WP 07/64)], 2009, Financial integration, capital mobility, and income convergence, Economic Policy April, 241-205.

Acemoglu, D., 2009, The crisis of 2008: Structural lessons for and from economics, http://econ-www.mit.edu/files/3722.

Adrian, T. and H.S. Shin, [2007 Working Paper Federal Reserve Bank of New York 328], 2010, Liquidity and Leverage, Journal of Financial Intermediation 19(3), 418–37.

Allen, F. and D. Gale, 2004, Financial intermediaries and markets, Econometrica 724, 1023-61.

Allen, F. and E. Carletti, 2008, The Role of Liquidity in Financial Crises, Jackson Hole Symposium http://www.kc.frb.org/home/subwebnav.cfm?level=3&theID=11442&SubWeb=10660.

Arestis, Ph. and A. Singh, 2010, Financial globalisation and crisis, institutional transformation and equitiy, Cambridge Journal of Economics 34(2), 225-38.

Arnold, L., 2009, Die Volkswirtschaftslehre steckt nicht in der Krise, ifo Schnelldienst 62(14), 3-5.

Ashcraft, A.B. and T. Schuerman, 2007, Understanding the securitization of subprime mortgage credit, Wharton Financial Institutions Center WP 07-43.

Baker, D., 2002, The run-up in home prices: Is it real or is it another bubble? CEPR, August 2002 www.cepr.net/index.php/publications/reports.

Baker, D., 2006, Recession looms for the U.S. economy in 2007, CEPR Reports and Issue Briefs 2006-29.

Baker, D., B. DeLong and P. Krugman, 2005, Asset Returns and Economic Growth, Brookings Papers on Economic Activity 2005(1), 289-330.

Bank of England, 2006, Financial Stability Report, July 2006.

Bank of England, 2007, Financial Stability Report, October 2007.

Bank for International Settlements, 2007, 77th Annual Report, Basle.

Bank for International Settlements, 2008, 78th Annual Report, Basle.

Barth, J.R. et al, [2009], 2010, Bank regulation in the United States, CESifo Studies 56(1), 112-140.

Beattie, A., 2008, Good question, Ma'am, Financial Times November 14 2008, http://www.garicano.com/index_files/ftqueen.pdf.

Ben-David, I., 2008, Manipulation of collateral values by borrowers and intermediaries, Job Market Paper, first draft, fisher.osu.edu/fin/dice/seminars/manipulation.pdf

Bernanke, B.S., 2005, The global savings glut and the U.S. current account deficit, Sandridge lecture, http://www.federalreserve.gov/newsevents/speech/bernanke20070911a.htm.

Bernanke, B. S., 2007, Opening Remarks, Jackson Hole Symposium http://www.kc.frb.org/home/subwebnav.cfm?level=3&theID=11442&SubWeb=10660.

Besley, T. and P. Hennessy, 2009, Letter to the Queen, http://media.ft.com/cms/3e3b6ca8-7a08-11de-b86f-00144feabdc0.pdf

Bezemer, D., 2009, "No one saw this coming": Understanding financial crisis through accounting models. MPRA Paper 15892.

Blanchard, O., 2009, The crisis: Basic mechanisms, and appropriate policies, IMF WP 09/80.

Blinder, A., 2007, Six fingers of blame in the mortgage mess, NYTimes Sept. 30, 2007.

Blinder, A., 2009, Economists explain how they missed warnings, PBS News Hour PPS News Hour 9.1.2009.

[15] The dates in square brackets refer to the first version available, which is relevant for the present paper, for considerations of priority.

Borchardt, K., 1979, Produktions- und Verwertungsbedingungen von Langfristprognosen in historischer Perspektive, Allgemeines Statistisches Archiv 63(1), 1-25.
Bordo, M. et al, 2001, Is the crisis problem growing more severe?, Economic Policy April 2001, 51-82.
Bordo, M. and O. Jeanne, 2000, Asset price reversals, economic instability, and monetary policy, Lecture, American Financial Association January 7, 2001.
Borio, C. and P. Lowe, 2002, Asset prices, financial and monetary stability: exploring the nexus, BIS Working Papers 114.
Borio, C., 2005, Monetary and financial stability: so close and yet so far?, National Institute Economic Review 192 (April), 84-101.
Borio, C. and M. Drehmann, 2009, Assessing the risk of banking crises – revisited, BIS Quarterly Review March, 29-46.
Brunnermeier, M.K. and L. Pedersen, [2007], 2009, Market liquidity and funding liquidity, Review of Financial Studies 22(6), 2201-2238.
Buiter, W.H., 2008, Central banks and financial crises, Jackson Hole Symposium, http://www.kc.frb.org/home/subwebnav.cfm?level=3&theID=11441&SubWeb=10660.
Caballero, R.J. and A. Krishnamurthy, 2001, International domestic collateral constraints in a model of emerging economies, JME 48(3), 513-48.
Caballero, R.J. and A. Krishnamurthy, 2008, Collective risk management in a flight to quality episode, JFin 63(5), 2085-2554.
Caballero, R.J. and P. Kurlat, 2009, The „surprising" origin and nature of financial crises: a macroeconomic policy proposal, Jackson Hole Symposium, http://www.kc.frb.org/home/subwebnav.cfm?level=3&theID=11441&SubWeb=10660.
Calomiris, Ch. and Ch.M. Kahn, 1992, The role of demandable debt in structuring optimal banking arrangements, AER 81(3), 497-413.
Case, K. and R. Shiller, 2006, Full house, Wall Street Journal, August 30, 2006.
Catte, P. et al, 2004, Housing markets, wealth and the business cycle, OECD Working Paper 394.
Cebenoyan, A.S. and Ph.E. Strahan, [2000 Working Paper], 2004, Risk management, capital structure and capital budgeting in financial institutions, Journal of Banking & Finance, 28, 19-43.
Chan, N. et al, [2005, NBER WP 11200] 2006, Systemic risk and hedge funds, in M. Carey and R. M. Stulz eds, The Risks of Financial Institutions, Washington: NBER.
Colander, D. et al, 2009, The financial crisis and the systemic failure of academic economics (Dahlem Workshop), http://www.irg-project.org/fileadmin/publications/PUBLIC/Events/Learning_from_Financial_Crisis.pdf
Cova, P. et al, 2009, Global Imbalances: The Role of Emerging Asia, IMF Working Paper No. 09/64.
Danielson, J. et al, 2001, An academic response to Basel II, LSE-ESCR Special Paper 130.
Dell'Ariccia, G., et al, 2008, Credit booms and lending standards: Evidence from the subprime mortgage market, Centre for Economic Policy Research, Discussion Paper No. 6683.
Diamond, D.W. and Ph.H. Dybvig, 1986, Banking theory, deposit insurance and bank regulation, JBus 59(1), 55-68.
Diamond, D.W. and R. Rajan, 2001, Liquidity risk, liquidity creation and financial fragility, JPE 109(2), 287-327.
Diamond, D.W. and R.G. Rajan, [2003, NBER Working Paper W10071] 2005, Liquidity shortages and banking crises, Journal of Finance 60(2), 615-647.
Dodd, R., 2007, Subprime: Tentacles of a Crisis, Finance and Development 44 (4).
Economist (US), 2005, Hear that hissing sound? Global house prices, 10.12.2005.
Economist (US), 2006, What's that hissing sound? America's house-price bubble, August 2006.
Economist, 2006, The dark side of the debt, 23.9.2006.
Economist, 2009, Efficiency and beyond, 16.7.2009.
Englund, P., 1999, The Swedish banking crisis: Roots and consequences, Oxford Review of Economic Policy 15, 80-97.
European Commission, 2008, Autumn economic forecast 2008-2010: GDP growth comes close to a stand-still in the EU and euro area, http://europa.eu/rapid/pressReleasesAction.do?reference=IP/08/1617.
EZB, 2005, Vermögenspreisblasen und Geldpolitik, Monatsbericht April, 53-69.
Feldstein, M., 2007, Overview and Concluding Remarks, Jackson Hole Symposium, http://www.kc.frb.org/home/subwebnav.cfm?level=3&theID=11441&SubWeb=10660.
Feldstein, M., 2007, Two top US economists present scary scenarios for US economy, Finfacts Sept 3, 2007, http://www.finfacts.com/irelandbusinessnews/publish.
Finanzgruppe Deutscher Sparkassen- und Giroverband, 2007, Vermögensbarometer 2007, Berlin.
Fischer, St., Concluding Remarks, Jackson Hole Symposium 2008, http://www.kc.frb.org/home/subwebnav.cfm?level=3&theID=11441&SubWeb=10660.
Flannery, M.J., 1994, Debt maturity and the deadweight cost of leverage: Optimal financing banking firms, AER 84(1), 320-31.

Franke, G. and J.P. Krahnen, 2005, Default risk sharing between banks and markets: The contribution of collateralized debt obligations, Center for Fin Stud WP 2005/06.

Franke, G. and J.P. Krahnen, 2009, Instabile Finanzmärkte, PWP 10(4), 335-66.

Gai, P. et al, 2008, Financial innovation, macroeconomic stability and systemic crisis, Economic Journal 118, 401-26.

Gallin J., 2004, The long-run relationship between house prices and rents; low level of rent-price ratio as a sign that we are in a house-price bubble, FedRes WP.

Geithner, T., 2007, Credit markets, innovations and their implications, Federal Reserve Bank of Richmond, Credit Markets Symposium (zitiert nach Spaventa 2008, 3).

Getmansky, M. et al, 2004, An econometric model of serial correlation and illiquidity in hedge-fund returns, Journal of Financial Economics 74, 529-609.

Giuliano P. and A. Spilimbergo, 2009, Growing up in a recession: Beliefs and the macroeconomy, NBER WP 15321.

Godley, W. and M. Lavoie, 2007, Fiscal policy in a stock-flow consistent (SFC) model, Journal of Post Keynesian Economics 30(1), 79-100.

Godley, W. and R. Wray, 2000, Is Goldilocks doomed?, Journal of Economic Issues 34: 201-206.

Godley, W. et al, 2007, Is there a way out of the woods? The Levy Economics Institute Strategic Analysis, November 2007, http://www.levy.org/.

Gramlich, E. M., 2007, Booms and busts: The case of subprime mortgages, Jackson Hole Symposium, http://www.kc.frb.org/home/subwebnav.cfm?level=3&theID=11441&SubWeb=10660.

Greenspan, A., 2005, Economic flexibility. Remarks to the National Association of Business Economics Annual Meeting, zitiert nach Franke und Krahnen 2009.

Hahn, F., 2000, EU-Konsultationspapier zur Überarbeitung der Eigenkapitalvorschriften für Kreditinstitute und Wertpapierfirmen – Kommentar aus makroökonomischer Sicht, BankArchiv 2000, 787-92.

Haldane, A., 2009, Rethinking the financial network, Bank of England Working Paper.

Hamilton, J., 2006, New home sales continue to fall, Econbrowser posted at August 24, 2006 09:37 AM http://www.econbrowser.com/archives/2006/08/new_home_sales.html.

Hamilton, J.D., 2007, Discussion, Jackson Hole Symposium, http://www.kc.frb.org/home/subwebnav.cfm?level=3&theID=11441&SubWeb=10660.

Harrison, F., 2007, House prices: expect the worst. MoneyWeek Nov. 7, 2007.

Heider, F. et al, 2009, Information asymmetries in the interbank market: theory and policy responses, ECB WP.

Hellwig, M.F., 2008, The systemic risk in the financial sector, An analysis of the subprime-mortgage financial crisis, MPI Collective Goods Reprint 2008/43.

Hilbers, P. et al, 2001, Real estate market developments and financial sector soundness, IMF Working Paper WP/01/129 (Sept).

Holmstrom, B. and J. Tirole, 2007, Financial intermediation, loanable funds, and the real sector, The Quarterly Journal of Economics 112(3), 663-691.

Holmstrom, Bengt, 2008, Discussion, Jackson Hole Symposium, http://www.kc.frb.org/home/subwebnav.cfm?level=3&theID=11441&SubWeb=10660.

Hudson, M., 2006b, The road to serfdom: An illustrated guide to the coming real estate collapse, Harper's Magazine, April.

Hudson, M., 2006a, Saving, asset-price inflation, and debt-induced deflation, in L. Randall Wray and Matthew Forstater eds., Money, Financial Instability and Stabilization Policy, Edward Elgar, 104-24.

IMF, 2007, Global Financial Stability Report, Washington, September.

IMF, 2010, Global Financial Stability Report, Washington, April.

Kaminsky, G.L.and C.M. Reinhardt, 1999, The Twin Crises: The Causes of Banking and Balance-of-Payments Problems, AER 99(3), 473-500.

Keen, S (2006) The lily and the pond. Interview reported by the Evans Foundations, http://evatt.org.au/news/445.html.

Keys B.K. et al, [2008], 2010, Did securitization lead to lax screening? Evidence from subprime loans, QJE 125(1), 307-362.

Kirchgässner, G., 2009, Die Krise der Wirtschaft: Auch eine Krise der Wirtschaftswissenschaften? PWP 10(4), 436-68.

Korinek, A., 2008, Systemic risk-taking: Accelerator effects, externalities, and regulatory response, http://www.eabcn.org/conferences/barcelona_2008/korinek.pdf.

Krahnen, J.-P. and C. Wilde, 2006, Risk transfer with CDOs and systemic risk in banking, Center for Financial Studies WP 2006-04.

Laperriere, A., 2006, Housing Bubble Trouble, Weekly Standard 11(28), April 10, 2006.

Leamer E., 1997, Housing is the Business Cycle, Jackson Hole Symposium, http://www.kc.frb.org/home/subwebnav.cfm?level=3&theID=11441&SubWeb=10660.

Leamer, E., 2006, Is economy headed for a soft landing?, US today 25.8.2006.
Lechner, C., Hg, 2009, Konsequenzen aus der Finanzmarktkrise: Perspektiven der HSG, St. Gallen.
Levy, F., 2009, Economists explain why hints of the economic crisis eluded them, PPS News hour 9.1.2009.
Lipsky, John, 2008, Discussion, Jackson Hole Symposium, http://www.kc.frb.org/home/subwebnav.cfm?level=3&theID=11441&SubWeb=10660.
Ludvigson, S.C., 2007, Discussion, Jackson Hole Symposium, http://www.kc.frb.org/home/subwebnav.cfm?level=3&theID=11441&SubWeb=10660.
Maddaloni, A. et al, forthcoming, Does monetary policy affect bank credit standards? ECB Working Paper forthcoming.
Mayer Ch.J., 2007, Commentary: Understanding recent trends in house prices and home ownership, Jackson Hole Symposium, http://www.kc.frb.org/home/subwebnav.cfm?level=3&theID=11441&SubWeb=10660.
Mian, A. and A. Sufi, 2008, The consequences of mortgage credit expansion: Evidence from the 2007 mortgage default crisis, NBER WP 13936.
Mishkin, F.S., 2007, Housing and the monetary transmission mechanism, Jackson Hole Symposium, http://www.kc.frb.org/home/subwebnav.cfm?level=3&theID=11441&SubWeb=10660.
Moody's, 2006, Moody's predicts big drop in Washington housing prices, Washington Business Journal October 5, 2006.
Mussa, M., 2004, Global economic prospects: bright for 2004 but with questions thereafter, Washington: Institute for International Economics.
Obstfeld, M. and K. Rogoff, 2004, The unsustainable US current account position revisited, NBER Working Papers 10869.
Petersen, M. and R. Rajan, 2002, Does distance still matter? The information revolution in small business lending, Journal of Finance 57(6), 2533-70.
Purnanandam, A., 2009, Originate-to-distribute model and subprime mortgages crisis, mimeo.
Rajan, R.G., [2005, NBER Working Paper 11728] 2006, Has finance made the world riskier?, European Financial Management 12(4), 499-533.
Rajan, U. et al, 2008, The failure of models that predict failure: Distance, incentives and defaults, Chicago Grad. School of Bus. Res.P. 122.
Reid, M., 1982, The secondary banking crisis 1973-75: Its causes and course, London: Macmillan.
Reinhart, C. and K.S. Rogoff, 2008, Banking crises: An equal opportunity menace, NBER WP 14049.
Roubini, N. and B. Setser, 2004, The US as a net debtor: The sustainability of the US external balances, mimeo.
Roubini, N., 2006, Global imbalances: A contemporary "Rashomon" saga, www.rgemonitor.com, November.
Sapir, J., 2008, Global finance in crisis, Real-world Economics Review 46, 82-101.
Schneider, F. and G. Kirchgässner, 2009, Financial and world economic crisis: What did economics contribute? Public Choice 140, 319-27.
Shiller, R.J., 2000, Irrational Exuberance, Princeton: Princeton UP; 2nd ed. 2005.
Shiller, R.J., 2003, The new financial order: Risk in the 21th century, Princeton: Princeton UP.
Shiller, R.J., 2007, Understanding recent trends in house prices and home ownership, Jackson Hole Symposium, http://www.kc.frb.org/home/subwebnav.cfm?level=3&theID=11441&SubWeb=10660.
Shiller, R.J., 2008, Challenging the crowd in whispers, not shouts, NYTimes 2.11.2008.
Shin, H.S., 2008, Financial intermediaries, financial stability and monetary policy, Jackson Hole Symposium, http://www.kc.frb.org/home/subwebnav.cfm?level=3&theID=11441&SubWeb=10660.
Smets, Frank, 2007, Discussion, Jackson Hole Symposium, http://www.kc.frb.org/home/subwebnav.cfm?level=3&theID=11441&SubWeb=10660.
Sørensen, J.K., 2006 The dynamics of house prices – international evidence, Social Science Research Network Paper at http://papers.ssrn.com/sol3/papers.cfm?abstract_id=1273183.
Spaventa, L., 2008, Avoiding disorderly deleveraging, CEPR Policy Insight 22.
Spaventa, L., 2009, Economists and economics: What does the crisis tell us?, CEPR Policy Insight 28.
Stein, J., 2002, Information production and capital allocation: Decentralized versus hierarchical firms, JFin LVII(5), 1891-1921
Stiglitz, J., 2007, House of cards, The Guardian, Oct. 9, 2007.
Stock, J.H and M.Watson, 2002, Has the business cycle changed and why?, NBER Working Papers 9127.
Tichy, G., 2009, Bankenkrise oder falsche Anreizsysteme in der Rentiergesellschaft, Manuskript.
White, W., 2006, Procyclicality in the financial system: do we need a new macrofinancial stabilisation framework? BIS Working Papers No 193.
Wyplosz, Ch., 2009, Macroeconomics after the crisis: dealing with the Tobin curse, The Walter-Adolf-Joehr Lecture, May 15.

Appendix

Survey 1: Prediction of sectoral crises

1992	Calomiris and Kahn	R[16]	"Borrowing short, lending long" requires sufficient equity
1994	Flannery	R	When new, unregulated financial institutions start taking in deposits, they expose themselves to runs, thus jeopardizing macro-stability
1997	Shleifer&Vishny	B	Arbitrage cannot prevent deviations of prices from fundamental values – the less, the greater the deviation
2000	Shiller	A	"Irrational exuberance": Consequential breakdown of housing- and stock markets
	Bordo and Jeanne	A	Reduction of speculative asset prices may turn out to be very expensive, because of falling output
	Godley and Wray	A	"Is Goldilocks doomed?" There is no such thing as mortgage-credit-induced growth
	Hahn	R	Weakness of regulation reform Basel II: merely technical reform, microeconomic, pro-cyclical, summation of individual risks instead
	Cebenoyan&Strahan	R/I/B	Weak capital structure, increasingly sophisticated risk-management strategies of banks may increase the volume of credits they can offer, but cannot reduce their risk
2001	Hilbers et al.	A	excessive rises of real estate prices frequently cause problems in the financial sector and should be taken account of in analyses of it
	Richebacher (IX; Bez. 09)	A/M	"The new housing boom is another rapidly inflating asset bubble financed by the same loose money practices that fuelled the stock market bubble ... will invariably implode in the foreseeable future, plunging the U.S. economy into a protracted, deep recession".
	Danielson et al.	R	Basle II enhances pro-cyclical effects and increases susceptibility to systemic crises
	Caballero&Krishnamurty	I/S	Significant negative surprise effect; networks have become too complex and opaque; Knightian uncertainty and panic followed
	Bordo et al.	R	Financial crises are becoming more frequent and deeper
	Diamond&Rajan	I	Credits are illiquid when granted debtor-specifically; therefore creditor has to call them in prematurely when in need of liquidity; problems when debtor and creditor have little capital
2002	Baker	A	Burst of mortgage bubble "will be extremely harmful, both to the economy as a whole, and to tens of millions of families".
	Stein	I	Bundling creates incentive problem: "soft information" cannot be checked / verified
2003	Shiller	A	"Infatuation with the stock market was fuelling volatility and distracting from more durable economic prospects of building up real, as opposed to financial assets".
	Diamond&Rajan	I	"Bank failures can be contagious...can shrink the common pool of liquidity, creating or exacerbating aggregate liquidity shortages".
2004	Gallin (Fed.Res.)	A	"Indeed, one might be tempted to cite the currently low level of rent-price ratio as a sign that we are in a house-price-bubble".
	Rogoff&Obstfeld	A	Bubbles bring with them danger of non-sustainable global expansion

16 Abbreviations: A = asset price bubble; B = Behaviour of finance industry; I = innovation/s; M = monetary policy; R= regulation; S = surprises; U = macro-imbalances.

Year	Author	Type	Statement
	Harrison	A	"The next property market tipping point is due at the end of 2007 or early 2008...The only way prices can be brought back...is a slump or recession".
	Madsen (Bez. 09)	A	"We are seeing large bubbles and if they burst, there is no backup. The outlook is very bad".
	Shiller	A	A catastrophic crash of housing and asset market imminent. Warning to regulators: "We are in middle of dangerous housing bubble".
	Baker et al.	A	"Asset prices are bound to fall in the medium term".
	Mussa	M	The exceptionally low level of interest rates is the basis of a non-sustainable rise of asset prices; this may bring about an asset market crisis and a recession.
	Allen&Gale	R	"We argue that there may be a role for regulating liquidity provision in an economy in which markets for aggregate risks are incomplete".
	Getmansky et al.	I	"The returns to hedge funds and other alternative investments are often highly serially correlated, in sharp contrast to the returns of more traditional investment vehicles such as equity portfolios and mutual funds".
	Roubini&Setser	U	USA: net debtors with long-term balance of payments problems: "The practical risk facing the United States is... that the U.S. will have to undergo a wrenching period of slow growth and a weak dollar (perhaps combined with high domestic interest rates...)".
	Bernanke (Fed.Res.)	U	Savings glut
2005	EZB (IV)	A	"From time to time asset prices rise above all reasonable levels ... boom-bust-cycles [may] damage the economy as a whole".
	Borio (BIS)	R	"... changes in the financial and monetary regimes may have made it more likely that financial factors in general and boom and bust in credit and asset prices in particular, act as drivers of economic fluctuations". "Since the 1970s, two major cycles have taken place and a third is under way...size and amplitude of the cycles may be growing".
	Chan et al.	I	"The banking sector is exposed to hedge-funds risky through proprietary trading activities, credit arrangements and structured products, and prime brokerage services"; "... the hedge-fund industry may be heading into a challenging period of lower expected returns, ... systemic risk is currently on the rise".
	Raghuram&Raghuram	I	Change of incentives problematic: risks are taken (esp. tail risks), but hidden from investors; self-enforcement in boom via lemming-effects and inexperienced managers and investors entering the market
	Economist	S	8.12.2005 and 24.8.2006: Fall in prices of AAA-rated securities was unexpected and unforeseen; they turned illiquid, and for long periods their prices did not correspond to fundamentals
2006	Baker	A	"... Plunging housing will likely push the economy into a recession".
	Godley&Lavoie	A	House price decline will lead to a "sustained growth recession somewhere before 2010".
	Hudson	A	"The bubble will burst...these factors will further shrink the 'real' economy, drive down those already declining real wages and push our debt-ridden economy into a Japan-style stagnation or worse".
	Sørensen	A	"The bursting of the housing bubble will have a severe impact on the world economy and even result in a recession".
	Richebacher (Bez.09)	A	"A recession and a bear market in asset prices are inevitable for the U.S. economy...All remaining questions pertain solely to speed, depth, and duration of the economy's downturn".

	Schiff (Bez.09)	A	"The US housing market [is]a bubble that will soon burst (May). "The United States economy is like the Titanic ... I see a real financial crisis coming for the United States"(August).
	Case&Shiller	A	"There is a significant risk for a very bad period with slow sales, slim commissions, falling prices, rising default and foreclosures, serious trouble in financial markets, and a possible recession sooner than most of us expected".
	Bank of England	A	The Stability Reports of 2006 and 2007 diagnose a bubble
	Hamilton	A	"The housing downturn is here now, and it's big. I have concerns that as the perception sets in that home prices are falling, we may see some significant shifts in consumer sentiment and budget constraints that could introduce a dramatic new dynamic to the current situation".
	Leamer	A	"This soft-landing scenario is a fantasy"
	Moody's	A	Forecast of a drastic fall in house prices in Washington; whether this will result in a hard landing, will depend on the secondary, indirect effects of the price slump
	Lapperiere	A	Even with constant house prices in the future, growth would be slowed down unless other sectors quickly step up their growth; a hard landing – a recession – is quite possible
	Krahnen&Wilde	R	Systemic risk may increase, but that should not be the problem of banks in the CDO-market; the government has to provide for costless insurance against a crisis of the system
	White (BIS)	R	"Numerous financial and other imbalances have emerged"; more attention should be paid to the emergence of such disequilibria.
	Economist	R/I	"The dark side of the debt": credit transactions opaque over the counter. "In a panic, incomplete paperwork could cause the whole system to collapse".
	Roubini	U	Crisis caused by U.S. deficits
	Keen	U	"Long before we manage to reverse the current rise in debt, the economy will be in a recession. On current data we may already be in one".
2007	Schiff (Bez.09)	A	"There will be an economic collapse".
	Janszen (Bez.09)	A	"US stock markets are likely to begin in 2008 to experience a 'Debt Deflation Bear Market'".
	Stiglitz	A	Restricted disclosure of who holds what in the OTD-chain
	Brunnermeier&Pedersen	A	"Mutually reinforcing link between market liquidity and funding liquidity"
	Feldstein	A	Formerly, slumps in housing construction announced 8 out of 10 recessions; inebriation by irrational expectations, cheap credits, changes in regulation, merely statistical assessment of risks, securitizations with prices not taking account of risks, and lowering of standards may easily bring about a recession
	Bernanke (Fed.Res.)	A	"Global financial losses have by far exceeded even the most pessimistic projections of credit losses on those loans".
	Shiller	A	"... it is not improbable that we will see such large real price declines extending over many years".
	Adrian&Shin (FedNY)	R	Changes of trader-repurchase agreements announce changes in risks on financial markets; market-to-market leverage is strictly pro-cyclical and reinforces the effect of shocks
	Gramlich (exFed)	B	Banks retain part of their mortgages in their balance; "independent lenders" do not do that, they have no deposits and little equity
	Blinder	B	Partial disclosure of who holds what in the OTD chain

	BIS-Ann.Report 2006/07	I/B	"Originators of the OTD-strategy may be stuck with a warehouse of depreciating assets"; "...banks have retained a significant degree of credit risk in their books"; "...growing complexity and opacity".
	IMF (IX)	B	"So far, despite significant ongoing contraction in financial markets, global growth remains solid, though some slowdown could be expected. Downside risks have increased significantly and, even if fail to materialize, the implications of this period of turbulence will be significant and far-reaching".
	Godley et al.	U	"Significant drop in borrowing is likely to take place in the coming quarters, with severe consequences for growth and unemployment, unless the U.S. dollar is allowed to continue its fall and thus complete the recovery in the U.S. external imbalance, and fiscal policy shifts its course – as it did in the 2001 recession.
2008	Shiller	A	Warning to regulators: "We are in the middle of a dangerous bubble".
	Shin (FedNY)	R	Balances of security brokers/dealers reveal problems much earlier than those of banks; their growth depends on interest rates policy; pro-cyclical leverage. Monetary policy and securing of financial stability are two sides of the same coin; bubbles must be fought (interest-sensitive). Intermediaries are in the centre of the transmission mechanism; crisis by de-leveraging.
	Lipsky (IMF)	R	Market-to-market assessment problematical; financial stress of considerable macroeconomic consequence; "arms-length financial system" transmits disturbances more quickly and more strongly
	Buiter	R	New and typical of this crisis: "Sudden and comprehensive closure of a whole range of financial wholesale markets".
	BIS Ann.Rep. 2007/08	R/I	"In the aftermath of a long credit-driven boom, it would not be surprising to see turmoil in financial markets, slowing real growth and temporarily rising inflation. The crucial questions at the present juncture have to do with the severity of these individual trends as they now appear and how they might interact. While difficult to predict, their interaction does appear to point to a deeper and more protracted global downturn than the consensus view seems to expect".
	Gorton	I	Structured products are opaque; opacity and innovation go hand in hand; opaque sectors must be monitored more strictly
	Allen&Carletti	I	Increasing vulnerability of the system
	Spaventa	I	"Risk of a fully fledged crisis...possibility that the whole financial system may be caught in a vicious circle of falling asset prices and insolvencies has loomed large."
	Holmstrom	I	Excessively complex contracts hide actual value of the mortgages concerned; more information is lost at each step of the transaction. The Synthetic Subprime Mortgage Index ABX, computed annually since 2006, showed much higher risks than those comprised in the prices
	Hellwig	I	Pricing system itself increases financial market problems
	Keys et al. (Fed.Res)	B	Securitisation entailed lax credit screening; warns of over-confidence in default models
	Eur.Comm. (Forecast XI)	B/S	"Economic standstill forecast in the wake of financial crisis ... which deepened and broadened rapidly"

For the sources cf. the list of References; as to the chronology, publications are listed according to the date of the first published version. When known, institutional affiliations are indicated next to names of non-academic authors.
Roman numerals in brackets refer to months of the year. For the abbreviation "Bez.09" next to an author's name read: "as quoted by Bezemer 2009".

Gunther Tichy*

Why did policy ignore the harbingers of the crisis?

Recent studies emphasised that financial crises are recurrent phenomena with obvious similarities (Bordo et al. 2001) and they are occurring with increasing frequency (Reinhart and Rogoff 2008). The likelihood of a financial crisis increases once capital markets have been liberalised (Caprio and Klingebiel 1997; Demirgüç-Kunt and Detragiache 1998) as a consequence of inadequate regulation and a lack of supervision. Capital flow bonanzas und large sustained current account deficits increase the likelihood of a financial crisis (Reinhart und Rogoff 2008, 26). The growth of real credit to households has also been found as a typical concomitant phenomenon (Kaminsky and Reinhart 1999). The constellation in 2005 could insofar have been regarded as a crisis waiting to happen. In fact Tichy (2010) found about one hundred studies pointing towards the untenable nature of the financial markets' design and development at that time. Not one of these studies, however, foresaw the depth and the global dimension of the recent crisis. This was due to two elements specific to this crisis: Firstly, it was not one single misalignment that provoked it but the concurrence of several ones. Secondly, it was triggered by surprise occurrence. This latter element has been found as typical of severe financial crises (Caballero and Kurlat 2009), and it is an outstandingly important element since a surprise is by definition an unpredictable factor.

Even if the depth and global dimension of the crisis could not have been foreseen, the warnings from theoretical and empirical studies were clear enough to call for policy action to prevent a crisis. But the warnings were ignored, in many cases by academia and fully by policy makers. This is all the more amazing as monetary authorities publish semi-annual Stability Reports, designed to investigate any impending risks. Why was there a benign neglect of the warnings? Did central banks and regulators fail to recognise the risks and did they ignore the relevant literature? Or did they recognise the risks, but considered them to be minor and trusted the market to solve the problems? Or, was it a communication problem between the staff recognising the problems and the board brushing them aside? Or, was it a problem of regulatory capture by powerful lobbies? A careful analysis of the publications by the monetary authorities suggests that the monetary authorities' experts analysed the risk factors more or less correctly, but vastly underestimated the probability that they would actually come to pass. Without inside information it is not easy to find out whether this was due to optimism, insufficient analysis, or an endeavour to calm the public. Some hints towards the latter could be found in the fact that the Annual Reports of the central banks downplay the risks even more than their Stability Reports and that the central banks are in general more cautious than the Bank for International Settlements or the International Monetary Fund.

Following a short description of the data basis, the next section will analyse the risks detected by the monetary authorities. Section three compares the risks inspected by the monetary authorities with those treated by the more academic studies. Section four asks whether the authorities detected the risks early enough to potentially ward them off, while section five speculates about the causes of the monetary authorities' benign neglect of the threatening risks.

* I am grateful for helpful comments by F. Hahn, M. Knell and G. Rünstler. The views expressed herein and any remaining errors are solely my responsibility.

1. The sources

This study is based on a careful analysis of the publications of the following monetary authorities in the period preceding the current crisis, specifically for the period 2005 to 2007: The Annual Reports of the European Central Bank (ECBY), the Bank of England (BoEY), the Board of Governors of the Federal Reserve System (FEDY), the Bank for International Settlements (BISY) and the International Monetary Fund (IMFY). The most information on financial-market risk could be found in the Annual Report of the BIS and the bi-annual Stability Reports of the European Central Bank (ECBSR),[2] the Bank of England (BoESR) and the International Monetary Fund (IMFSR). The Annual Reports of the FED and the BoE contained very little information on risks within the financial system, so that they were substituted by the Federal Reserve Board's "Monetary Policy Report[s] submitted to the Congress" (FED) and BoESR respectively. Table 1 gives a compact overview over the number of risks examined in the respective sources. The risks are counted per report, so that the same risk is deliberately counted twice, if the same authority refers to it in two reports of the same or another year. The reason is that if a specific risk is emphasised year after year by the same institution, it is apparently considered important.

Table 1: Number of risks stated

	Number of risks
Annual Reports	
European Central Bank (ECBY)	5
Bank of England (BoEY)	–
Board of Governors of the Federal Reserve System (FEDY)	–
Bank for International Settlements (BISY)	19
International Monetary Fund (IMFY)	2
Stability Reports	
European Central Bank (ECBSR)	21
Bank of England (BoESR)	16
International Monetary Fund (IMFSR)	15
Monetary Policy Report, submitted to the Congress (FED)	2

As can be seen from Table 1, Annual Reports are more close-lipped about risks than the Stability Reports which are addressed to a more restricted audience; BIS appears to be an exception, but it does not publish separate Stability Reports and it addresses a more restricted audience as well.

2. Risks debated by the monetary authorities

The evidence clearly shows that the monetary authorities do recognise risks. The question is which are the risks of which they are most aware, i. e. which specific risks do the reports mention most often during the emergence of the crisis? As Table 2 indicates it is not actually, as could have been expected with the help of hindsight, asset bubbles or the bundling of subprime mortgages, or the overextended leverage of deregulated financial institutions, but global imbalances which are mentioned most frequently.[3]

[2] As ECBSR is published in December (and June), the December-2004 report has been included.

[3] Table 2 neglects – as almost all reports of monetary authorities and academia – the interdependence of risks. For instance, behaviour towards risks is to some extent a result of over-optimism, and the credit expansion to US households is closely related to US monetary policy and global imbalances. This paper does not aim at discussing these relationships but takes a descriptive approach in analysing the wordings used in the various reports.

2.1 Macro-imbalances

Already in December 2004 the European Central Bank argued that "[l]arge and growing US current account deficits have generally been perceived as posing a significant risk for global financial stability, at least since 2000", and "[i]f the recent widening of global imbalances is not corrected over the medium term, important risks would remain" (ECBSR 12/04, 9f). The BISY (6/05, 103) emphasised half a year later the impact of "reserve accumulation and the 'Asian bid'". For Bernanke (2005) these Asian surpluses and increased savings in Europe create the global imbalance of the "savings glut". In 2006 the ECB affirmed the order of risks: "The greatest medium-term risk for global financial stability continues to be the possibility of an abrupt unwinding of global imbalances, especially because these imbalances have widened further. While the likelihood of this occurring still appears small, the materialisation of such an event would represent a challenging test of the risk management systems and loss absorption capacities of financial institutions" (ECBSR 6/06, 16). All in all, global imbalances are mentioned 12 times as significant risks in the reports and make up 15 % of all references, half of them stemming from the ECB.

Table 2: Character of risks stated by monetary authorities

	ECBY	ECBSR	BoESR	IMFY	IMFSR	BISY	FED	Σ
Macro-imbalances Global imbalances	06,07	04,05,06,06	04,06	05,06	06	05	–	12
Globalisation	–	04	–	–	–	06	–	2
Financial innovation and behaviour towards risk Financial innovation	07	04	06	–	05,05,07	05,06,07	–	9
Bubble/household behaviour	06	05,07	04,06	–	07	06	06,07	9
Repricing	–	04,04,05	06	–	05,05	06	–	7
Increased risk taking	–	04	04,05	–	–	05,07	–	5
Shift of risk	–	07	05	–	07	05,07	–	5
Quest for yield	–	04	05	–	05	05	–	4
Control problems	–	–	07	–	05	06	–	3
Hedge funds	06	04,06	05	–	–	07	–	5
Monetary policy Monetary policy	–	–	–	–	07	06,06,07	–	4
Liquidity	–	07	–	–	05,06	–	–	3
Over-optimism Combination of risks	–	07	06,07	–	05	–	–	4
Surprise	–	07,07		–	05	–	–	3
Over-optimism	–	–	05	–	–	07	–	2
Other	–	07	07	–	–	05	–	3
Σ	5	21	16	2	15	19	2	80

The numbers indicate the year in which the report was published

Very similar to the risks resulting from global imbalances are the risks arising from *globalisation.* Disturbances in the US market are reckoned to spill over quickly into Europe: "In the event of an unexpected disruption in the US Treasury market, it is unlikely that the euro area financial system would be left unperturbed" (ECBSR 12/04, 11). Developments in the US on the other hand are frequently of foreign origin: "Strong foreign demand for US securities is another reason frequently cited for declining term premia in the United States. Foreign governments and central banks – particularly from Asia – have continued to channel funds into US Treasuries and other US quasi-government securities, largely as a result of intervention in the foreign exchange markets" (BIS 6/06, 103). Global imbalances and globalisation together account for 18 % of all perceived risks.

2.2 Financial innovation and behaviour towards risks

Risks resulting from *financial innovation* directly are perceived and recorded nine times, two thirds of them by the international organisations IMF and BIS. "An increasingly relevant contributor to this liquidity risk is the recent proliferation of complex and leveraged financial instruments, including credit derivatives and structured products such as collateralized debt obligations (CDOs). While secondary trading for these products exists, these instruments still rely on quantitative models for relative value assessment, investment decisions, and pricing. Therefore, there is a risk that models that are overly similar in their construction could cause investors to rush to exit at the same time, leading to market liquidity shortages" (IMFSR 4/05, 3).

Risk evaluators in the IMF nevertheless calm themselves by believing in the risk-diversification model of financial innovation: "Demographic changes and ensuing pension reforms increase the size and importance of institutional investors such as pension funds and life insurance companies relative to more short-term-oriented investors. To the extent that these long-term institutional investors need to match their assets to long term liabilities, their corresponding asset liability management has shown a strong commitment to strategic asset allocation; such allocation is largely guided by long term fundamentals as opposed to day-to-day noise in the markets. This type of investor is usually very large and can, by definition, move markets, especially if the markets are small and narrow. In addition, institutional investors' reallocations are typically infrequent and implemented at a rather deliberate speed. In short, the fast growth of assets under management of this type of investor will probably have a stabilizing effect on financial markets" (IMFSR 9/05, 4).[4] The Bank for International Settlements is more sceptical in this respect, observing that "possible worry, linked to the 'originate and distribute' strategy, is that originators might be stuck with a warehouse of depreciating assets in turbulent times" (BISY 6/07, 144f) and that "[m]uch of the risk is embodied in various forms of asset-backed securities of growing complexity and opacity" (BISY 6/07, 145). The central banks recognise the risks of financial innovation, if at all, seldom and rather late. Even the terms denominating specific financial innovations are infrequently used, and specific glossaries do not appear in the reports before 2007.

The risks emerging from asset bubbles, especially *house-price bubbles and household behaviour* are mentioned nine times in the reports surveyed, much less than would have been expected given the evidence from academic studies or public debate. Interestingly the reports are less concerned with bubbles but more with household debt: "Current elevated levels of household expenditure in countries like the United States are not sustainable" (BISY 6/06, 5); and: "Within the euro area, the substantial increase in household sector indebtedness together with signs of vulnerability in some housing markets adds to the credit risk facing euro area banks in the short to medium term" (ECBSR 12/07, 18). In contrast to household debt, the reports rarely mention house-price risks; ECBY (4/06,

[4] That the IMF considers an institutional setup of very large investors on small and narrow markets which can, by definition, move markets, as stabilising is in any case surprising.

118) is the only European reference, saying that "[i]n addition, household balance sheets remain vulnerable to the possibility of corrections in house prices in some countries". Even the FED appeared not to be overly concerned with the house-price bubble in 2006: "Some of the uncertainty is centred on the prospects for the housing sector. On the one hand, some observers believe that home values have moved above levels that can be supported by fundamentals and that some realignment is warranted. Such a realignment – if abrupt – could materially sap household wealth and confidence and, in turn, depress consumer spending" (FED 6/06, section 1). A year later, however, the risks had become more visible to the FED (6/07, part 1): "If home values were to depreciate sharply, the resulting erosion of household wealth could impose appreciable restraint on consumer spending"; note: solely on US consumer spending, not even on US demand in general.

Economists would probably tend to subsume the risk of *repricing asset values* (7 observations) under the heading "bubbles" as well. The risk evaluations of the monetary authorities typically subsume them under the heading "search for yield": "To the extent that this search for yield took asset prices above intrinsic values in some corporate, emerging economy debt and other securities markets, vulnerabilities to a reappraisal and re-pricing of risk may be present" warned ECBSR (12/04, 10) already at the end of 2004. The IMF worried that this "general reassessment of risk appetite of large investors and intermediaries, due to a worsening of the general economic and financial situation, could have knock-on effects for related asset classes due to relative value considerations" (IMFSR 4/05, 2). Financial markets were left more "vulnerable to global liquidity conditions and unexpected credit events. A disorderly correction could potentially disrupt the intermediation of funds through global capital markets, which would have implications for the euro area. Moreover, some euro area financial institutions, including banks, would likely endure losses – at least in the short term – from any upturn in long-term interest rates" (ECBSR 6/05, 14).

The quest for yield (mentioned four times in the reports) and *increased risk taking* (five times) are mainly observed by the Bank for International Settlements, and the Bank of England. BoE (12/05, 9) "noted the continuing accumulation of debt by many borrowers and the aggressive 'search for yield' across financial markets. That has fuelled a rapid increase in highly leveraged financial products – a trend which, if anything, has intensified since June [2005]. The relaxation of lending criteria in some markets and increased appetite for potentially illiquid instruments suggest that financial discipline may also have weakened somewhat. Previous experience suggests that such developments could herald future problems if assessments of risk were to change sharply." And "[t]he continued 'search for yield' could be leading some investors to underestimate risk" (BoE 12/05, 10). As a consequence BIS observed "overstretched corporate and household balance sheets" (BISY 6/05, 6), a "growing willingness on the part of virtually all investors, including pension and mutual funds, to take on more risk as a way of raising returns" (BISY 6/07, 9), and a "trend towards higher risk-taking ... in the investment banking sector" (BISY 6/05, 133). "Why this appetite for risk? ... [BIS refers to] relatively low risk-free rates, increased competition among providers of funding" (BISY 6/07, 9), and added that "[t]here seems to be a natural tendency in markets for past successes to lead to more risk-taking, more leverage, more funding, higher prices, more collateral and, in turn, more risk-taking" (BISY 6/07, 144). This, of course, was a consequence of what was widely felt as the Great Moderation, the NICE(st) – non-inflationary, continuously expanding – situation for about a decade.

According to monetary authorities' reports, further risks could result from a *shift of risk* to households (BISY 6/05, 133) or "to other parts of the financial system. Greater emphasis on the 'originate and distribute' business model by banks has been possible in a relatively benign credit market environment. However, there are uncertainties about how all of the counterparties in this process would be collectively affected if the CRT [credit risk transfer] markets were to be subjected to severe stress, possibly triggered by an adverse turn in the credit cycle" (ECBSR 6/07, 15). Contrary to the promises of its innovators, the credit-risk-transfer model need not reduce the banks' risks: "Financial innovation and macroeconomic stability do not necessarily mean, however, that the financial system has become intrinsically less risky. Although banks have transferred some risks to other investors, they often retain residual exposures and have additional counterparty exposures. They could also retain indirect exposures if they are extending finance to purchasers of the transferred risk. Furthermore, banks might be holding risky assets in preparation for subsequent securitisation and could face significant losses if asset prices moved abruptly. Given strong competitive conditions and greater demand from end-investors for risky assets and bespoke financial products, financial intermediaries have sometimes taken on more exposures that may be difficult to hedge in wholesale markets" (BoESR 12/05, 10).

Some risk reports hold that these uncertainties are amplified by *control problems.* BIS mentions "frequent shortcomings in the supporting legal documentation and to other operational risks" (BISY 6/06, 10) and that "[u]nanticipated losses could also arise from shortcomings in risk management" (BISY 6/06, 116). The Stability Report of the Bank of England adds that "vulnerabilities may arise if some firms in the financial sector pay inadequate attention to operational controls in the present environment. For example, the confirmation and assignment backlogs in structured credit markets raise the prospect of settlements problems that could complicate risk management should a major risk crystallise" (BoESR 12/05, 11).

A gloomy view is taken by the monetary authorities with regard to *hedge funds.* "There has also been growing unease about the extent of CRT outside the banking system, especially concerning the extent to which hedge funds may have taken on greater credit risk exposure. Again, this is not so much because of doubts about the risk management capacities of hedge funds, which are often quite advanced, but because very little is known about how CRT markets would function under stressed conditions" (ECBSR 12/06, 15–16). "Hedge funds might be most exposed, since many have tended to specialise in purchases of the riskiest sorts of these instruments, and their inherent leverage can in consequence be very high" (BISY 6/07, 145). The European Central Bank correctly recognised the close relationship of banks and hedge funds and concluded in the typical overcautious way: "Banks with links to hedge funds may also be indirectly exposed to market risks" (ECBSR 12/04, 13), and "it cannot be ruled out that, should credit markets endure further volatility, banks could be exposed to future losses from their activities with hedge funds" (ECBY 4/06, 118–19).

2.3 A surprising result as to monetary policy

Interestingly, and in contrast to academic studies, central banks did not consider (expansive) *monetary policy* as an impending risk. Only BIS and the IMF did so. BIS regarded the financial market problems as manifestations of the extended period of easy credit conditions: "This combination of relatively accommodative monetary policy and a substantial appetite for portfolio investments – purchases by the private sector of emerging market securities, and even greater purchases by reserve managers of bonds issued by the major industrial economies – seems to have put downward pressure on term premia everywhere" (BISY 6/06, 8), and it suspected that it "could eventually lead to future inflation, or financial imbalances, or both" (BISY 6/06, 10). The IMF, on the other hand, identified a *liquidity risk* already in 2005: "The question of a liquidity shortage as a potential amplifier for market price shocks is still one of the major 'blind spots' in our financial market landscape. The interactions of liquidity risk and other potential amplifiers of market shocks with changes in global capital flows will have to be at the forefront of all future effort to further improve the global financial architecture" (IMFSR 4/05, 3). This potential risk is insofar interesting as both the IMF and BIS felt uneasy as regarded the *high* level of *actual* liquidity resulting from an expansive monetary policy: "Low interest rates and healthy corporate balance sheets have spurred an increase in private equity buyouts. This has led to a substantial rise in leverage in the acquired firms, potentially making such firms more vulnerable to economic shocks. The increased use of leveraged loans as part of financing also poses risks to some intermediaries that provide bridge financing to leveraged-buyout transactions" (IMFSR 4/07, ix), "[a]nd it remained unclear what firms intended to do with the substantial amount of cash they have accumulated in recent years: invest it in profitable projects or return it to shareholders" (BISY 6/06, 115).

2.4 Over-optimism

A major risk exposure is implied as a result of the *combination of several vulnerabilities,* and this is in fact mentioned four times by the monetary authorities. Already in 2005 the IMF wrote that "[t]he combination of low risk premiums, complacency, and untested elements of risk management systems dealing with complex financial instruments could ultimately become hazardous to financial markets" (IMFSR 4/05, 1). The British Central Bank observed: "When gauging the future resilience of the UK financial system, it is important also to consider what would happen if several vulnerabilities crystallised in combination. The *Report* discusses two extreme but plausible scenarios: (•) A sharp turn in the credit cycle and (•) a substantial further fall in asset prices" (BoE 7/06, 11), while ECBSR (6/07, 15) added that "some asset price valuations could prove vulnerable to several potential adverse disturbances, especially if they were to materialise simultaneously." After the Bear-Sterns calamities in June 2007 the Bank of England analysed: "Most of the individual ingredients of recent stress in the UK financial sector had been highlighted in advance, including by the Bank in previous Reports – for example, the impact of the search for yield and risk transfer markets on credit risk assessment standards and the risks to those financial institutions with a growing dependency on wholesale funding markets of impaired market liquidity. But few had predicted that these ingredients would combine in such a way and with such force" (BoE 10/07, 9).

Most astonishing are three propositions in the reports indicating a risk exposure resulting from a shock, or in the terminology of modern theory: a *surprise.* Already in April 2005 the International Monetary Fund (IMFSR 4/05, 1) indicated that there was the likelihood of a shock in a period of complacency: "If history is any guide, the single most important risk factor for financial markets in good times is complacency. ... The combination of low risk premiums, complacency, and untested elements of risk management systems dealing with complex financial instruments could ultimately become hazardous to financial markets. ... At present, it is not easy to see which single event could possibly trigger a sharp and abrupt reversal of this positive assessment. However, because we are more advanced in the economic profit and credit cycles, disappointments or negative surprises are more likely to occur. Possibly, a combination or correlation of several less spectacular events might cause markets to reverse their course, and create a less hospitable environment for investors and borrowers who have become accustomed to low rates." In June 2007, still before the Bear-Sterns shock, the European Central Bank was concerned that "several of the previously identified main potential sources of risk and vulnerability have remained and some have grown in the past six months. Against this background, low-probability but plausible and challenging risk scenarios for financial systems could be triggered by adverse disturbances which resulted in unexpected changes in global market liquidity conditions or by unanticipated credit events" (ECBSR 6/07, 15). After the first shock in the summer of 2007 the bank analysed that "the most probable outcome seemed to be that the effects of the shock would be limited. However, the effects on financial systems were amplified considerably for two main reasons. First, several vulnerabilities – many of which had been identified previously in this Review and elsewhere – arising from the ways in which risks were assessed, valued and distributed within financial systems where the 'originate and distribute' banking model has increasingly taken hold were brought to light. Second, these vulnerabilities combined in unanticipated ways, causing risks that some large banking groups in several mature economies had seemingly transferred off their balance sheets to unexpectedly flow back onto them" (ECBSR 12/07, 11).

The seven statements dealing with the risk resulting from a combination of several vulnerabilities and the risk of a surprising shock are highly relevant for two reasons: First, because hindsight reveals that these were in fact the dominating causes of the present crisis (Hellwig 2008; Acemoglu 2009; BISY 2008; BISY 2009), and second, because modern theory emphasises that *severe* financial crises result from a combination of a negative surprise, an excessive concentration of aggregate risks and a slow policy reaction (Caballero and Kurlat 2009).

Concerning the remaining assessments of risks by the monetary authorities, two statements refer to *over-optimism.* "Current conditions may have generated a degree of over-optimism about the underlying risk of some financial products", the Bank of England (BoE 12/05, 12) analysed already in 2005, and the Bank for International Settlements added that the "perception that the risks involved had in fact diminished, given a more benign macroeconomic environment" (BISY 6/07, 9). Three other statements concerned *various items:* BISY (6/05, 6) suspected a "recurrence of credit, asset price and investment booms and busts" and the central banks saw structural risks: "The structure of institutions' balance sheets and, in particular, their funding is more fragile than previously. And ongoing uncertainties about the valuation and location of exposures means that financial market expectations are sensitive to further shocks" (BoE 10/07, 13). The European Central Bank (ECBSR 6/07, 15) felt "growing unease about rapid releveraging in some parts of the corporate sector – especially concerning LBOs."

In summary, the survey of the monetary authorities' risk assessment shows at least four important results. First, that the authorities – at least collectively – were aware of all the important risks, but, as will be documented below, they grossly underestimated their probability. Second, the Stability Reports addressing professional readers are much more explicit about risks than the more widely distributed annual reports. Third, that the central banks do not mention any risks resulting from over-expansive monetary policy. Not even the rather restrictive European central banks refer to the over-expansive US policy, while the IMF and BIS definitely do. The fourth important result addresses a major flaw. Almost all the risks assessed by the monetary authorities address exclusively the financial sector. The problems which the real sector faces if the risks identified actually come to rise, are completely neglected, with the unique exception of the risk of inflation (BISY 6/06, 10; IMFSR 9/06).

3. Risk appraisal: monetary authorities versus 'academia'

Contrary to frequent current perceptions (see e. g. Colander et al 2009; dissenting e. g. Kirchgässner 2009) the instability of the financial system in the years before the crisis developed in 2007, was certainly discussed: Tichy (2010) assembled dozens of theoretical and empirical studies from 'academia' (including a few from financial journalists and practitioners[5]) discussing important instabilities with the potential to trigger a break in economic development, even if the studies did not predict a severe worldwide crisis. To what extent did the risks assessed by the monetary authorities resemble those emphasised by 'academia'?

Due to the different weight given to the intrinsic characteristics of risks by the two groups, the classifications differ. In order to make the classifications in this study comparable to the one in Tichy (2010) the following adjustments were made: Bubble/Household Behaviour and Repricing (as in Table 2) were aggregated to "Bubbles", Financial Innovation and Hedge Funds to "Financial Innova-

[5] This is why the term 'academia' is put in quotes.

tion", Control Problems were subsumed under "Behaviour of Financial Institutions", Global Imbalances and Globalisation under "Macro-imbalances", Monetary Policy and Liquidity were aggregated to "Monetary Policy", and a new category "Behaviour Towards Risk" was introduced.

The most important difference between the two groups is the greater importance that 'academic' literature assigns to the risks of *Bubbles, Regulation,* and *Behaviour of Banks,* especially to the rise of a "shadow financial system". Two explanations may exist for this different assessment. In economic theory the existence and cause of bubbles on the one hand, and of market failures calling for regulation on the other, represent a major challenge. Financial markets are frequently regarded as the least imperfect markets, reacting quickly and efficiently. More than half of all risks, detected by 'academia', refer to bubbles and regulation, compared to a mere fifth by the monetary authorities. The benign neglect of these types of risks by the authorities may be due to several preoccupations: First, an articulate conviction that bubbles cannot be distinguished from normal market behaviour (Assenmacher-Wesche and Gerlach 2010). Second, the conviction that risks in general are unlikely to actually occur engenders little demand for regulation. Policy makers forcefully deregulated financial markets in an endeavour to improve their effectiveness. Quite contrary to this hypothesis the 'academic' studies actually pinpoint *Deregulation* as one of the dominating causes of the crisis. Specifically the formation of a shadow financial system, strongly emphasised by 'academia', is almost completely ignored in the monetary authorities' risk assessments. Amongst the monetary authorities the central banks see more risks from *Bubbles* than the IMF and BIS. This may be due to selfish attitudes. Central banks tend to shift the problematic risk-generating attitudes to *Global Imbalances* and to *Household Behaviour,* both outside their control, while the IMF and BIS emphasise central banks' policy.

Table 3: Composition of risks

	IMF and BIS		Central Banks		Monetary authorities		'Academia'	
	number	%	number	%	number	%	number	%
Bubbles	5	*14*	11	*25*	16	*20*	38	*40*
Regulation	–	–	–	–	–	–	16	*17*
Financial innovation	7	*19*	7	*16*	14	*18*	16	*17*
Behaviour of fin. institutions	2	*6*	1	*2*	3	*4*	16	*17*
Macro-imbalances	5	*14*	9	*20*	14	*18*	5	*5*
Surprise	1	*3*	2	*5*	3	*4*	3	*3*
Monetary policy	6	*17*	1	*2*	7	*9*	2	*2*
Behaviour towards risk	7	*19*	7	*16*	14	*18*	–	–
Other	3	*8*	6	*14*	9	*11*	–	–
	36	*100*	44	*100*	80	*100*	96	*100*

Differences due to rounding

Source: Table 2 above and Tichy 2010, Survey 2 (see p. 17)

The second major divergence pertains to *Macro-Imbalances.* For the monetary authorities macro-imbalances contain the greatest risks, while they are hardly mentioned in 'academic' risk assessments. This does not mean that the 'academic' literature is not full of concern about these imbalances, but in most cases they are not identified as a decisive causation of this crisis. The third difference may appear paradoxical at first sight: *Monetary Policy* is seen as an important risk by the IMF and BIS (6 out of 26 entries), while hardly mentioned as a cause of the crisis in 'academic' literature. Moreover, the IMF has been worried about the difference between the excessive actual liquidity (in 2005) and the potentially insufficient future liquidity (IMFSR 4/05, 3). Central banks, understandably, did not identify any risks in their policy, not even the European ones, which pursued a rather restrictive policy.

A fourth divergence in assessment between the monetary authorities and 'academia' concerns the *Behaviour towards Risk,* which is not explicitly mentioned in the 'academic' studies at all, whilst it comprises almost one fifth of the authorities' concern. The difference, however, is, to some extent, more apparent than real: Quest for Yield, increased Risk Taking and Shift of Risk, which are prominently quoted as potential sources of risks by the authorities, are hidden behind the categories Financial Innovation and Behaviour of the Financial Institutions in the risk assessments of 'academia'. Nevertheless, the different classifications indicate different points of view: For the 'academic' studies the causation runs from financial innovation to investors' behaviour, while for the monetary authorities the financial system reacted to investors' increased risk appetite with financial innovations. A fifth difference, last but not least, are the low *probabilities* allotted to the *expected risks* by the monetary authorities which are in striking contrast to the assessments in the 'academic' studies.[6]

It is somewhat startling that the academic studies dealing with the instability of the financial system are almost completely ignored by the monetary authorities.[7] If academic studies are referred to at all, it is in the "Features" sections or in boxes. An intensive examination does not take place in any one of the reports. One should not, however, forget the *published scholarly work of the top economists of the IMF and BIS.* Addressed to a scientific audience they are less reticent and address the problems more explicitly. Their research appears to be the basic cause of the superior quality of their organisations' analyses.[8] Three examples: The outstanding study of the IMF's then Chief Economist Rajan (2005), demonstrating that financial development had made the world riskier, will be discussed in section 5. Borio (2007), Head of the Monetary and Economic Department of BIS, in a similar vein indicated that "despite this [financial] revolution, some fundamental characteristics of the financial system have not changed and that these hold the key to the dynamics of financial instability". He highlighted the evaporation of market liquidity as a consequence, due to structural change and the paradoxical concurrent increased reliance on the availability of funding liquidity. White (2006), 1995–2008 Head of the Monetary and Economic Department of BIS, confronted the "more orthodox explanation" of the financial crisis with his "less orthodox" one, giving more weight to inflation reducing competition from South-East Asia, expansive monetary policy, and liberalisation of the global financial system. He discussed the crisis' possible "significant effects on output growth".

4. Did authorities detect the risks early enough?

The analysis of the published risk assessments of three important Central Banks and two international financial institutions demonstrated that all of them were well aware of the impending risks. Central banks' actions must, nevertheless, be characterised as benign neglect. One potential explanation for their repose could be a time lag, the fact that they detected the risks too late. Table 4 clearly shows that this was not the case. Specifically the IMF and BIS were critical already in 2005, and the number of risks discussed by the central banks was almost equally distributed over the years. The risk awareness of monetary authorities in 2005 was even higher than that of 'academia', though one should not forget that the warnings of 'academia' have a longer history: From the early nineties up to 2004 Tichy (2010) counted 34 statements emphasising the lack of stability and sustainability of the system.

[6] This is the main reason why different risk classifications had to be used in the studies.

[7] Partial exceptions are the IMF's Stability Reports, citing references in journals, but not necessarily the rather critical ones.

[8] This refers even more to BIS, as the IMF reports appear to be more subject to editorial revision.

Table 4: Timetable of risk detection

	IMF and BIS		Central Banks		Monetary authorities		'Academia'	
	number	%	number	%	number	%	number	%
2005	17	*47*	16	*36*	33	*41*	5	*13*
2006	10	*28*	14	*32*	24	*30*	19	*49*
2007	9	*25*	14	*32*	23	*29*	15	*38*
	36	*100*	44	*100*	80	*100*	39	*100*

Differences due to rounding
Source: Table 2 above and Tichy 2010, Survey 2 (see p. 17)

The bare numbers, however, reveal one potential cause of the authorities' hesitancy to act in time. They appear to have been fooled by a temporary improvement. In 2006 the financial system appeared healthier to them and more able to handle external shocks than before. In the words of the IMF (IMFSR 4/06, 1): "The positive assessment contained in the September 2005 GFSR [Global Financial Stability Report] that 'the global financial system has yet again gathered strength and resilience' has been validated by recent developments. However, a number of cyclical challenges appear to be gathering on the horizon, which necessitates a more nuanced view of the financial outlook for the remainder of 2006 and beyond. As this report has argued earlier, globalization and financial innovations have advanced the scope for capital markets to channel credit to various users in the economy. In particular, the emergence of numerous, and often very large, institutional investors and the rapid growth of credit risk transfer instruments have enabled banks to manage their credit risk more actively and to outsource the warehousing of credit risk to a diverse range of investors." This misleading optimistic view was shared by the ECB, which stated in December 2005 (ECBSR 12/05, 9): "The strength and resilience of the euro area financial system has further improved over the past six months, contributing to a positive outlook for financial stability", and was reiterated half a year later: "The strength and resilience of the euro area financial system continued improving in the six months following the finalisation of the December 2005 Financial Stability Review (FSR). However, during these six months financial imbalances also continued expanding, primarily at the global level, but also in the euro area. Although shock-absorption capacities have been improving, the fact that risks and vulnerabilities have remained and that some have grown and increased further means that there is no room for complacency: the financial stability outlook still rests upon a delicate balance" (ECBSR 6/06, 10).

Even in April 2007 the economic situation still appeared 'non-threatening' to the monetary authorities. Financial market stability continued to be underpinned by favourable global prospects. Despite bouts of nervousness in May/June 2006 and again in February/March 2007, market volatility generally remained at low levels (IMFY 4/07, 12). The IMF's Stability Report was somewhat less pleased with the overall economic situation. "Favorable global economic prospects, particularly strong momentum in the euro area and in emerging markets led by China and India, continue to serve as a strong foundation for global financial stability. However, some market developments warrant attention, as underlying financial risks and conditions have shifted since the September 2006 Global Financial Stability Report" (IMFSR 4/07, ix). Looking back, BIS analysed that "[t]he performance of the global economy over the last few years has been extraordinary, and this includes the period April 2006 to May 2007, ... real growth has been maintained, ... inflation levels have generally remained subdued,... real interest rates and risk premia of all sorts have remained uncharacteristically low,... record global trade imbalances have thus far been easily financed and exchange rates have been generally quite stable. ... [T]he combination of developments is so extraordinary that it must raise questions about the source and, closely related, the sustainability of all this good fortune" (BISY 6/07, 3). But, the BIS continued in its analysis: "However, as the period under review wore on, concerns began to mount that the US economy might slow excessively, with potential implications for growth elsewhere. In the United States, consumption spending began to falter only after very rapid gains. While some deceleration was then to be expected, the fact that income and employment growth had not kept up, and that much consumption was financed through debt and lower saving, probably also played a role. A particular concern was a possible link with the US housing cycle, which began to turn down sharply in early 2006" (BISY 6/07, 5).

The temporary, at least presumed stabilisation in 2006 was a "[s]urprise, because a whole set of imbalances, which some thought had clear potential to eventually threaten that good performance, had still not done so" (BISY 6/06, 3). The surprise that this (positive) surprise of 2006 had been wrong appears to have been one of the most important reasons for the psychic trauma sparked by the negative surprise shocks from mid 2007 onwards.[9] The most important of these surprises was, of course, that of practitioners (and regulators) when in summer 2007 they became aware of the enormous leverage of financial institutions and the firesale-induced crack-up of markets, which forced the central banks to extraordinary measures to re-establish order in the interbank market.

5. Why did monetary authorities not react to repel the identified risks?

It is true that a *severe* financial crisis cannot be predicted, due to one of its inherent characteristics, namely the element of surprise and the non-linear and variable interaction of numerous components. However, even if the monetary authorities could not predict the depth and the global level of the crisis, surely the risks they themselves had specified in their publications as looming should have forced them to react. Why did they twiddle their thumbs? Six hypotheses are conceivable: Authorities' erroneous interpretation of the development in 2006, the popular laisser-faire fallacy of self-regulating financial markets, authorities' notions about the impact of monetary instruments, communication problems between the presidents of the monetary authorities and the (scientific) staff, regulatory capture, and last but not least the perception of risk assessment as an intellectual game rather than an analysis of reality and a basis for action.

5.1 Erroneous interpretation and laisser-faire ideology

The monetary *authorities' erroneous interpretation* of the development in 2006 may have been one of the reasons why they underestimated the risks. It does, though, not explain the continuous benign neglect of the risks in 2007 and to some extent even in 2008. Furthermore this erroneous interpretation appears more as a consequence of wishful thinking than of careful analysis. The 'academic' assessments became even more pressing in 2006 (Tichy 2010, table 2) and insofar proved superior as has now become apparent.

Another cause of benign neglect may have been the *laisser-faire ideology of self-regulating markets* and a general hesitation to disturb their efficiency. President Bush was quite clear on this subject. Even after the Bear-Sterns troubles, on Aug. 8, 2007, he "struck a reassuring tone ... about recent turbulence on Wall Street, saying he believes the markets will work their way through safely and achieve a 'soft landing'" (S.C. Bush 2007).

The monetary authorities' ideological position is less easy to document, as their policy on providing information is rather cautious (Geraats 2007), and they express themselves less explicitly in this

[9] The first shock was the Bear-Sterns disaster in August 2007, the second one the refusal to bail out Lehman Brothers in September 2008, the third the realisation of the enormous leverage and the sheer quantity of CDOs outstanding, and the fourth the crack-up of the markets.

regard. Governor Greenspan (2005, 8), nevertheless, clearly stated his position that "[t]he more flexible an economy, the greater its ability to self-correct in response to inevitable, often unanticipated disturbances" and affirmed his view of the impotence of monetary policy to fight markets: "Such data suggest that nothing short of a sharp increase in short-term rates that engenders a significant economic retrenchment is sufficient to check a nascent bubble. The notion that a well-timed incremental tightening could have been calibrated to prevent the late 1990s bubble is almost surely an illusion. Instead, we noted in the previously cited mid-1999 congressional testimony the need to focus on policies 'to mitigate the fallout when it occurs and, hopefully, ease the transition to the next expansion'. It seems reasonable to generalize from our recent experience that no low-risk, low-cost, incremental monetary tightening exists that can reliably deflate a bubble. But is there some policy that can at least limit the size of a bubble and, hence, its destructive fallout? From the evidence to date, the answer appears to be no" (Greenspan 2002).[10] ECB-President Trichet (2005, 532–33), three years later, accepted, that "[l]ong-term expectations, thus, may overreact to a shock. They may drift endogenously reflecting the impact that the unprecedented disturbance exerts on agents' own reassessment of the key structural features of the economy. ... An aggressive policy adjustment in reaction to detected signs of expectations instability can help head off the risks one might see associated with the manifestations of such a phenomenon". But he shied away from the consequences: "However, any unexpected and possibly unprecedented action that the central bank takes in response to these risks might disorient the market. ... By maintaining a steadier posture the central bank embracing this policy views its role as that of a light house ... in a storm" (Trichet 2005, 533).[11] Geithner (2007), President of the Federal Reserve Bank of New York, refused to act even in 2007 "as of now ... there are few signs that the disruptions [in the subprime mortgage segment] of the credit markets will have a lasting impact on credit markets as a whole". Like Trichet, he warned about the possibility of "positive feedback dynamics".

Another piece of evidence about the position of the monetary authorities can be gained from the 2005 Symposium of the Federal Reserve Bank of Kansas City (Jackson-Hole Symposium): "The Greenspan era – Lessons for the future", devoted to the retirement of Alan Greenspan. R. Rajan, Director of Research at the IMF, disturbed the ceremony with a contribution: "Has financial development made the world riskier?" He elaborated that the growing disintermediation in the financial sector had changed managerial incentives which in turn have altered the nature of risks undertaken by the system, with some potential for distortions. "Even though there are far more participants today able to absorb risk, the financial risks that are created by the system are indeed greater" (Rajan 2005, 318). "This is why it is so critically important to get incentives right. Given the possibility of perverse incentives coming together in some states, a risk management approach to financial regulation will be important to attempt to stave these states through the judicious operation of monetary policy and through macro-prudential measures. I argue also that some thought should be given to influence incentives of financial institution managers lightly, but directly" (Rajan 2005, 360).

At first sight this looks rather similar to what Greenspan himself said in his opening remarks to this symposium about his "policy of risk management": "In this approach, a central bank needs to consider not only the future path of the economy but also the possible distribution of outcomes about that path. ... Our forecasts and, hence, policy are increasingly driven by asset price changes. ... To some

[10] This says indeed that the Fed will not intervene to burst a bubble, and that it will support a new expansion if the bubble bursts; this led to a promise of a long period of low interest rates, and necessarily induced banks' excessive leverage and risk transformation.

[11] In its monthly reports ECB (2005, 53) analysed that in fact "sometimes asset prices tend to exceed the level which corresponds to an adequate evaluation", and even dared to publish that "[b]oom-bust cycles of asset prices can hurt the whole economy" (my translation G.T.). This may be one of the few hints that the higher ranks are more resistant to adjust policy than the staff.

extent, those higher values [house prices] may be reflecting the increased flexibility and resilience of our economy. But what they perceive as newly abundant liquidity readily can disappear" (Greenspan 2005, 5–7). But the first insight is wrong. Participants "disagreed about whether financial markets had become riskier and about whether new forms of deregulation were desirable", the Vice President of the Federal Reserve Bank of Kansas concluded (Kahn 2005, xxvii), and Kohn, a member of the Federal Reserve Board, heavily posed a challenge:[12] "[T]he action of private parties to protect themselves – what chairman Greenspan has called private regulation – are generally quite effective. Government regulation risks undermining private regulation and financial stability by distorting incentives by moral hazard ... I do not share Raghu's [Rajan] nostalgia for systemic risk-implications of bank-dominated finance. ... most asset managers are employees of institutions – mutual funds families, bank holding companies – that are in the market for long haul. It is not in their interest to reach for short-run gains at the expense of long-term risk, to disguise the degree of risk they are taking for their customers, or otherwise to endanger their reputations" (Kohn 2005, 372–5). And he concluded: "In my view, such policies would result in less accurate asset pricing, and reduce public welfare on balance" (Kohn 2005, 378). Hyun Song Shin (2005, 386) from the London School of Economics admitted that Rajan touched an important problem but "throwing out the baby with the bath water... his proposal is a non-starter, at least under current circumstances". Therefore, much more pronounced than in the official documents, IMF-Research Director Rajan elaborated on the risks which began to actually emerge two years later; but his arguments were definitely rejected at this conference and didn't have any effect on policy. Even the Stability Reports ignored Rajan's paper.[13] The central banks steadfastly trusted self-correcting markets.

One should not forget, however, that even the academic community, two years later, was still divided as to the possibility and helpfulness of interventions. At the Jackson-Hole Conference in August 2007, devoted to "Housing, Housing Finance, and Monetary Policy", the contributing professors Shiller (2007) of Yale, Leamer (2007) of UCLA, Mishkin (2007) of UC San Diego and Feldstein (2007) of Harvard provided evidence of an exaggerated bubble, and called for policy action, even if they foreboded only an American recession, not a worldwide crisis. But almost all the other participants downplayed any danger: Mayer (2007), professor at Columbia, rated the price decline of houses as neither stronger nor more problematic than earlier ones. Gramlich (2007), Senior Fellow of the Urban Institute, emphasised the positive aspects of the housing boom. Ludvigson (2007), professor at NY University, saw only a limited effect even of a considerable house-price decline on private consumption, and Hamilton (2007), professor at UC San Diego, indeed argued for regulation of the mortgage market, but was against any action of monetary policy.[14] Even today (May 2010) non-standard actions of central banks, as e. g. the lengthening of maturity of refinancing operations or the exten-

[12] Rajan (2010, 3) describes the situation: "I exaggerate only a bit when I say I felt like an early Christian who had wandered into a convention of half-starved lions."

[13] The only exception is ECBSR's (12/07, pp. 164–67) chapter "Features" with the title "The impact of short term interest rates on bank credit risk taking": "Empirical evidence indicates that low short term interest rates encourage bank risk-taking. ... Despite this increased risk-taking, low short term interest rates reduce credit risk in the very short run since they reduce refinancing costs, thereby lowering the credit risk of outstanding bank loans. As the volume of outstanding bank loans is larger than that of new loans, low interest rates may make banks safer in the very short run. In the medium run, however, interest rates that are too low encourage bank risk-taking and increase credit risk in banks, thereby threatening financial stability, especially if they then return to or rise above normal levels. It is also found that banks which are less well monitored – and therefore more subject to moral hazard – take on excessive risk when interest rates are low, thus suggesting that better banking regulation and corporate governance reduce the impact of low short term interest rates on risk-taking." This, however, had not been the main objective of Rajan's provoking article.

[14] Hamilton, however, was one of the analysts predicting worse times ahead in his blog, even if the probability of recession kept changing in his assessments.

sion of the eligible collateral list, are heavily criticised inside (Freiberger 2010) and outside the monetary community (Aebersold Szalay 2010).

Ideology and ideology-enhanced interpretation of reality have to be distinguished from the third hypothesis about the authorities' benign neglect of the risks: *Authorities' notions about the impact of monetary instruments*. It is widely held that a proper setting of interest rates to achieve the inflation target will promote stabilisation of asset prices (Bernanke and Gertler 2000). This is even more relevant as central banks consider it as extremely difficult to distinguish bubbles from 'normal' market developments.

5.2 Communication problems and the perception of risk assessment as a purely intellectual game

Whether the monetary authorities failed to act because they really believed in self-correcting markets (in the absence of market externalities) and therefore underestimated the risks, or whether it was detrimental factors such as e.g. regulatory capture by powerful lobbies which over-rode the experts' warnings and thus kept the authorities from acting cannot actually be decided here. It is beyond the ability of economists, given the available information. One potential reason for inaction can, however, be excluded with certainty: *Communication problems between the president/boards of the central banks and the (scientific) staff.* This can be excluded definitely, as all the risks cited in this study are quotes from monetary authorities' published reports; and no member of staff of a monetary authority is free to publish even a single line without explicit authorisation.

The most likely reason – besides ideological preoccupations – for the monetary authorities' benign neglect of the risks, correctly diagnosed in their publications, is that they apparently considered risk assessment as an *intellectual game rather than an analysis relevant for policy.* The assessments identified all the risks that had been raised in academic literature, even the systemic ones and they identified the joint occurrence of risks and the consequences of a surprise, but they attached an extremely low probability to their actual realisation. Apart from the BIS they appear to strongly believe in the stability of the financial system: "At present, it is not easy to see which single event, short of a 'major devastating geopolitical incident or a terrorist attack' as highlighted in the September 2004 issue of the Global Financial Stability Report (GFSR), could possibly trigger a sharp and abrupt reversal of this positive assessment" (IMFSR 4/05, 1).

Most interesting in this respect is the BoE's summer 2006 report, discussing individual and joint incidence of risks. "The Bank's responsibility is not just to consider the most likely outcome but also to assess major downside risks. By their nature, these risks are likely to be low probability events in the tail of the distribution of possible outcomes. The fact that these risks are unlikely does not mean, however, they should be ignored." (BoE 7/06, 6). "In this *Report,* six main sources of vulnerability are explored. None of them is new and most are of long standing. Although these vulnerabilities are unlikely to crystallise, either individually or in combination, the consequences for the UK financial system if they did *could be material. (1) ... Far and away the most likely outcome in the near term is that none of the vulnerabilities crystallise.* Moreover, even if these vulnerabilities were to crystallise individually, they would be unlikely to erode to any significant extent the capital base of the UK banking system. (10f)... When gauging the future resilience of the UK financial system, it is important also to consider what would happen if several vulnerabilities crystallised in combination. (11)... The severe crystallisation of credit, market and liquidity risk could plainly represent a serious shock to the UK financial system. Such extreme scenarios could be sufficient to more than absorb the annual profits of the UK banking system and therefore cause some material erosion of capital. Although such an outcome is very unlikely, given its potential impact, it merits consideration in *financial firms' risk management planning*" (12, my emphasis G.T.). Relevant for "financial firms' risk management planning" only, and, even more, unlikely to erode even their "capital base" – this is far away from any effects on the real sector! Nobody could express more clearly that the analysed risks should they come about at all are considered neither as problematic nor as dangerous. In this respect monetary authorities' assessments clearly diverge from those of 'academia'. Most of the latter are pretty sure of negative consequences, even to the real sector, within a rather short period (Tichy 2010, exhibit 1). But if the analysed risks, should they come about at all, are considered neither as probable nor as dangerous by monetary authorities why should monetary policy or regulation agencies act and disturb the markets' supposed "ability to self-correct in response to inevitable, often unanticipated disturbances"?

This reaction, plausible as it may be, raises the question of the responsibility for the (undocumented) assumption of a low probability that the assessed risks would come to pass. On the one hand it could be argued that not the experts were responsible for these guesses, but the censorship of their supervisors. Three observations provide some arguments for this interpretation. Firstly, there is the wide discrepancy between the Stability Reports' careful analysis and description of the risks and the generous rejection of their probability. Secondly there is the fact that the Annual Reports of the central banks downplay the risks even more than their Stability Reports, and the fact that the central banks in general are more cautious than the Bank for International Settlements or the International Monetary Fund. Thirdly there is the fact that the economists of the IMF and BIS are less risk pacifying in their scientific work than the respective reports of their organisations.[15] Although these differences could be due to the monetary authorities' endeavour not to alarm the public, a definite conclusion cannot be drawn from the material at hand.

It should, however, be borne in mind that it is an established fact that experts tend to underestimate the risks of rare but hazardous events – nuclear and bio-technology are well known examples[16] –, while the public overestimates them (Kahneman and Tversky 1972; Jungermann and Slovic 1993). The Stability Reports resemble expert assessments as to their results, but not as to their technique. Experts estimate risks in terms of the amount of damage or loss multiplied by its probability. However, not a single assessment of the amount of damage in terms of potential losses can be found in any one of the Stability Reports, and there is no effort to seriously appraise quantitatively any probability of loss.[17] This, however, is not without cause. For complex technical systems – tight coupling of system components and their complex non-linear interaction[18] – risk assessment is extremely complicated and considered as practically impossible by most observers (Perrow 1984). Therefore, failure-avoiding strategies are recommended as being better suited to achieve the desired results than risk assessment. It goes without saying that financial systems are highly complex systems, so that the assessment of risks, if feasible at all, requires extraordinarily complex techniques to account for the tight coupling of system components and their complex interaction. Insofar it is highly questionable if the Stability Reports will ever succeed in correctly assessing the risks; a sharp-cut reduction of the system's complexity could be more promising (Tichy 2011). Insofar Rajan (2005) turned out to be on the right side in his Jackson-Hole lecture.

---

[15] They, therefore, strongly emphasise that the respective papers reflect the authors' views and not necessarily those of the International Monetary Fund, its management or its board, or of the BIS respectively.

[16] M. Prisching (personal correspondence) argues that this may be due to the experts' trust in their technical skills, their closeness to the risk, or that admitting high risks could endanger their job. Financial experts, additionally, may have been proud of their success in coping with past crises – see 2006 (see the reports cited above) or the dot.com crisis.

[17] White (2005, 13), Head of BIS's Monetary and Economic Department, is at least aware of this problem.

[18] The correlations between the risks are almost completely neglected in the Stability Reports, but this is true for the 'academic' studies as well.

Summary

An analysis of the monetary authorities' annual reports as well as stability reports for the period 2005 to 2007 clearly reveals that the central banks were well aware of the risks which caused the recent financial crisis. They, however, tended to overemphasise the risks outside their control (global imbalances and risk taking as well as households', firms' and banks' quest for yield) and to neglect those at least partially under their control (over-expansive monetary policy, deregulation and financial innovation). Even if severe financial crises cannot be foreseen, since a (naturally unpredictable) surprise is an indispensable element of their character, monetary authorities should have acted already in 2005. Academic studies and their own assessments clearly indicated an accumulation of risks. Why didn't they act? Four reasons probably came together: Monetary authorities' belief in the laisser-faire fallacy of self-regulating markets, their beliefs about the impact of monetary instruments on the economy, and their tendency to enumerate a long list of potential risks whilst assigning them an extremely low probability. This is not untypical for expert assessments. Technical experts, however, are increasingly aware that risk assessment for complex technical systems is extremely complicated if not impossible. It goes without saying that financial systems are highly complex systems so that the assessment of risks, if feasible at all, would require extraordinarily complex techniques to take into account the tight coupling of system components and their complex interaction. These instruments will not be available in the foreseeable future. As a result reducing the system's complexity appears to be the only way to reduce the probability and the severity of future financial crises.

References

Aebersold Szalay, Cl., Wenn die Politik der EZB nicht mehr richtig ankommt. Berechtigte Sorgen um den Transmissionsprozess in der Euro-Zone, *Neue Zürcher Zeitung* 1.6.2010, http://www.nzz.ch/finanzen/nachrichten/wenn_die_politik_der_ezb_nicht_mehr_richtig_ankommt

Acemoglu, D., 2009, The crisis of 2008: Structural lessons for and from economics, http://econ-www.mit.edu/files/3722.

Assenmacher-Wesche, K. and St. Gerlach (2010), "Monetary policy and financial imbalances: Facts and fiction." *Economic Policy* 25 (63), 437–482.

Bank for International Settlements (BISY), 2005, *75th Annual Report,* Basle.

Bank for International Settlements (BISY), 2006, *76th Annual Report,* Basle.

Bank for International Settlements (BISY), 2007, *77th Annual Report,* Basle.

Bank for International Settlements (BISY), 2008, *78th Annual Report,* Basle.

Bank of England (BoESR), 2005, *Financial Stability Review,* December 2005.

Bank of England (BoESR), 2006, *Financial Stability Report,* July 2006.

Bank of England (BoESR), 2007, *Financial Stability Report,* October 2007.

Bernanke, B., 2005, The global saving glut and the U.S. current account deficit, *Homer Jones Lecture, St. Louis, Missouri,* http://www.federalreserve.gov/boarddocs/speeches/2005/200503102/

Bernanke, B. and M. Gertler, 2000, Monetary Policy and Asset Price Volatility, *NBER Working Paper 7559.*

Bordo, M. et al, 2001, Is the crisis problem growing more severe?, *Economic Policy April 2001,* 51–82.

Borio, Cl., 2007, Change and constancy in the financial system: implications for financial distress and policy, *BIS Working Papers 2007.*

Bush, Scott Conroy, 2007, Wall Street will make "Soft Landing". President tries to reassure wary investors about stock market's strength, http://www.cbsnews.com/stories/2007/08/08/politics/main3147926.shtml?source=RSSattr=Business_3147926

Caballero, R.J. and P. Kurlat, 2009, The "surprising" origin and nature of financial crises: a macroeconomic policy proposal, *Jackson Hole Symposium,* http://www.ko.frb.org/home/subwebnav.cfm?level=3&theID=11441 &SubWeb=10660.

Caprio, G. and D. Klingebiel, 1997, Bank insolvency: Bad luck, bad policy, or bad banking? In B. Pleskovic and J. Stiglitz, eds, *Annual World Bank Conference on Development Economics,* Washington DC: The World Bank, 79–104.

Colander, D. et al, 2009, *The financial crisis and the systemic failure of academic economics,* 98th Dahlem Workshop.

Demirgüç-Kunt, A. and E. Detragiache, 1998, The determinants of banking crises in developing and developed countries, *IMF Staff Papers 45,* 81–109.
European Central Bank (ECBY), *Annual Report 2005,* Frankfurt
European Central Bank (ECBY), *Annual Report 2006,* Frankfurt
European Central Bank (ECBY), *Annual Report 2007,* Frankfurt
European Central Bank (ECBSR), 2004, *Financial Stability Review December,* Frankfurt
European Central Bank (ECBSR), 2005, *Financial Stability Review June,* Frankfurt
European Central Bank (ECBSR), 2005, *Financial Stability Review December,* Frankfurt
European Central Bank (ECBSR), 2006, *Financial Stability Review June,* Frankfurt
European Central Bank (ECBSR), 2006, *Financial Stability Review December,* Frankfurt
European Central Bank (ECBSR), 2007, *Financial Stability Review June,* Frankfurt
European Central Bank (ECBSR), 2007, *Financial Stability Review December,* Frankfurt
Federal Reserve Board (FED), 2006, *Monetary Policy Report submitted to the Congress on February 15, 2006, pursuant to section 2B of the Federal Reserve Act* http://www.federalreserve.gov/boarddocs/hh/2006/february/ReportSection1.htm
Federal Reserve Board (FED), 2006, *Monetary Policy Report submitted to the Congress on February 14, 2007, pursuant to section 2B of the Federal Reserve Act,* http://www.federalreserve.gov/monetarypolicy/mpr_20070214_part1 .htm
Feldstein, M., 2007, Overview and concluding remarks, *Jackson Hole Symposium,* http://www.kc.frb. org/home/subwebnav.cfm?level=3&theID=11441 &SubWeb=10660.
Freiberger, H., 2010, Bundesbank: Axel Weber Ein Falke bringt sich in Stellung, http://www.sueddeutsche.de/geld/bundesbank-axel-weber-ein-falke-bringt-sich-in-stellung-1.940011.
Geithner, T., 2007, Credit markets, innovations and their implications, *Federal Reserve Bank of Richmond, Credit Markets Symposium,* zitiert nach Spaventa 2008, 3.
Geraats, P.M., 2007, The mystique of central bank speak, *International Journal of Central Banking* 3(1), pp. 37–80.
Gramlich, E. M., 2007, Booms and busts: The case of subprime mortgages, *Jackson Hole Symposium,* http://www.kc.frb.org/home/subwebnav.cfm?level=3&theID=11441 &SubWeb=10660.
Greenspan, A., 2002, Opening remarks, Federal Reserve Bank of Kansas City, Jackson Hole Symposium Aug. 29–31, 2002, "Rethinking Stabilisation Policy" http://www.kansascityfed.org/publications/research/escp/escp-2002.cfm
Greenspan, A., 2005, Opening remarks, Jackson Hole Symposium, http://www.kansascityfed.org/publicat/sympos/2005/sym05prg.htm
Hamilton, J.D., 2007, Discussion, *Jackson Hole Symposium,* http://www.kc.frb.org/home/subwebnav.cfm?level=3&theID=11441 &SubWeb=10660.
Hellwig, M.F., 2008, The systemic risk in the financial sector, An analysis of the subprime-mortgage financial crisis, *MPI Collective Goods Reprint 2008/43.*
International Monetary Fund (IMFY), 2005, *Annual Report,* Washington.
International Monetary Fund (IMFY), 2006, *Annual Report,* Washington.
International Monetary Fund (IMFY), 2007, *Annual Report,* Washington.
International Monetary Fund (IMFSR), 2005, *Global Financial Stability Report.* Market Developments and Issues, Washington, April.
International Monetary Fund (IMFSR), 2005, *Global Financial Stability Report.* Market Developments and Issues, Washington, September.
International Monetary Fund (IMFSR), 2006, *Global Financial Stability Report.* Market Developments and Issues, Washington, April.
International Monetary Fund (IMFSR), 2006, *Global Financial Stability Report.* Market Developments and Issues, Washington, September.
International Monetary Fund (IMFSR), 2007, *Global Financial Stability Report.* Market Developments and Issues, Washington, April.
International Monetary Fund (IMFSR), 2007, *Global Financial Stability Report.* Market Developments and Issues, Washington, September.
Jungermann, H. and P. Slovic, 1993, Charakteristika individueller Risikowahrnehmung, in: W. Krohn und G. Krücken eds., *Riskante Technologien: Reflexion und Regulation,* Frankfurt, 79–100.
Kahn, G.A., 2005, Symposium introduction, *Jackson Hole Symposium,* http://www.kansascityfed.org/publicat/sympos/2005/sym05prg.htm
Kahneman, D. and A. Tversky, 1972, Subjective probability: A judgement of representativeness, *Cognitive Psychology 3,* 430–54.

Kaminsky, G.L. and C. Reinhart, 1999, The twin-crises: The causes of banking and balance of payment problems, *American Economic Review 89(3),* 473–500.

Kirchgässner, G., 2009, Die Krise der Wirtschaft: Auch eine Krise der Wirtschaftswissenschaften? *PWP 10(4),* 436–68.

Kohn, D.L., 2005, Commentary: Has financial development made the world riskier? http://www.kansascityfed.org/publicat/sympos/2005/sym05prg.htm

Leamer E., 2007, Housing is the business cycle, *Jackson Hole Symposium,* http://www.kc.frb.org/home/subwebnav.cfm?level=3&theID=11441 &SubWeb=10660.

Ludvigson, S.C., 2007, Discussion, *Jackson Hole Symposium,* http://www.kc.frb.org/home/subwebnav.cfm?level=3&theID=11441 &SubWeb=10660.

Mayer Ch.J., 2007, Commentary: Understanding recent trends in house prices and home ownership, *Jackson Hole Symposium,* http://www.kc.frb.org/home/subwebnav.cfm?level=3&theID=11441 &SubWeb=10660.

Mishkin, F.S., 2007, Housing and the monetary transmission mechanism, *Jackson Hole Symposium,* http://www.kc.frb.org/home/subwebnav.cfm?level=3&theID=11441 &SubWeb=10660.

Perrow, Ch., 1984, *Normal accidents: Living with high risk technologies,* Basic Books

Rajan, R.G., 2005, Has financial development made the world riskier? http://www.kansascityfed.org/publicat/sympos/2005/sym05prg.htm

Rajan, R.G., 2010, *Fault lines: How hidden fractures still threaten the world economy,* Princeton: Princeton UP.

Reinhart, C. and K.S. Rogoff, 2008, Banking crises: An equal opportunity menace, *NBER WP 14049.*

Shiller, R.J., 2007, Understanding recent trends in house prices and home ownership, *Jackson Hole Symposium,* http://www.kc.frb.org/home/subwebnav.cfm?level=3&theID=11441 &SubWeb=10660.

Shin, Hyun Song, 2005, Commentary: Has financial development made the world riskier? http://www.kansascityfed.org/publicat/sympos/2005/sym05prg.htm

Spaventa, L., 2008, Avoiding disorderly deleveraging, *CEPR Policy Insight 22.*

Tichy, G, 2010, War die Finanzkrise vorhersehbar? *Perspektiven der Wirtschaftspolitik* 11(4), 356–382. For English translation see p. 9ff of present publication.

Tichy, G., 2011, Reicht Bankregulierung zur Vermeidung schwerer Finanzkrisen? In: Kubon-Gilke et al., Hg., *Jahrbuch Normative und institutionelle Grundfragen der Ökonomik Band 10: Ökonomik in der Krise,* 65–91. For English translation see p. 48ff of present publication.

Trichet, J.-Cl., 2005, Monetary policy strategies: A central bank panel, http://www.kansascityfed.org/publicat/sympos/2005/sym05prg.htm

White, W.R., 2006, Procyclicality in the financial system: do we need a new macrofinancial stabilisation framework? *BIS Working Paper 193.*

Gunther Tichy

Regulation of the banking sector

Could stricter regulation of the banking business help avoid a major financial crisis?

The recent financial crisis came as a shock not only to the public, to academic economists and regulation authorities, but also to the banking profession. The tenet of "Great Moderation" had built up both confidence in the capacity of markets to absorb shocks quickly and efficiently and the conviction of being in full control of the system. The expansion of US subprime problems into a veritable global economic (not only financial) crisis came as a surprise even to those who had never been quite so sure about the inherent stability of the system. The shortcomings of theory, regulation, and politics – all of them incapable of either explaining the crisis or overcoming its effects – caused not only an extensive public discussion, but also intensified research efforts, just as in the aftermath of the Great Depression.[1] They resulted in a flood of literature that analysed not only earlier crises and the causes of the recent one but also contained a wealth of suggestions for improving both analysis and predictability of financial crises and for more efficient regulation.

In what follows I propose to analyse whether the remedies discussed at present both by theorists and practitioners in the pertinent fields could stabilize the system and help avoid severe financial crises. Section 1 considers the predictability of severe crises; for, counter to what has been made public, numerous research papers had pointed out the instability of certain elements of the system, while the stability reports of national and international monetary authorities presented painstakingly detailed analyses of the various risk components even before the crisis broke. Neither academic economists nor monetary authorities, however, were able to summarize or see in their entirety the many and various risk elements whose combination was responsible for the extent of the crisis; still less did they succeed in assessing the probabilities of those risks. Nor is there, considering the complexity of the systems, much chance that they will do so in the future. But if major financial crises are highly unlikely to become predictable, which makes their prevention improbable indeed, improving the stability of the system would seem the better strategy. Section 2 briefly reviews the causes of the recent crisis and of the instability of the system, thus providing the starting point for section 3, an analysis of the possible consequences of improved regulation for the stability of the system. It seems that the regulation of *individual* banks (i. e. microprudential regulation) could be improved; what we need, however, is the regulation of the *system* (i. e. macroprudential regulation), and instruments for that are sadly lacking; nor does there seem a serious chance of creating such instruments any time soon. Furthermore, from the regulation of technological systems we know that in general complex systems are very difficult to control; and one of the major causes of the crisis, viz. the over-supply of funds to be invested, does not lend itself to regulation

[1] See e. g. the works of Keynes (1936) or Haberler (1937) – fundamental for both theory and policy.

at all. Therefore, section 4 suggests that we should start thinking about simplifying the complex financial system and thus reducing the susceptibility of the real sector.

1. Predictability of major financial crises: experience and hopes

According to recent analyses, (even major) financial crises are not at all rare events (Reinhart and Rogoff 2008), and they also show certain similarities (Bordo et al 2001).[2] In fact, they have become more frequent ever since capital markets were liberalized: for reasons of deregulation and insufficient control (Caprio and Klingebiel 1997; Demirgüç-Kunt and Detragiache 1998). The oversupply of investment-seeking funds on "western" financial markets as well as the significant, continued disequilibria in current account balances increase the probability of financial crises (Reinhart and Rogoff 2008, p.26), while the expansion of (real estate) loans to households turned out to be a typical symptom of such crises (Kaminsky and Reinhart 1999). In view of such regularities one would not think it too difficult to predict even severe crises. And indeed, numerous elements of instability of the financial system and many potential risks had been recognized long before the crisis broke: More than eight dozens of *research papers* had stressed the present financial system's tendency to instability, had stressed that the developments on financial markets could not continue for long, while a turnabout would have costly consequences (Tichy 2010b). None of those analyses, however, foresaw the intensity and the global dimension of the pending crisis.[3] Two decisive facts had not been recognized at that time: the fact that the crisis did not have one single cause, but was brought about by several factors acting in combination, and that the crisis had been triggered by a surprise, in fact several successive surprises. Caballero and Kurlat (2009) pointed out that this was typical of major financial crises. By definition, one cannot foresee surprises – and even less the kind and extent of the panic they cause; severe financial crises are unpredictable on principle.

But not only theoretical economists studied the risks that might endanger the stability of the financial system; the *stability reports of central banks, of the International Monetary Fund (IMF), and of the Bank of International Settlements (BIS)* were concerned with this topic. They recognized and actually described all of the potential risks – most of them soon to become reality –, but by a wide margin underestimated their probability (Tichy 2010c). There were several reasons for this grave mistake. Of these, Tichy (2010c, sect.5) mentions the (financial) markets' capacity for self-regulation, a capacity typically overestimated by the financial sector; the (narrow) ideas of the monetary authorities on the effects of monetary instruments; difficulties of communication among the presidents of the monetary authorities and their (research) staff; regulatory capture by lobbyists; the tendency of experts to underestimate rare, but highly risky events,[4] and, last not least, the not at all negligible tendency of monetary authorities and banks to consider the assessment of financial risks an intellectual duty rather

---

[2] Goetzmann and Newman (2010) pointed out the similarities between the US building boom in office skyscapers in the 1920s and the recent crisis. Then, too, overinvestment was financed by securitized mortgages; when demand and prices slumped, the price of those securities dropped to a quarter of their original value.

[3] In his blog, Roubini – already in 2005 – predicted a drop of house prices by about 30%, and in 2006 considered this drop sufficient "to trigger a US-recession"; but in his opinion such a recession would be caused not by a financial crisis, but by the current account deficits of the USA vis-à-vis China, while the international diffusion mechanism would be shrinking US demand; he did not predict a break-down of the financial markets. Rajan (2005, p.317f) clearly recognized that financial innovations, liberalization and institutional change "may create a greater (albeit still small) probability of a catastrophic meltdown", but – perhaps in view of his position in the IMF – played down the probability of such a development and would say nothing about the consequences for the real sector.

[4] This would depend above all on the experts' trust in their own know-how; it is in striking contrast to the public's overestimation of the dangers of such events (Kahneman and Tversky 1972; Jungermann and Slovic 1993); nuclear and bio-technologies are well-known pertinent examples.

than an analytical tool, helpful in decisions. This last reason may have to do with staffs knowing from experience that we lack reliable methods of assessing the volume of damage and the probability of risks in complex systems – i. e. systems characterized by the rigid coupling of its components and their complex interaction, e. g. the financial system. As far as technological systems are concerned, this lack of instruments is well known and has resulted in the suggestion to look for solutions preferably in the direction of lessening risks by reducing the complexity of a system (Perrow 1984) rather than unpromising attempts to assess the risks. In view of the importance of surprises as a cause of crises, our experience with stability reports and their incapacity to assess, even ordinally, the probability of a risk occurring (to say nothing at this point of estimating the amount of damage) would suggest a strategy of complexity reduction in the financial sector as well.

Thus we arrive at our first conclusion: The analysis of financial crises of the past shows that financial crises, even severe ones, are recurrent phenomena; the recent one is not at all a singular event. Both theoretical analysis and historical experience have shown that, with some probability, one may realize in time the danger of a pending financial crisis, but not its intensity or scope. Instead of desperately searching for better methods of forecasting and risk assessment it may be better to put one's efforts into improving a system's crisis resistance and to increase its capacity to fight a crisis. This brings us to the question if and how regulation could help us achieve this. Before this can be answered we must briefly survey the causes of the recent crisis.

2. A combination of many factors caused the crisis

The vast literature shows increasing agreement that it was not *one single cause* that brought about the crisis, but the *combination of various causes.*[5] It was triggered by US subprime problems, which in turn had been created by various bubble-generating factors: low interest rates due to the lax interest policy (Taylor 2009; Maddaloni et al, forthcoming), oversupply of investment-seeking (foreign) funds, and distorted incentives.[6] A second group of causes, bunched together in the literature, are changes in the US financial system due to globalization and deregulation: *Globalization* expanded the networks of banks and increased their opacity, even for those concerned.[7] The new system was better in dealing with frequent small risks, but did worse on rare big risks (Acemoglu 2009); it destabilized because – according to network theory – the stability of closely interconnected systems decreases with their size. On the other hand, *deregulation* (Tichy 2010a, 480ff) encouraged banks dramatically to increase the leverage of their transactions and helped bring into existence a powerful shadow financial system skirting any and all regulation.

A third group of causes consists in *financial innovations* and consequent changes in the dynamics of the system. Standardization and automation of (mortgage-) loan contracts – a prerequisite for bundling credits and the sales of such bundles – changed the incentives of creditors,[8] increased the opacity of the system and contributed substantially to the enormous expansion of the shadow finan-

[5] For a survey see Adams (2009) or Rajan (2010); the subsequent passages follow i.a. Tichy (2010b), where additional literature is listed as well.

[6] Above all, mortgage debtors were not personally liable and in many cases did not even have to make a down-payment.

[7] According to Arnold (2009), in October 2007 the IMF had estimated the depreciation allowance with respect to mortgage credits at 200 bill. dollars, while in April 2009 that figure had been raised to 4000 billions.

[8] At first, subprime mortgages were written by newcomers looking for new business opportunities (Dell'Ariccia et al 2008); these people replaced the traditional screening of debtors by a simple formal credit information (Keys et al 2010; Tichy 2010b) – thus substantially increasing the credit risk; but that would not concern them as long as they bundled those credits and sold off the bundles.

cial system. Nor must we forget that opacity made for a considerable underestimation of risks, for opportunism (moral hazard) and in many cases for criminal activities.

A last group of causes is denoted as *information deficits and surprises,* often of a shock-like nature.[9] Spaventa (2008, 2) stresses the "deep information gap, affecting supervisor no less than market participants, as to the extent and location of risks: it came as a surprise that at least half of the credit risk that had been ostensibly transferred had directly or indirectly flown back to the banking system through conduits, SIVs [special investment vehicles], asset management entities, proprietary trading desks. ... It is a fact, in any case, that the extent of leverage and risk exposure of banks, hedge funds, and other investment vehicles that came to light during the crisis was far larger than anybody – market participants as well as regulators – had realized". The discovery that risks had ended up in places quite different from what theorists, regulators and practical economists had supposed, was not the only surprise, however; there were five, in fact, one positive, four of a negative kind. The positive surprise, in early 2006, was the unexpected non-appearance of serious problems that had been dreaded as an effect of international disequilibria; thus, agents convinced themselves that, after all, they were masters of the situation. Eventually this may have been one of the major causes of the psychological problems created by the negative surprises[10] since mid-2007.

Composition of risks

	Monetary authorities		"Academic" studies	
	number	%	number	%
Bubbles	16	20	38	40
Regulation	–	–	16	17
Financial innovations	14	18	16	17
Behaviour of financial institutions	3	4	16	17
Macro-imbalances	14	18	5	5
Surprises	3	4	3	3
Monetary policy	7	9	2	2
Attitudes to risk	14	18	–	–
Others	9	11	–	–
	80	100	96	100

Rounding-off differences
Source: Tichy 2010c, Table 2 (see p. 31)

Most of those causes of the crisis pointed out *ex post* in the literature had already been identified *ex ante* both in theoretical studies and in the stability reports of monetary authorities, although as isolated arguments only (Tichy 2010b; 2010c). None of the analysts had realized the destructive potential of the simultaneous interaction of at least some of those elements; they recognized and analysed individual risks and ignored the systemic perspective. Academic economists considered creation and effects of bubbles as particularly risky while monetary authorities thought macro-disequilibria and

[9] The specific problem here is this: in a panic "economic agents behave as if the likelihood of a catastrophe were much higher than it actually is (at least in the absence of the panic itself)" (Caballero and Kurlat 2009).

[10] The second surprise was the shock of the Bear-Sterns disaster in August 2007, the third the discovery, on the part of practitioners and regulators, of the enormous leverage of financial vehicles and the huge volume of outstanding CDOs, the fourth was the refusal to save Lehman Brothers in September 2008, and last not least the fifth shock was the breakdown of interbank markets caused by emergency sales of assets (see also p. 40 of this volume).

the big "risk appetite" of financial vehicles as well as of non-financial firms and of households just as risky; expansionary monetary policy was of minor importance to them.

Two causes of the crisis were rather neglected in the standard literature: the complexity of the financial system and the over-supply of investment-seeking funds on "western" financial markets. The various surprises of experts since the summer of 2007 revealed that even bankers with first-hand experience of the markets were unfamiliar both with the characteristics and with the practices of their network partners, nor did they understand the workings of the system, which had become overly complex.[11] Regulators and monetary authorities found both the network and the workings of the system even more opaque: They could enumerate the various risks, but would have been unable to assess either their probabilities or the effects of their coming to pass simultaneously (Tichy 2010c).

The second element neglected by analysts, viz. the over-supply of investment-seeking funds on "western" financial markets,[12] is related to several other factors acting as triggers of the crisis: Glaringly low interest rates caused banks and their customers, eager for higher returns, to accept higher risks; the frantic search for higher returns caused bubbles – first in the mortgage markets, subsequently on the markets for shares, gold, natural resources etc. Furthermore, the small returns (due to the low interest rates) forced banks to extend their leverage in order to offer appropriate returns to their shareholders (BIS 2010, 74).[13]

As yet, causes and effects of the oversupply of investment-seeking funds have not been thoroughly analysed; so far, attention has been focussed on the macro-disequilibrium of the USA-China current account balance. But that is only a partial view. Not only China saves excessively, i. e. produces far more than it can absorb; the same holds true for all of Southeast Asia and increasingly also for South America. These imbalances in foreign trade caused capital flows to change direction: "Capital flows uphill" (Prasad 2008), from low income to high income countries. In addition, the volume of capital flowing into "western" economies is expanded by semi-illegal and illegal capital from all parts of the world, as well as by investments on the part of the newly rich in countries with as yet underdeveloped capital markets (especially in Asia). A third cause of the over-supply of capital is to be found in the high and – partly – still increasing household savings in most of the high income countries.

As yet it is not clear how much of this over-supply is merely temporary, how much of it is the result of structural changes that become effective at least in the medium term, how much is due to "oversaving" (Bernanke 2005), and how much to an "investment draught" (Cova et al 2009). The following may be rather temporary phenomena: today's worldwide uncertainty, the South East Asian countries' dislike of indebtedness after their experience of the debt crisis of 1997/98, or the (perhaps cyclical?) investment restraint, as proved by the voluminous re-purchases of shares by the respective corporations beween 2004 and 2007 (BIS 2010, 39). What may result in structural changes, on the other hand, are the mercantilist policies of South East Asia and the extremely high savings rates of many emerging economies; these have been caused by the breakdown of social insurance and the enormous costs of education. In rich countries, too, increasing provision for old age (due to demographic factors) and increasing disparities in the distribution of income and wealth lead to an increase of savings (and thus a decline in consumer demand).

---

[11] "Each market participant and policymaker knows their own local world, but understanding all the possible linkages across these different worlds (...) is too complex. This change in paradigm, from irrelevant to critical linkages, triggers massive uncertainty" (Caballero and Kurlat 2009, 2).

[12] But see the discussion on "savings glut" (Bernanke 2005) versus "investment draught" (Cova et al 2009) and on "capital flows uphill" (Prasad 2008); cf. the summaries in Tichy (2010a, 2010c).

[13] From 1995 to 2009, the banks' return on assets was 0.6% and thus far below that from non-financial corporations (3.2%), while the 12.2% return on equity was slightly higher than with those firms (11.7%) (BIS 2010, 74).

How to remove or master which causes of the crisis? How to reduce the probability of future crises or at least attenuate their effects; how to improve the stability of the system? What could stricter regulation of banking activities contribute?

3. Would regulation of the banking sector solve the problem?

Regulation of financial markets as well as of financial institutions is indispensable, as has been shown by recent developments: Reputation-driven "private regulation" (Greenspan) of banks has been, at best, sporadic (Acemoglu 2009), and financial markets have proved to be short-sighted.[14] Already in 2005, Borio (2005, 84) had asked for a "strengthening of the macroprudential orientation of regulatory and supervisory frameworks". But at present, the discussion on reforms is above all concerned with two aspects of the matter: micro-regulation of the financial system and setting right the US-China current account deficit. As to the latter, no effective instrument has been found as yet; a sufficient appreciation of the Chinese currency is not in view – its effects being disputed, anyway (Evenett and Francois 2010). The discussion about regulating the banking sector has taken a new turn, however: After a quarter century which "mistakenly equated free markets with unregulated markets" (Acemoglu 2009) and was characterized, particularly in the USA, by massive deregulation of the financial sector, re-regulation is being debated again. But: both pertinent political discussion and practical reform efforts run in traditional grooves – "more of the same regulation" –, while still neglecting systemic aspects and the limited possibilities of government. Theoretical discussions, however, came to the conclusion[15] that regulation of the banking sector by itself will at best be a partial solution; with respect to three of the causes mentioned above, viz. macro-disequilibria, complexity of the system, and surprises, it will be ineffective. In section 4 we will come back to this point.

So far, regulation of banking activities has been restricted to the microprudential one-to-one approach of controlling individual banks. There is no macroprudential (= systemic) regulation, and the micro-regulatory instruments have proved insufficient – in fact, counterproductive – in warding off a severe crisis. They amplify cyclical fluctuations, pertain to only a segment of financial institutions, thus encouraging the growth of a powerful shadow system, and they bring in the wrong incentives: by offering risky investment opportunities without the risk of loss. Thus, they encourage risky behaviour instead of regulating it. It is the main purpose of this paper to make clear that regulation of banking activities is insufficient when wielded as the only instrument for avoiding a severe financial crisis and/or alleviating its effects. Therefore the next section will discuss regulation only briefly.

3.1 Micro-regulation

As its foremost objective, a reform of micro-regulation would have to diminish "leverage", i. e. the relation of a financial institution's assets and liabilities to equity. As permitted at present, leverage is far too big: (1) Many financial institutions, above all the entire shadow system, are not subject to any capital requirements at all. (2) Even for regulated banks present-day capital requirements are insufficient, particularly with respect to risky short-term transactions and to the banking-book. (3) Banks are allowed to go to the limits any time, so they may have nothing to fall back on in an emergency. (4) Furthermore big banks are allowed to use their own risk assessment models, which tend to underestimate risks, thus again increasing the leverage. Together with the rules of the International Financial Reporting Standard (IFRS), which requires valuation at respective market prices, present-day

[14] In the returns on government bonds, the rather diverse developments in EU-countries began to show up in mid-2008 only, but from then on were rather too overshooting.

[15] See e. g. Hellwig (2008), BIS (2010) or the analysis in section 2.

regulation acts pro-cyclically: During the upswing, low risks and high asset prices allow banks to construct a high credit pyramid on the basis of given equity, which pyramid will have to be dismantled in the downturn when equity no longer suffices, due to increasing risk and falling asset prices. In that situation, emergency sales of assets may easily start a vicious circle of asset prices dropping even further and diminishing the equity ratio.[16]

It must be pointed out, though, that the efficiency of the usual risk-based equity rules has been called in doubt: According to the regulation paradox, minimum equity is not available in a crisis, because otherwise committed, and for a dynamic context Blum (1999) has shown that risk-based equity rules have frequently led to even riskier investments. Lately, flexible rules, relating to periods instead of points in time, have been advocated as a solution for this problem; precommitment is another such suggestion.[17] Alternatively, minimum reserves on the assets of all financial institutions have been proposed (Palley 2004; Holz 2007); they would dampen the cyclical fluctuations and would allow for different national requirements. As to the hotly debated question of the appropriate size of the equity ratio, periodical stress tests might be helpful; although those, too, have been put in doubt (Borio and Drehmann 2009).

The second important objective of a reform of micro-regulation is its extension to all financial institutions. So far, the powerful shadow system has evaded regulation. Consequently, the leverage of hedge funds by far surpasses the leverage of traditional banks, while that of SIVs and conduits exceeds even that of hedge funds; in addition, both invest long-term and refinance themselves short-term, in other words: they are especially sensitive to rising interest rates. Their emergency sales caused by risen interest rates are among the major systemic risks. Therefore strict regulation of the transactions of banks with hedge funds and private equity firms is recommended.

Thirdly, any reform of regulation will have to improve incentive structures. The present-day system follows more or less the motto: "Heads I win, tails my creditors lose" – and those creditors are increasingly identical with the general public. In many instances, US-American mortgage debtors do not have to make a down-payment nor are they personally liable; they profit if house prices happen to rise, but do not lose when house prices fall below the amount of credit, because they can leave the house to the bank and thus rid themselves of all responsibilities. In the same way big financial institutions – those "too big to fail" or "too system-relevant to fail" – profit from highly risky investments or an insufficient equity ratio: Whenever those risks come to pass, it is the general public that suffers. In the last resort it is the general public that has to bear the consequences. Mortgage creditors and financial institutions that bundle credits can also let the purchasers bear the risk; therefore they are not at all interested in carefully screening their debtors. The debtors, on the other hand, put their trust in the evaluation of rating agencies; these, however, cannot fulfil their task properly as theirs are conflicting interests (their business is both to evaluate and to consult!); apart from that, rating agencies tend to neglect systemic risks.

Fourthly, excessive transformation of credit terms must be restricted. Of course, that is one of the original obligations of the banking system, and the danger of a "run" has always been present; but whenever the central bank managed to provide the appropriate volume of liquidity, the situation was soon brought back to normal. It was deregulation that caused excessive term-transformations, especially in the shadow system; and the liquidity shortage was not caused by a "run" on the part of bank

---

[16] In addition, the IFRS valuation results in paper profits in the upswing and in paper losses in the downturn; those paper profits are frequently distributed and thus decrease equity.

[17] With the precommitment approach, financial institutions estimate their maximum losses themselves and commit themselves to hold equity to that amount (Kupiec and O'Brien 1997; Hahn 2000).

customers, but by financial institutions running into liquidity problems in consequence of rising interest rates. This systemic risk can only be dealt with by stricter credit rules.

Less clear are the scope and methods of regulation of *financial innovations.* Hardly anyone has recommended their general prohibition; with certain derivatives, however, disadvantages considerably outweigh the advantages, e. g. with phased securitization: CDO^2s (a CDO^2 is made up from the risky tranches of earlier CDOs; from this bundle still another tranche with an AAA-rating can be squeezed).[18] Even for "ordinary" CDOs there are no reliable models of risk assessment and pricing (Duffie 2007), and even less so for such extreme derivatives; the fact that the risks of these latter ones simply could not be rationally assessed contributed not a little to the opacity of the markets. The use of credit default swaps (CDS) is just as questionable as the possibility of selling even the CDO-Junior (i. e. high risk) tranche; this distorts the incentive structure as the bundling entity usually divests itself of all liability. It will also be necessary to devise rules for securitization, above all for some standardization of products and the establishment of organized markets.

The discussion on how to improve micro-regulation has gone on for two years now, without substantial results. Too many influential people profit by the present system; consequently, there is strong resistance against changes (Rajan 2010, 1). Some of the reform proposals, like higher taxation of banks, do seem counterproductive indeed: Contrary to what has been published, the returns on assets (RoAs) of banks are comparatively modest, while the (average) returns on equity (RoEs) result from excessive leverage, in other words from an inordinate risk appetite (BIS 2010, 74f).[19] Thus, an additional tax would probably result in still higher leverage and even riskier transactions, especially if the tax were to be raised on the balance sheet total instead of on "risky" transactions only. But a definition of "risky" that is economically reasonable and also watertight with respect to tax laws certainly seems a tall order, because economically speaking many "risky" transactions are actually quite useful.

Whatever the What and How of a reform of micro-regulation, from now on regulators will have relentlessly to disclose and punish criminal practices such as undoubtedly contributed to bring on the recent crisis.

3.2 Macro-regulation

Even if the massive resistance of financial lobbies could be overcome and substantial improvements in traditional micro-regulation achieved, such improved rules might keep individual banks from defaulting, but they could not prevent the break-down of the system. In other words, they could not alleviate severe financial crises, to say nothing of preventing them. The US subprime problems have shown how deficiencies in the system's design can turn an economy's domestic problems into a major global crisis. In addition to "one-to-one" micro-regulation we need macro-regulation that must deal with the deficiencies inherent in the system, such as wrong incentive structures and encouragement of opportunistic behaviour; we need rules that will improve the elasticity, flexibility, and stability of the system – although, of course, this is more easily said than done: In contrast to micro-regulation, which (merely) needs to be improved, there has been hardly any macro-regulation so far; it will have to be devised from scratch – taking account of the pro-cyclical behaviour of the system and

[18] For the details of this method see Hahn 2008.

[19] "In this respect, Herr Ackermann is correct when he says that 25 % RoE are the standard by which he is measured. One talks less about risks – they do not make such a good topic of public discussion as returns achieved. So it is hardly ever asked at what risks a high return was achieved. And it is not asked at all whether the 25 % return on equity is not merely a proof of the general undercapitalization of the entire sector" (Hellwig 2010, 29). The problem is not at all new: "In England e. g. the ratio of equity and liabilities is exceedingly low; in the London and Country Bank, an excellently managed institution, that ratio was 4.38 : 100 in 1900. On the other hand, this ratio explains the size of the dividends of English deposit banks" (Hilferding [1919] 1968, 114).

the complex interrelations among financial institutions, the interrelations being responsible for the risks of joint exposure and (consequent) joint failure.[20]

The *pro-cyclical effect* of recent regulation was already mentioned in the previous section: The combination of IFRS evaluation rules[21] and fixed, insufficient equity ratios, which – furthermore – the banks stick to, necessarily cause transactions to expand quickly during the upswing and to contract in the downturn. When top managers are promised bonus payments for the short-term profits they achieve, such promises also encourage pro-cyclical, i. e. short-term oriented, speculative, and risky behaviour. Such tactics can easily be stopped, however, and in fact have been stopped in several cases.[22] Other incentives for pro-cyclical transactions are harder to remove. In addition to more flexible IFRS evaluation rules cyclical variation of equity requirements has been discussed, i. e. the proposal that for brief periods of time equity requirements may be lowered if and when destabilising emergency sales are to be prevented (Drehmann et al 2010).

The other externality presents an even bigger problem, viz. *involvement in joint risks and collective failures.* The complex network of financial entities is a major factor in transforming local difficulties into global crises. This problem is hard to tackle, as the international linkages among banks are known only in rudiments and are altogether insufficiently documented in figures. It would not be at all trivial to aggregate the interrelations among the diverse branches (of differing importance) of the banking sector, but the requisite cooperation on the part both of the institutions themselves and of national political institutions is unlikely to be forthcoming: Financial institutions are not at all keen on revealing to regulators and/or competitors their connections with foreign branch offices, daughters and corresponding banks, especially those located off-shore or in tax havens. National regulatory authorities insist on their sovereignty and tend to support their national champions in their activities abroad; in this respect, they find opacity quite useful.

The danger of being hit by risks common to all exists both when the *financial system* is one of *perfect competition* – i. e. when it consists of a large number of small financial institutions of identical structure,[23] sharing identical risks –, and when it consists of a *small number* of huge institutions.[24] Once such institutions can no longer be supported – which they should when they are either too big to fail or too closely interconnected to fail –, there arises the danger of all of them defaulting. In either case it is hard to devise counteracting measures and even harder to enforce them. This is true with respect to one of the central causes of such uniform behaviour, the computerized trading systems,[25] as well as the dividing up of system-relevant banks into several smaller ones or their being split into a commercial bank and an investment bank. Nor is still another suggestion being seriously discussed, viz. the suggestion altogether to prohibit foreign branches and to put foreign subsidiaries completely under the control of the country they are based in ("ring fencing"; Carletti 2010); this suggestion has been rejected by the financial institutions as counterproductive and unfeasible.

Another group of measures would have to limit follow-up costs and spill-over effects of bank crashes. If it were possible to perceive a concentration of risks beforehand – and that would ask more

---

20 For a more general discussion see e. g. Hellwig (2008), Pellens et al (2009) or BIS (2010, ch.7).

21 Such an evaluation is based on the current market value – even if that does not exist, as happens in severe crises when no transactions take place.

22 Bonuses have been made to depend on longer-term success, and payment has been significantly deferred.

23 Haldane (2009) showed that the homogenization of financial institutions is conducive to the creation of bubbles and increases the system's vulnerability.

24 At the end of 2007 the assets of 13 banks were even higher than their respective country's gross domestic product, those of 30 banks amounted to at least half the GDP (Wehinger 2008, 24).

25 With a market share of about one half they increase the probability of a crisis; for they rely on the same models and result in uniform (lemming) behaviour.

of regulators than merely reliable and internationally cooperative supervision of banking activities – the follow-up costs could be made to be borne by those responsible for them; what is being discussed as more reasonable are payments of banks into a fund out of which to cover follow-up costs. *Spill-over effects and panics* usually result from asymmetrical information, e. g. about the risks of certain investments or the soundness of business partners. Therefore it has been suggested that assets should be priced not at their respective market values, but at their average over the entire cycle, in order to avoid cascades of devaluation in the wake of emergency sales. The information basis could be improved by requiring big banks to reveal their risk positions as well as by standardizing financial innovations and their being traded on stock exchanges.[26] In addition, bundling of risks – as exemplified by monoline-insurers e. g.[27] – should not be allowed in the future; and the relationship between banks and their SIVs and conduits – if at all permitted – should be put on an unequivocal legal footing. In order to suppress the risk appetite of financial entities, incentive systems would have to be designed anew: Insolvency of banks and governments as well as conversion of debts would have to be permitted – under strict rules – and in case of over-indebtedness liability should in the first resort rest with the creditors.[28]

The demand for instruments of macro-regulation is much higher than their supply; so far very little has been done to create and enforce new instruments. Effective macro-regulation would require simple and unequivocal rules *plus* additional discretionary measures (Drehmann et al 201), new institutions, intensive international cooperation both among regulating authorities themselves and among the authorities and those responsible for monetary and competition policies. None of this exists and one may (and should) doubt that it will come in sight even in the medium run.

4. Could the crisis resistance of the system be improved?

The period of Great Moderation from the mid-1980s up to the recent crisis, governed by the conviction that "the era of aggregate volatility has come to an end" (Acemoglu 2009), turned out to be a rather untypical interlude. Off and on, there have always been financial crises, even severe ones, and there is no reason why that should change in the future – on the contrary: The ever deeper international involvement of financial institutions and the spread of globalization increase both scope and likelihood of crises; after all, the recent crisis was more or less confined to the USA and Europe. Better, i. e. stricter micro-regulation is an indispensable, but certainly not a sufficient prerequisite for avoiding and/or mitigating crises, while macro-regulation is in its infancy yet. Apart from that, both micro- and macro-regulation are on the whole ineffective with respect to three major causes of crises: complexity of the system, macroeconomic disequilibria and surprises. Further efforts are needed if we want to improve the crisis resistance of the economic system and/or to smooth the consequences of unavoidable financial crises. What could be done in this respect is to adapt monetary policy, to reduce the complexity of the financial system, to decrease the flow of investment-seeking funds, and to enhance the crisis resistance of the industrial/producing sector. The following considerations are

26 So far, CDOs are based exclusively on individual contracts that are traded over the counter, i. e. individually; indeed, that is in the interest of investment banks, which thus enjoy customer-specific rents. The differentiation in the dealings with big customers makes an interesting contrast to the standardization of mass business, e. g. the subprime business.

27 Subprime credits were generally insured against default, although by (monoline-) insurers specializing in that business; and those could not offer protection against systemic risks.

28 Under the present system, potential losses from speculation with highly risky investments promising appropriately high returns can be passed on to the general public: Commerzbank, Belgian Dexia and the German Postal Bank held Greek sovereign bonds to the extent of resp. 62, 54, 47 % of their equity; their risks were considerably reduced, i. e. socialized, with the help of purchases by the European Central Bank.

intended to stimulate the discussion on reforms, which has made very little progress since the memorable summer of 2007.[29]

The *adaptation of monetary policy* should involve two elements: (1) Apart from the rate of inflation it would have to watch the development of asset prices in order to preclude the creation of bubbles. Monetary authorities disagree: bubbles cannot be recognized, there is no need to suppress them ("markets would take care of themselves"), and there are no instruments to fight them; they also assert that anti-inflation policies counteract bubbles anyway (Tichy 2010c, sect.5). None of these arguments is convincing: Numerous studies did point out the bubbles that led to the recent crisis (Tichy 2010b) and suggested instruments for early recognition of bubbles even before this crisis (e. g. Borio and Lowe 2002). The ECB (2005) actually considered including asset prices in the monetary policy indicator; but Trichet (2007) shied away from it.[30] Buiter (2008) proposed that in the interest of asset price regulation one should distinguish between liquidity policy and interest policy; suggestions of requiring minimum reserves on the part of creditors tend in the same direction (Palley 2004). (2) Monetary policy has to avoid abrupt changes of direction and thus of interest rates. In the years before the crisis, the Federal Reserve obviously misinterpreted this tenet; for too long, it fostered the illusion of a period of low interest rates (Rajan 2010, ch.5) and thus misdirected expectations and dispositions.

Reduction of the complexity of the financial system seems of major importance, for the system has become quite opaque not only for monetary authorities and regulators, but even for market participants themselves, to say nothing of the fact that complex close-knit systems tend to be instable. But reduction of complexity must not reduce efficiency. The suggestions mentioned, viz. prohibition of overly complex products and/or fighting the opacity of derivatives markets by standardization and trading on organized markets would, on the contrary, improve efficiency. The same would hold for lessening intermediatization, if it were not for the lack of appropriate instruments. On the other hand, competition policy will have to have a considerable part in all this. At this point, of course, it is not at all clear whether the problem of "too big to fail" and/or "too interconnected to fail" could be sufficiently abated by means of micro-regulation, i. e. by stricter equity requirements for big or "system-relevant" banks;[31] the same holds true for dividing up such banks into a commercial and an investment bank. In the first case the required differentiation is difficult to enforce and would have considerable effects as regards competition, in the second case the close interconnections of the various lines of business would make a division difficult and might reduce efficiency. But at least economic policy could refrain from promoting size and competitiveness of its respective national champions and prevent their growth abroad by prohibiting mergers and encouraging the sale of peripheral lines of business.

The *reduction of the flow of investment-seeking funds* is a topic as yet not properly discussed by policymakers. Paramount topics of discussion have been China's mercantilist policy and the resulting surplus in her balance on current account; but that sort of policy is hardly applicable in the "West". It could be useful, however, to try and build up practicable banking systems in Asia. For potential investors, such banks would offer an alternative to New York or London markets; this strategy has worked quite well in the EU accession countries (Abiad et al 2009). In "western" industrial economies the problem of insufficient absorption, so-called "oversaving", must be tackled: savings promotion, low and decreasing taxation of incomes and wealth accompanied by increasing income disparities, as well as the tendency to change from a pay-as-you-go system to a funding system with respect to old-age

[29] In fact, since 2005, when various authors (Tichy 2010b) as well as the stability reports (Tichy 2010c) questioned the adequacy of the system.

[30] "However, any unexpected and possibly unprecedented action that the central bank takes in response to these risks might disorient the market" (Trichet 2005, 533).

[31] According to Lannoo (2010, 158f) stricter micro-regulation automatically leads to subdivision and specialization.

pensions[32] tend to depress consumption and further enlarge the volume of investment-seeking funds, while slack consumer demand and slow growth tend to deter potential investors from actually going into debt. The problem will become even more pressing if and when governments stop incurring debts – because of EU-rules and over-indebtedness: As soon as governments no longer incur further debts – in a situation of a balance on current account equilibrium –, firms will have to incur bigger debts or households will have to save less (Tichy 2009).[33] In view of the slow growth expected for the foreseeable future, firms will hesitate to incur debts; thus, other things remaining equal, the macro-imbalance of "over-saving" could become even more pronounced. In times of an urgent search for profits no amount of bank regulation will keep actors away from excessive risks nor will it prevent new bubbles.

Proposals for restructuring the financial sector and reducing global disequilibria are indispensable, but they would not suffice; in order to contain future financial crises and mitigate their effects, policies must be more broadly based. Prasad (2008) used the simile of correcting tectonic faults around which enormous stress has built up. The following suggestions focus on measures for improving the crisis resistance of the economy and for increasing survival probabilities of firms in case of shocks.

The measures in the first group would have to target the *financing of the non-financial sector.* As financing activities are shifted more and more from the banks to the capital market and in view of additional intermediatization entities, creditors and debtors move ever farther apart; their only connection are the quarterly statements, and the signals sent out by those are excessive, due to IFRS requirements. Furthermore, actors on the capital market are mainly agents, who are under pressure from their principals to prove themselves successful; thus, the system inclines to very short-term decisions. Profits of firms have to be kept at a constantly high level in order to satisfy shareholders; therefore these firms necessarily adapt to shocks by adjusting volumes of production and costs – frequently with dubious long-term consequences. The firms' rather narrow equity base makes them even more vulnerable; many of them, however, are not interested in a sound equity base even in "normal" times.[34] In times of crisis when the firms' existence is in jeopardy, those disadvantages will become obvious – too late though. The following measures could encourage firms to increase their equity ratio: ending tax deductibility of interest paid on debt, tax benefits for increasing equity (fictitious interest on equity), and/or making public subsidies dependent on a minimum equity requirement. One could also create incentives for savers to invest more and directly in business firms. Removal of the various disincentives named must also be mentioned here.

Another way to strengthen the crisis resistance of business and to contain the damage to the real economy would be to make firms switch from short-term to longer-term strategies. Over the last decades those strategies have been more and more targeted at short-term optimization – not only under the pressure of the financial markets and competition, but also under the influence of consultants and fashions; by reacting to profit slumps by massive layoffs (Oliner et al 2007) a firm diminishes its crisis resistance and its survival chances and jeopardizes its future. Longer-term measures would be strategic diversification of production and customer portfolios to relieve an over-concentration on core activities, maintenance of buffer stocks instead of relying on just-in-time-delivery, and/or building up a stock of qualified personnel that will allow and ensure the development of firm-specific "immobile, unique, non-replicable created assets". Of course, in these respects economic policy could act only

---

[32] See e. g. Kirchgässner 2009.

[33] According to accounting rules, savings must always equal debts incurred. As a rule, household savings equal debts of firms plus sovereign debt, when the balance on current account is in equilibrium.

[34] The leverage of financing by debt enables them to maintain a high return on equity and to shift some of the risk to their creditors.

indirectly; what it could do, however, as mentioned above, is to regulate both the taxation of manager bonuses and the time-spans over which these may be paid.

Thirdly, competition policy with respect to mergers will have to be reconsidered. Many governments as well as the EU Commission still put their trust in sheer size and think they can improve their competitiveness by way of economies of scale up to tolerating national or European champions. The results, at best, have been corporations "too big to fail" whose survival in times of crisis has to be ensured by public subsidies. "When a firm is bailed out because it is too big to fail, it is evidence that competition laws have not been effectively enforced" (Stiglitz 2009, sect.1, no.6). In this respect, too, a portfolio of diverse, medium sized firms is considerably more resistant to crises than one single firm or a few big ones.

Last not least, most governments will have to revise their *consumption policies* – in different directions. Let us take the USA and Germany as contrasting examples. US policymakers believe in boosting business activities and employment by private and public consumption, both financed via deficits; Germany relies exclusively on exports. Apart from the fact that both strategies cause imbalances in international trade and current accounts, neither one of them is sustainable. German concentration on exports at the expense of domestic consumption has been possible only by restrictive wage policies; instead of catering to the welfare of the population this policy increases foreign engagements by German banks, amplifies cyclical fluctuations and makes Germany highly dependent on demand fluctuations abroad. When one considers these measures one realizes that Germany's particular concern over the crisis is far from accidental.

References

Abiad, Abdul et al (2009): Financial integration, capital mobility, and income convergence, *Economic Policy* April, 241–205.

Acemoglu, Daron (2009): The crisis of 2008: Structural lessons for and from economics, http://econ-www.mit.edu/files/3722.

Adams, F.Gerard (2009): The World Financial Crisis: New Economy, globalization and old-fashioned philosophy, *World Economics 10,* 45–58.

Arnold, Lutz (2009): Krise der Wirtschaftswissenschaften: Braucht die VWL eine Neuausrichtung? *Ifo Schnelldienst 14,* 3–5.

Ben-David, Itzhak (2008): Manipulation of collateral values by borrowers and intermediaries, *Job Market Paper,* first draft, fisher.osu.edu/fin/dice/seminars/manipulation.pdf

Bernanke, Ben S. (2005): The global savings glut and the current U.S. current account deficit, *Sandridge Lecture,* http://www.federalreserve.gov/newsevents/speech/bernanke20070911a.htm.

BIS – Bank for International Settlements (2010): *80th Annual Report,* Basle.

Blum, Jürg (1999): Do capital adequacy requirements reduce risks in banking? *Journal of Banking and Finance 23,* S. 755–71.

Bordo, Michael et al (2001): Is the crisis problem growing more severe? *Economic Policy* April 2001, 51–82.

Borio, C. and Lowe, Philip (2002): Asset prices, financial and monetary stability: exploring the nexus, *BIS WP 114.*

Borio, Claudio (2005): Monetary and financial stability: so close and yet so far? *National Institute Economic Review 192* (April), 84–101.

Borio, Claudio and Drehmann, Mathias (2009) Towards an operational framework for financial stability: "fuzzy" measurement and its consequences, *BIS WP 284.*

Buiter, William H. (2008): Central banks and financial crisis, *Jackson Hole Symposium,* http://www.kansascityfed.org/publicat/sympos/2008/Buiter.03.12.09.pdf

Caballero, Ricardo J. and Kurlat, Pablo (2009): The "surprising" origin and nature of financial crises: a macroeconomic policy proposal, *Jackson Hole Symposium,* http://www.kc.frb.org/home/subwebnav.cfm?level=3&theID=11441&SubWeb=10660.

Caprio, Gerard and Klingebiel, Daniela: (1997): Bank insolvency: Bad luck, bad policy, or bad banking? In Pleskovic, Boris and Stiglitz, Joseph, eds, *Annual World Bank Conference on Development Economics,* Washington DC: The World Bank, 79–104.

Carletti, E. (2010). Financial regulation going forward, in: OeNB, Central Banking after the Crisis, 38th Conference, 136–156.

Cova, Pietro et al (2009): Global Imbalances: The Role of Emerging Asia, *IMF Working Paper No. 09/64.*

Del'Ariccia, Giovanni et al (2008): Credit booms and lending standards: Evidence from the subprime mortgage market, *Centre for Economic Policy Research, Discussion Paper No. 6683.*

Demirgüç-Kunt, Asli and Detragiache, Enrica (1998): The determinants of banking crises in developing and developed countries, *IMF Staff Papers 45,* 81–109.

Drehmann, Matthias et al (2010): Countercyclical capital buffers: exploring options, *BIS WP 317.*

Duffie, Darrell (2007): *Innovations in credit risk transfer: Implications for financial stability,* http://www.Stanford.edu/~duffie/BIS.pdf.

Evenett, Simon J. and Francois, Joseph (2010): Will Chinese revaluation create American jobs? http://www.voxeu.org/index.php?q=node/4931

EZB – Europäische Zentralbank (2005): Vermögenspreisblasen und Geldpolitik, *Monatsbericht April,* 53–69.

Goetzmann, William and Newman, Frank (2010): Securitization in the 1920s, *National Bureau of Economic Research WP 15650.*

Haberler, Gottfried (21955 [1937]): *Prosperität und Depression,* Tübingen: Mohr-Siebeck.

Hahn, Franz R. (2000): EU-Konsultationspapier zur Überarbeitung der Eigenkapitalvorschriften für Kreditinstitute und Wertpapierfirmen, *Bankarchiv 48 (9),* 787–792.

Hahn, Franz R. (2008): Internationale Bankenkrise und die Rolle von Finanzaufsicht und Finanzinnovationen, *Monatsberichte des Österreichischen Instituts für Wirtschaftsforschung 81 (8),* 593–606.

Haldane, Andrew G. (2009): Rethinking the financial network, *Bank of England Working Paper.*

Hellwig, Martin (2008): Systemic risk in the financial sector: An analysis of the Subprime-Mortgage financial crisis, *Preprints of the Max Planck Institute for Research on Collective Goods,* Bonn 2008/43.

Hellwig, Martin (2010): Finanzkrise und Reformbedarf, *Preprints of the Max Planck Institute for Research on Collective Goods,* Bonn 2010/19.

Hilferding, R. ([1910] 1968): *Das Finanzkapital,* Frankfurt: Europäische Verlagsanstalt.

Holz, M. (2007): Asset-Based Reserve Requirements: A New Monetary Policy Instrument for Targeting Diverging Real Estate Prices in the Euro Area. *Intervention,* Bd. 4, 331–351.

Jungermann, Helmut and Slovic, Paul: (1993): Charakteristika individueller Risikowahrnehmung, in: Krohn, Wolfgang und Krucken, Georg, Hg, *Riskante Technologien: Reflexion und Regulation,* Frankfurt, S. 79–100.

Kahneman, Daniel and Tversky, Amos (1972): Subjective probability: A judgement of representativeness, *Cognitive Psychology 3,* 430–454.

Kaminsky, Graciela L. and Reinhart, Carmen, M. (1999): The Twin Crises: The causes of banking and balance-of-payments problems, *AER 99 (3),* 473–500.

Keynes, John M. ([1936] 1964): *The general theory of employment, interest and money,* New York: Harbinger.

Keys, Benjamin J. et al (2010): Did securitization lead to lax screening? Evidence from subprime loans, *QJE 125 (1),* 307–362.

Kirchgässner, Gebhard (2009): Die Krise der Wirtschaft: Auch eine Krise der Wirtschaftswissenschaften? *Perspektiven der Wirtschaftspolitik 10 (4),* 436–68.

Kupiec, P. H. and J. M. O'Brien, The Pre-Commitment Approach: Using Incentives to Set Market Risk Capital Requirements. *Finance and Economics Discussion Series 1997-14,* Federal Reserve Board, Washington DC.

Lannoo, Karel (2010): Agenda 2020 and the financial crisis, *Intereconomics 45 (3),* 156–59.

Maddaloni, Angela et al (forthcoming): Does monetary policy affect bank credit standards?, *ECB Working Paper,* http://www.cepr.org/meets/wkcn/1/1693/papers/MaddaloniFinal.pdf

Mian, Ativ and Sufi, Amir (2008): The consequences of mortgage credit expansion: Evidence from the 2007 mortgage default crisis, *NBER WP 13936.*

Oliner, Stephen P., Sichel, Daniel E. and Stiroh, Kevin D. (2007): Explaining a productive decade, *Brookings Papers on Economic Activity (1),* 81–137.

Palley, T. (2004): Asset-Based Reserve Requirements: Reasserting Domestic Monetary Control in an Era of Financial Innovation and Instability. *Review of Political Economy 16,* 43–58.

Pellens, Bernhard et al (2009): Bilanzierungsstandards im Kontext der Finanzmarktkrise, *Perspektiven der Wirtschaftspolitik 10 (4),* 413–35.

Perrow, Charles (1984): *Normal accidents: Living with high risk technologies,* New York: Basic Books.

Prasad, Eswar S. (2008): Financial globalization: What to think when capital flows uphill, *The Milken Institute Review, 2nd Quarter,* 36–43.

Rajan, R.G., 2005 Has financial development made the world riskier? http://www.kansascityfed.org/publicat7sympos/2005/sym05prg.htrn

Rajan, G. (2010): *Fault lines: How hidden fractures still threaten the world economy,* Princeton: Princeton UP.

Reinhart, Carmen and Rogoff, Kenneth S. (2008): Banking crises: An equal opportunity menace, *NBER WP 14049.*

Spaventa, Luigi (2008), Avoiding disorderly deleveraging, *CEPR Policy Insight 22.*

Stiglitz, Joseph E. (2009): Principles for a new financial architecture, *The Commission of Experts of the President of the UN General Assembly of the International Monetary and Financial System.*

Taylor, John B. (2009): *Getting off track: How government actions and interventions caused, prolonged and worsened the financial crisis,* Stanford, CA: Hoover Institution Press.

Tichy, Gunther (2009): Einige unkonventionelle Gedanken zum Leben nach der Krise, *Wirtschaft und Gesellschaft 35 (4),* 501–14.

Tichy, Gunther (2010a): Bankenkrise oder falsche Anreizsysteme in der Rentiergesellschaft, In: Christian Brünner et al, Hg, *Mensch – Gruppe – Gesellschaft: Von bunten Wiesen und deren GärtnerInnen. Manfred Prisching zum 60. Geburtstag.*

Tichy, Gunther (2010b): War die Finanzkrise vorhersehbar? See p. 9ff of present publication.

Tichy, Gunther (2010c): Why did policy ignore the harbingers of the crisis? See p. 29ff of present publication.

Trichet, Jean-Claude (2005): Monetary policy strategies: A central bank panel, *Jackson Hole Symposium* http://www.kansascityfed.org/publicaVsympos/2005/sym05prg.htm

Wehinger, Gert (2008): Lessons from the financial market turmoil: Challenges ahead for the financial industry and policy makers, *OECD Financial Market Trends,* 2–40.

Erich W. Streissler

Saving and Investment in the Long Run

1. The present dominance of saving intentions

1.1 Since the year 2000, macroeconomic development has to be seen as the aftermath of the great boom of the years 1995–1999, particularly in the USA, up to recently the per capita richest and the leading developed nation. This boom manifested itself in the stock market and was above all an industrial boom led by the development of the computer hard- and software-industries. I regard it as the fifth Kondratieff boom in world history. [J.A. Schumpeter (1939) named the long-term waves of modern-time industrial innovations, which he takes to recur cyclically every 40 to 50 years, after a Russian statistician.[1]] In consequence of the re-introduction of unrestricted international mobility of capital around 1990, financial markets had begun to become more important and became ever more so during this boom. By various measures the banking sector more or less doubled in several economies and continued to flourish even after the actual boom ended in 2000. It seems clear now that US central bank policy tried to rekindle and prolong that boom from 2001 onwards[2] and that banks frantically tried to place profitable financial investments and stimulate the world economy by diverse types of speculation.

I propose, however, (thesis 1) that centering attention on finance and banking is lop-sided. Above all, the world-wide problem was one of too extensive world saving intentions chasing too few world investment opportunities: The problem since 2001 has been a disequilibrium between intended (i.e. ex ante) world savings and real investment opportunities – too extensive savings intentions constantly being frustrated.

An investigation of long-run saving and investment intentions provides the key to all real economic development.

1.2 A curious feature of standard global financial market analysis is its complete disregard of the real economic background of financial markets. According to the national accounting identities, which are generally used and have to be generally used because they have been standardized by the United Nations' "System of National Accounts", accomplished world savings are identically equal to world (net) investments. This identity is the logical consequence of the fact that our "world" is a closed economy as long as it does not trade with other worlds in the universe.

Only in a world without trade and without international capital movements would the identity of savings and investments also hold for any one single economy. In his *General Theory of Employment Interest and Money* (1936) Keynes ignored exports (and a function of capital movements) and made the savings-investment identity appear to be a general feature. That was a fitting simplification in 1936 when international trade had nearly ceased due to national protectionism on all sides. At the

[1] See Joseph A. Schumpeter, *Business Cycles*, London 1939.

[2] Note the reduction in bank rate, as sharp as never before: From 6,5 to 1,75 % in 2001 alone and soon to 1 %. Furthermore the interest reduction has been criticized for being continued much too long.

very high point of national autarkies, i. e. when international trade was nearly stifled by high tariffs, and international capital movements were largely forbidden, Keynes in writing his *General Theory* could assume that each single economy was a closed economy.

General economic text-books retained this closed economy perspective nearly up to the year 1990, when the approximate realism of this view of national economies was long out of date: Thus still in 1993 the Nobel Laureate Krugman, and also R. Gordon, deplored that standard text-books tended to glance at international economic relations at best at their very end.[3]

But even when we fully recognize that for each single economy savings and investments can be substantially different, we have to remember that they can only differ if other economies take the requisite complementary position. Thus an excess of investments over savings for one country is also identically equal with that country's current account deficit; or the other way round an excess of savings over investment is identically equal to a current account surplus. But a current account deficit can only arise if other countries lend the requisite sums to the deficit country, and lend them either voluntarily or involuntarily because of just not being paid, at least not paid in time. And a current account surplus has to find willing borrowers. This crucial bilateral constellation is regularly forgotten.

To take a typical and very prominent example: At the turn of 2010 into 2011 the United States had a current account deficit of $460 billion for the last 12 months which nearly corresponded to the current account surplus of $316 billion of China, their main creditor. Therefore we might say that the USA can run such a current account deficit only as long as China is willing to lend accordingly, its total financial loans to foreign amounting to 2.9 trillion dollars or more than eight times the present yearly additional sum. Or, alternatively, we might say that China can only lend those 6.1 percent of its social product that it did lend recently as long as there were willing borrowers to take up its loans.

To put it differently: One type of country finds it self-evident that the rest of the world is eager to borrow from it and is surprised when the eventual returns on its loans are often low or when it even suffers capital losses. And another type of country finds it self-evident that the rest of the world should unfailingly be willing to lend to it, apparently indefinitely, and is then highly surprised, if not indignant, when the lenders suddenly wish to reduce their current lending or even want their "money back". For these curious contradictions in perception take, on the one hand, Germany and, on the other, Greece as an example. To conclude: A world-wide balance between saving and investment can very easily be fraught with surprises for creditors and debtors, if not to say with international conflicts. Equilibrium (more precisely an identity) is necessarily achieved ex post, but is not at all easy to find ex ante.

1.3 Savings are internationally transferred by international capital movements. International capital movements had been controlled down to relative insignificance by the Bretton Woods (1944) regime of world trade and finance, which broke down in March 1973 at the latest. Each subsequent decade increased the importance of international capital movements.

For the Nobel Laureate Robert Mundell the crucial event for the re-emergence of the full mobility of international capital – after their break-down in 1914 – is the demise of the Soviet Empire in 1989[4]. This is a good generalization, but in the case of such a continuous rise in the importance of interna-

[3] "It is now more important than ever before that basic training include a solid grounding in the principles of international trade": Paul R. Krugman, "What Do Undergraduates Need to Know About Trade?", Amer. Econ. Rev. 83/2 (May 1993), pp. 23–26, here p. 26. [Robert] Gordon, "Why the Principles Course Needs Comparative Macro and Micro", Amer. Econ. Rev. 83/2 (May 1993), pp. 17–22. P. 18 says: "International Economics is often buried in a back-of-the-book ghetto in many Principles texts".

[4] Robert A. Mundell, "A Reconsideration of the Twentieth Century", Amer. Econ. Rev. 90/3 (June 2000), pp. 327–340 (Nobel Prize Lecture).

tional capital movements one could just as well argue for earlier or later time points of decisive change. In particular, international capital movements, which Mundell had stressed so appropriately and with great foresight, rose to their greatest importance shortly after his Nobel Lecture in 1999: the first decade of the 21st century was characterized by a surge in South East and South Asian savings, in particular those of China, and a great increase of the appetite for foreign capital in the USA.

But such appetite for foreign capital without a concomitant willingness to invest causes a deep misunderstanding in the banking industry: Banks tend to believe that the savings they put on the market will eventually create investments with positive returns, while actually such savings may generate only consumption loans without any increase in the aggregate ability to repay. Turning from a real world with a dearth of investment opportunities to its financial counterpart we witness lots of merely redistributive financial speculation, where the financial "investor" loses and the gains of his counterparts are minimal because the middlemen, those who place the financial "investments", earn large placement fees. Any gains would but completely disappear if banks were, as is contemplated now, additionally taxed on their transactions.

1.4 There is a second profound misunderstanding. In 2002 a new international currency was created, the Euro. It corresponds to the historic gold currency in its not being the currency of any one nation. The advantage of adopting such an international currency is achieving a lower level of real interest rates, as Carl Menger had already argued in 1892 (with respect to the gold standard)[5]. But such an international currency cannot be used as an instrument of national fiscal policy; nor does it have to be complemented by an internationally run fiscal policy, which could not easily be devised. With conflicting national preferences a common fiscal policy would just be an exploitation of one country by the other. Hankering after a common fiscal policy is a misunderstanding on the part of figures like Soros or Sarkozy and would simply mean transferring former national priorities to an international level too heterogeneous and confusing.

1.5 Historically there were <u>two ways</u> of looking at the savings-investment identity for the world as a whole, or, if economies are assumed to be closed, for each separate economy. And they also correspond to two different historical "climates" or situations: Adam Smith in the *Wealth of Nations* assumed that (scarce) savings determine investments. In this scenario higher savings pull up investments to a higher level. This is the scenario typical for poor economies but also in rich economies in boom periods: There is an unsatisfied investment demand which can be satisfied if savings increase.

Keynes in his *General Theory* assumed the opposite: There is a lack of any (further) investment opportunities. Therefore a low level of realizable investment limits savings. This is typical for already saturated rich economies; and it is typical for depression periods after booms. It was typical for Keynes' Europe (and the USA!) in the 1930s and has become once more typical for the world as a whole since the year 2001: China and other South East Asian countries were increasing their savings heavily, while there was little demand for business investment world-wide.

But an increase in Chinese savings does not yet mean that there is any increase in world savings – all might be consumed by other nations: and an increase in savings now does not mean there will be any wealth creation eventually. The attempt to invest too much in housing made US (and Spanish) house prices crash so that finally little investment value was realized and the use of (intended) savings for speculative purposes created no real investment but only caused redistributions of wealth. In such a scenario – and it is not infrequent – we might see in realizable and sufficiently profitable investment

[5] Carl Menger, "Beiträge zur Währungsfrage in Oesterreich-Ungarn", Jahrbücher für Nationalökonomie und Statistik, Dritte Folge, vol III, Jena 1892, pp. 109. Reprinted in *Carl Menger, Gesammelte Werke,* F. A. Hayek (ed), vol. IV, Mohr-Siebeck, Tübingen 1970, pp. 125, here p. 138f.

(i. e. investment not of zero or negative profitability and not with falling asset values) the determinant of additional wealth creation.

To clarify: Lately, China had a current account surplus of + $316 billion, but the United States an even larger current account deficit of – $460 billion. A current account deficit means that a country either invests or consumes more than what it produces and therefore imports so much. And as US investment is rather on the low side, we might simply say that the USA consume too much, and this excess consumption – and not investment which might easily be financed at home by the USA – is financed by China. Thus the USA figure as a merry-go-round for the destruction of Chinese savings, which just finance US consumption: China is merely providing consumption loans to the USA but, apart from what it is investing at home, does not stimulate much investment outside China.

But consumption loans are not costless: On the $2.9 trillion dollars which China holds as its accumulated foreign trade surplus it earns interest income, of course! The interest income China earns from the USA is constantly mounting with all these US current account deficits. Of course, China's interest income is at present not very high because it earns the current low interest rates on its predominant short term loans. But short term loans are also extremely dangerous for the USA because China might demand repayment at any time – more precisely might not renew short term loans or might demand higher interest rates. The USA represent the Greece of China, fully at its mercy. The question is (as everything has two sides): Or, as is typical for all large creditors, is China at the mercy of the USA to get its money back?

1.6 The upshot of these arguments is: It is misleading to look only at finance. Without due regard to real investments and the relation of savings to investments one is apt not to realize that mere finance is likely to end only in speculative breakdowns of financial markets.

2. Are investments or are savings the key to long-term development?

2.1 At present, investments limit and determine savings. That it is investments that are dominant in the savings-investment identity was the vision of Karl Marx. In *Capital,* vol. I, 1867 he presented the first analysis of the innovation process as the source of development.[6] And innovation led to investment: According to Marx it is the innovation process that is the decisive factor manifesting itself in any investment successful in the long run. This view tends to push savings to backstage. But my question is: Does innovation just drop exogenously from heaven or is it not partly created purposely in order to earn an appropriate rate of return on savings, i. e. is it not much rather endogenous? And, furthermore do not intended savings in the very long run often by themselves create the investment opportunities? Do intended savings search for investments to implement them? Even in an identity one side or the other may be the prime cause!

2.2 It is mainly intended savings of entrepreneurs that create investments: Owners of firms find it would be a good idea to increase their firm's capital and they produce savings in order to invest in their firm. This is particularly likely during long-run recessions: Smaller and medium sized firms find they do not get any or at least not sufficient loans from banks or only at very high rates of interest. This is particularly so if banks are mainly financing governmental budget deficits and are not at all interested in loans to private firms, as they cannot well judge their credit-worthiness in recessionary

[6] The very important, purely analytical and value free parts of the theoretical analysis of Marx can be found in chapters 4, 10 and especially the huge chapter 13 ("Maschinerie und grosse Industrie"), about 140 pages of the 800 pages in all, and chapter 23, about 100 pages; in: Karl Marx, *Das Kapital* – Kritik der politischen Oekonomie, vol. I, Hamburg 1867.

periods. But the private firm thinks it can judge the chances of the likely profitability of its investments better than the bank, and it turns to self-finance.

But unless the firm has from the past large financial reserves, it can only invest if it saves more on its own. Around the year 1900 savings, in particular British savings, were largely those of the upper middle class, in particular the higher civil servants, for retirement or for starting out children. Now, however, savings of business firms (incorporated or not) have become much more important, and simultaneously also the self-finance of firms. The desire or the necessity to self-finance firms thus frequently creates additional savings, which stimulate investment.

2.3 This point might also be made another way round. Periods of drawn out recessions and stagnations have frequently shown high interest rates on loans by banks, due to the perceived riskiness of business investments; while, on the other hand, firms find the interest rates for their savings deposits in banks to be very low. Due to this unusually large discrepancy between borrowing rates and deposit rates of interest in times of depression firms discover that it pays them to self-finance: The expected rate of return for an investment is likely to be higher than the deposit rate but lower than the borrowing rate of interest. In one word: the desire to increase the volume of self-finance increases the amount of saving. The consequence is: if business firms cannot increase their savings, they will frequently remain undercapitalized and underinvested. And that again may stimulate them to achieve higher savings.

2.4 As he explicitly stated in a personal communication, Robert Solow in his theory of economic growth[7] saw economic growth as exogenously given by the exogenously given rate of technical progress. This also makes "technical progress" highly technical and not due to organizational effort or human learning processes. Technical progress is then typically one of big jumps, just as it is in the thought of Marx. Hayek, on the other hand, in "The Use of Knowledge in Society"[8], sees advances in production techniques of an entrepreneurial economy as typically occurring in numerous small steps. And whether in large steps or in small steps the question is if technical advance does not quite often come about endogenously – created by a firm intent on surviving – rather than exogenously?

What happens if a firm finds itself suddenly out-competed by another firm, in a globalized economy most likely out-competed by a foreign firm with quite different factor and input commodity prices? Two options remain for it (I do not take account here of a third option, that of immediately running to the government for subsidies or protective tariffs, which I consider to be only short-term stop gaps). The two options are: either close down the firm or turn more competitive by a bout of innovation. As Wolfgang Weigel has shown empirically[9] such bouts of innovation might also occur even before taking up a new line of business in order to comply with rigorous governmental production standards. And endogenous innovation is also typical for regional or even world-wide monopolies, which innovate to ward off potential competition. (Often such dominating, but potentially threatened monopolies are actually highly competitive.[10])

2.5 And here we are once more faced with savings causing investment: If we adopt Solow's view of exogenously occurring technological advances we are puzzled: Why do advances occur at such an

---

7 Robert Solow, "A contribution to the theory of economic growth", Quart. Journ. Econ. 70 (Feb 1959), pp. 65–94. The exogeneity was stressed in oral communication.

8 Friedrich A. Hayek, "The Use of Knowledge in Society", Amer. Econ. Rev. 35 (Sept. 1945), pp. 519–530.

9 Wolfgang Weigel, "How Well are Authorities Suited to Prevent Damage to the Environment?", European Journal of Law and Economics 4 (1997), pp. 23–39. Also the same, "Wie wirkungsvoll sind Genehmigungsverfahren für Betriebsanlagen?", Wirtschaftspolitische Blätter 5/1995, pp. 325–333.

10 An example of such a world monopoly in Austria is Metallwerke Plansee, producing special metals: Threatened for once by a foreign firm it made a big jump in its constant innovation process, thus preserving its technological lead and world monopoly.

even rate over time that average growth rates stay relatively constant and, even more so, average long run rates of return (i. e. 10 yearly average government bond returns) stay to such a degree more or less constant over time?

From the 1750s onwards, British government bond rates remained nearly constant at 3 percent and only rose to 3.3 percent in the mid-1780s with the start of the industrial revolution.[11] Similarly 3 percent was the predominant rate of interest during the 19th century – witness Galsworthy who tells us that at the death of Queen Victoria (1901) his fictitious Forsytes had become rentier capitalists and were earning those very 3 percent.[12] For the USA, E.R. McGrattan and E.C. Prescott show[13] that "estimates of returns on long-term, high-grade bonds in the post-war period" were on "average for 1960–2002 ... 3.72 percent". Thus for fully developed nations real interest rates of 2.5 percent on the low side up to 4.0 percent on the high side have for long been the real rates of return, even during mildly inflationary periods, which eventually tend to push up real returns. Why is such a stability achieved? That purely technological advances should stay so constant over time, appears highly implausible, in particular as these are sometimes capital saving, sometimes capital using.

My explanation is: It is the savers who dominate and determine rates of return. Normally, they just do not accumulate private savings if the real rate of return is not at least about 2.5 percent (only governments save at even lower real rates, vide China, which by the way now has also an average rate of return on foreign investment of around 4.0 percent). This is so because savers "demand" at least such returns; they are the minimum rates of return still noticeable over a very long period. At a 2.5 percent interest rate an invested capital sum increases just noticeably over time, doubling in 29 years; and at 4 percent capital doubles over 18 years. 18 to 29 years are the average life time of savings held from maturity to retirement, say from 40 years of age till about 60–65 years. This is the reason for the noted stability of long-term interest rates: It is savers that demand them in order to achieve a still noticeable accumulation. And investors have to adjust their innovations in such a way that savers get the desired minimum return. This is so even in the case of long-term foreign investment. Quite in contrast to Marx it is innovation that adjusts to savers' demands!

I repeat: the real rate of return, i. e. the inflation-corrected rate of return, on safe loans is determined by savers as the rate at which their long-term savings still accumulate noticeably, i. e. doubling within 18 to 29 years. Business firms have to adapt their rates of innovation in such a way that they earn at least these real rates of return of 2.5 to 4 percent a year, actually mostly even within a narrower band of 3 to 3.5 percent. If they do not earn such returns on average they have to close down.

But this also means that governments cannot set long-term interest rates at lower rates than these for any length of time. In the *General Theory* Keynes quotes[14] Bagehot's saying "John Bull can stand many things, but he cannot stand 2 percent". This is a footnote to Keynes' own remark, which is in exact conformity to my above statements: "The most stable, and the least easily shifted element in our

[11] See T. S. Ashton, *An Economic History of England: The 18th Century,* London 1955, ed. 1966, passim. "On the whole, eighteenth century England was blessed with cheap money", p. 29. See Table XIII for prices of 3 % Annuities and 3 % Consolidated Stock.

[12] In *The Forsyte Saga* (1922) John Galsworthy has *The Man of Property* (1906), the solicitor Soames Forsyte, reflect at the funeral of Queen Victoria (1901) that over her long reign British investment opportunities shrank and shrank and only 3 percent government bonds remained. Galsworthy does not mention that therefore before the First World War the British financially invested in foreign, particularly in South American bonds (e. g. Argentinian city and railway bonds), while the French found it "patriotic" to invest in Russian government bonds, a "patriotism" which they rued when the Russians after the revolution ceased payment.

[13] Ellen R. McGrattan and Edward C. Prescott, "Average Debt and Equity Returns: Puzzling?", Amer. Econ. Rev. 93/2 (May 2003), pp. 392–397, here p. 395.

[14] John M. Keynes, *The General Theory of Employment Interest and Money,* London 1936, p. 309.

contemporary economy has been hitherto, and may prove to be in future, the minimum rate of interest acceptable to the generality of wealth owners".

2.6 Governments can set, in particular, short-term interest rates at very low rates, at 1 p.c. (both Greenspan after 2002 and the European Central Bank now) and even at practically zero (B. Bernanke since 2008 or Japan for long periods). But then Greenspan suffered the disappointment of losing all contact with the long-term, i. e. 10-year government bond rate. This now at the turn of 2010 into 2011 stands at 3.48 percent for the USA, higher than in Germany with 2.94 percent and nearly the same as the Austrian rate of 3.35 percent. (The low German rate is explained by the country's shifting three fifths of its savings abroad.) All these rates are within the stated range of 2.5 to 4 percent, the latter being typical only for long term booming periods.[15] The corresponding real rates are within this range in particular when we take account of today's slightly deflationary expectations. Only Japan has a much lower rate (1.16 percent), but that country experiences decided deflation with an – underestimated – measured rate of –0.8 percent. This low rate also means that private investors are forced out of the country.

Lower rates than these are only achievable when all investment is simply state-financed. Then, of course, the calculation of my average long-term saver – or, what amounts to the same thing, that of "John Bull" – no longer counts. Then we are in a kind of "planned" economy, which has always had low interest rates. Present-day China, by the way, is not one of them, having at present 4.06 percent interest on 10-year bonds, a figure which has shifted up by 1.1 percent within the last half year (up to the turn of 2010 to 2011).

Actually short-term interest rates at near zero percent or even at 1 percent for long periods of time, as bank rates are now, are nothing but a form of subsidizing privately owned banks – at the taxpayers' cost. As banks in general do not hand on these subsidized credits to private individuals, charging them risk-determined high rates, the question is why banks should be so generously subsidized for long periods at all.

2.7 Of course, in market economies with free capital mobility the rates of return on savings always have to be above the rate of economic growth. This is so because at rates below the growth rate everyone would be offered a Ponzi game, if s/he invests in any enterprise which, together with its profits, grows at the average rate of growth of the economy: Earnings would become infinite in sum at real interest rates below the growth rate! And rates of return have to be higher than the growth rate because there always is a (substantial) risk even in the safest investments.

For that reason Nicholas Lord Kaldor had suggested as a rough estimate that average rates of return on capitals had to be about double the growth rate of the economy; and the rates of return achieved by well established viable business firms once more about double the average rate of return on capital, as the average rate of return on capital is lowered by business failures, especially those of new start-ups. And 2.5–4.0 percent interest rates are close to double the correctly estimated long-run growth rates of developed economies, 1–1.5 percent growth on average at historically the lower levels and 2–2.5 percent at higher levels. Lower interest rates can only be achieved under unusual circumstances. The present interest rate of Japan of 1.16 percent fits in this picture because it is a nominal interest rate for a deflationary economy of 1 to 2 percent deflation per year. Thus the real rate comes within my interest band of 2.5–4 percent; possibly it is a rate below Japan's equilibrium as so many Japanese savings leave the country. Japan also has a growth rate unusually low in the long run. The other nominal rates quoted above are nearly real rates because the correctly calculated rate of inflation is actually zero in many countries now.

[15] Within half a year, from mid 2010 to its end, i. e. during writing, these interest rates, originally rather at the low side, have shifted up by some 0.5 to 0.8 percent; and most of all for the USA.

There were only two periods when long-term US interest rates were below the rate of economic growth: (1) the period 1945–1955, when capital mobility was severely restricted and investors therefore had to stay in the USA and there were, on the other hand, mostly only highly risky currencies outside the USA; (2) the 1970s, when both inflation and the (falling) growth rate were evidently miscalculated. (Similarly Swiss investments promise unusually "safe havens" and therefore have low rates of return, 1.61 percent at present, but Switzerland also has very low growth rates and slight deflation.)

2.8 To conclude: In periods of roughly foreseeable growth and inflation and with unrestricted international capital mobility, as guaranteed within the EU since July 1st 1990, real long-term interest rates below the rate of growth of the economy are only a chimera. Other than by compulsory measures it is not possible to push the real rate of interest below the range of 2.5 – 4 percent for any length of time. But it is possible to increase the nominal rate of interest to levels above that by government policies which are seen to cause very high financial risk: vide the example of present-day Greece.

In general, however, it is the readiness of savers to save that determines interest rates in the long run. And their readiness to save has its limit at a rate of return still noticeable and considered just sufficient in the long run.

Erich W. Streissler

Using Economic Theory for Forecasting

(A) Economic forecasts of practical import are extremely hazardous. The forecaster is confronted with the self-serving propaganda of a vast number of financial market agents. And all too frequently his forecasts are misjudged as simply willfully spoiling the best hopes of hundreds of thousands of worthy savers. Financial market advisors – by politicians all too frequently confused with economists – tend to paint a rosy picture of easily available profit opportunities for everyone, or at least for those who become their own clients. This tendency will be magnified if legal safeguards are defective. Then financial sales persons will attempt to herd as many investors as feasible into the riskiest projects, because their own fees tend to increase with the risk of the product sold. Furthermore the essential learning process of the investing public will be seriously impeded if in every crisis politicians step in and promise a safer world of regulation, safer that is not only for the regulators. Somehow the public is made to believe that all financial mishaps have to be due to sinister anonymous forces, but never due to the faulty judgment of the investors themselves, or those who sell financial investments to them.

(B) I have made a name for myself by long-run macroeconomic forecasts. You cannot publish forecasts in book form, however, because they are inherently "ad hoc"; nor are there any academic journals for forecasts. Thus, my most important scientific work was published in weeklies or even daily newspapers, well-known to the interested public and even among academic economists, but not among scientists outside of economics.

My best-known forecast was that on the likely success of German reunification, published in the biweekly Austrian journal *Wochenpresse*[1] in a two-part article in April 1990 – written after I had been witness to a mood of hysterical triumph at the German Bundesbank in February 1990, well before actual unification took place on October 3rd of that year. Without any noticeable exceptions the general opinion in Germany was then that you merely had to abolish economic planning and all sorts of administrative regulation, whereupon gross domestic product would immediately surge upwards – a notion without any economic foundation, or, at best, just an idealistic notion unsupported by facts.

For my part, I employed the elementary theoretical notions behind <u>growth theory</u>: The rate of economic growth, measured over a certain period of time, is equal to the rate of increase in physical capital plus the rate of increase in productivity, where the productivity increase in capital is largely due to the increase in the efficiency of labour using it; or alternatively to the rate of increase in labour employed plus the rate of increase in labour productivity, where the latter increase is once more largely due to the increase in the quality and quantity of the capital that labour uses. This equation, expressed in rates of change over time, can easily be expressed also by the corresponding notion of levels: the level of the social product of a certain period is identically equal to the amount of capital used times its productivity; or, alternatively, the volume of labour employed times labour productivity.

This was standard economic theory at that time. But in a triumph of hope over experience German economists devised their own pseudo-theory, quite forgetting that economics describes time-dependent processes or, in other words, a necessarily <u>slow process of learning</u>. Sudden jumps in labour efficiency

---

1 Wochenpresse Nr. 14, 6. April 1990, "Deutschland, Deutschland über Alles?", p. 48ff, Nr. 15, 13 April 1990, "Deutschland, Deutschland über Alles? 2. Teil", p. 42ff.

just don't happen. Thus, economic productivity must be understood as primarily caused by material conditions: labour and capital employed and their technical advances. Mere ideological changes matter at best only by and by, in the very long run.

I calculated the volume of capital it would require to raise to the West German level of productivity (and therefore of income) the average East German labourer, whose productivity was estimated at only 40 or at best 50 percent of his West German counterpart. I concluded that the amounts of capital needed would either make West Germans despair over the size of the burden imposed upon them to modernize East German production or would make East Germans resent the insufficient amount of capital they would receive in order to raise their income levels. With the most likely outcome – viz. large, but still quite insufficient transfers – both sides would become unhappy and social tensions would dangerously increase. I spoke of East Germany as a newly arising "Mezzogiorno", a remark which the German Chancellor Kohl came to consider as the acme of insult. A German undersecretary of state was dispatched to Vienna explicitly to contradict my analysis.

As it turned out, I proved to be correct in nearly everything I had forecast. (The German undersecretary, by the way, eventually became President of the Republic of Germany. His name was Horst Köhler.)

You will have noticed that my analysis made use of a notion of Karl Marx: Under "capitalism", the productivity of an economy – more precisely, its "surplus value" – depends on the amount of capital the economy employs. Actually it is the capitalist innovation process – this, too, a process that was first analyzed in depth by Karl Marx – that has little chance in a state-run planning system as the East German Democratic Republic had been. For, if and when a possibly successful innovative production process offers itself, it is usually too risky and not sufficiently profitable for mere state managers to implement it: If it should fail they would be found at fault, while if it succeeded they would not get anything from it. Furthermore, new = innovative industries would not even be looked for or even planned. Thus after breaking away from "capitalism" planned socialist economies become progressively less efficient – and eventually quite inefficient.

After the publication of the two articles in *Wochenpresse,* I discussed my vision in late May 1990 extensively with Wilhelm Krelle, then one of Germany's foremost economic theoreticians. Krelle, who had originally come from Madgeburg (then GDR), disagreed with me and used the "sudden productivity jump" theory for East Germany in a slightly more sophisticated way: He pointed out that there was so much capital "lying around" unused in Eastern Germany, just waiting to be productively employed! But after two years, which he spent in Eastern German university administration, Krelle changed his mind and came to take exactly the opposite view (a view close to my own): It was the upper echelons of the East German labour force who had been completely ruined as to their economic perceptions, never having learned any useful new ideas or techniques of production.

(C) My second important forecasting success came in 2002: After the fifth great Kondratieff boom of 1995–1999, the computer hard- and soft-ware boom, and after the US recession of 2001 I forecast a banking and financial market crash within a few years. I stuck to this forecast and recently had the satisfaction that a former CEO of the Austrian National Bank told me that after my repeated forecast in the year 2006 he sold all his stocks and shares, which then proved to be the ideal moment for sale. The actual crash, as everybody knows, only came in 2008.

The theory behind my forecast was one taken from economic history: booms and busts repeat themselves, in particular on financial markets. After identifying the 1995–1999 boom as the fifth Kondratieff boom and one that, as usual, had been blown up by excessive speculation,[2] I forecast a

[2] See "The Financial Market Crisis", p. 91ff.

crash: one in which the stock market crash would eventually be followed by a crash of banks and other financial institutions. Normally, the crashes of Kondratieff booms occur every 40 to 50 years. This time, the crash had been deferred twice by economic reconstruction after two world wars. But to think that because a crash had been deferred by political action it would never come, was deplorably wrong. Once more, my forecast ran counter to what was then near-general opinion: It was vociferously claimed that "this time is different", a claim wrong, as usual. My analysis rested on the vision that business cycles have in general monetary causes, the vision of Joseph Schumpeter in his notion of secular or Kondratieff booms (1939), which notion in the last analysis rests on Karl Marx.

In one respect you may say I was wrong: In the 1930s the time span between the first stock market crash, in 1929, and the eventual banking crisis of 1931, was less than two years. From 2001 to 2007/08, however, a full seven years lapsed. On the one hand this was to be expected: financial reaction periods lengthen in time the wealthier economies become. On the other hand monetary policy in the past decade of the USA, both under Greenspan, who expertly chose his retirement date in February 2006 – nicely before the probable crash – and then under Ben Bernanke, was the opposite of that from 1929 till early 1933: The highly expansionary policies with interest rates held at 1 percent or lower and then close to zero for long periods, stimulated the suicidal house purchase boom. With house credits up to 120 percent of a property's value, home-owners tended to misjudge the length of time very high house prices would last: It has been estimated that at present one quarter of all US homeowners possess a property of negative net value!

Thus monetary policy deferred the crash but also made it more lethal when it came. Then, in 2008, the Federal Reserve increased cash money, i.e. M_0, as violently as never before, viz. by a full 150 percent (from 900 billion to 2.3 trillion dollars) within one single month. As yet, we still do not know what the eventual effects of that step will be! But what is most likely to result from it is the Japanese scenario ever since 1990. There will be one relatively small decline of social product after another without any marked recovery, i. e. it will be less painful than one really big crash, but the pain will last much longer.

(D) A third successful forecast of mine referred to Italy's ability of joining the Euro – or rather the pre-Euro scenario – at its inception in 1996. Arguably the "Maastricht criterion" for the acceptability of an EU member country's budget deficit was fixed purposely at 3 percent of that member's annual GDP as the upper limit in order to keep Italy out: Influential German circles considered Italian fiscal policy to be so irresponsibly in deficit that it would endanger the "soundness" of a European common currency. The Italian budget deficit was then well over 10 percent of GDP. It was assumed that in the short time available Italy would not be able to achieve the target of at the most a 3 percent deficit.

I saw that actually nothing would be easier for Italy. To understand that one has to remember that then the primary Italian budget, i. e. the current budgetary inflow and outflow, leaving out debt charges, was actually in substantial surplus: current government expenditure was considerably less than current budgetary intake, in particular from taxes. The deficit was only due to the huge interest load on the very large Italian government debt of some 125 percent of GDP. For many years Italy had frequently depreciated its currency so that it had to pay interest on its debt at the ruling real rate of interest plus the expected rate of inflation plus – because of the high uncertainty about the country's future monetary policy – a big risk premium. Thus, actually its real rate of interest was oppressively high (similar to the situation of present-day Greece). The introduction of the Euro, which then (and largely now still) was just another name for the continuation of the highly stable Deutsche Mark, offered a unique opportunity for Italy: Quite plausibly, it could suddenly *de facto* adopt the D-Mark, whose stability would be controlled outside Italy. (The mere promise that one will adopt a much more stable monetary policy of an unknown kind, is nowhere near as convincing!) Thus the plausible assurance alone that Italy could link its currency to the Deutsche Mark made Italian interest rates plummet and approach German levels – which they promptly did. At German interest rates on Italian national debt most of the Italian budget deficit was gone. There would be a further effect: Italian long-run fixed interest bonds, which had been issued at former high interest rates, would shoot up in value due to the much lower interest rates then beginning to prevail. For at low ruling interest rates the sum of high promised interest charges discounted to the present is high. Therefore, there was a huge inflow of financial capital into Italy: All long-run financial institutions wanted to buy long-run Italian bonds, hoping they would appreciate. Italian financial markets thus became both cheap and highly liquid, and Italy would easily meet the Maastricht criterion. Unfortunately, by now, 14 years later, Italy has once more dissipated that initial advantage of entering the Euro.

Early in 1996, I explained this likely scenario to the then minister of foreign affairs, Wolfgang Schüssel, who understood my argument within a few minutes: Correct forecasts are not theoretically complicated, they just have to employ the appropriate analytical framework. In August 1996, I explained the same ideas to a conference of top Austrian financiers (many of them CEOs of insurance companies) and top industrialists. Here I made a mistake: Asked whether profitable buying opportunities for Italian bonds were still ongoing, I thought: no; the opportunity had gone. Actually I underestimated the time-span needed for adjustments.

(E) I close this essay by recounting a marvelous forecast of a great friend of mine, a former foreign member of the Austrian Academy, Béla Csikos-Nagy (1915–2005). Csikos-Nagy entered the Hungarian Ministry of Finance in 1943 and stayed on top of the political topsyturvy for the rest of his life – with just one year in prison, whence he was released to be appointed director general of a large Hungarian firm. For many years, he was secretary of state for price policy and after 1989 he became an influential political advisor and a member of the Hungarian Academy of Sciences. Thus he was first a nationalist, then a communist party member, then a socialist – his mother, a former head of the union of Roman-Catholic women of Southern Hungary, ignoring the fact that her son was a communist of sorts. Csikos-Nagy's talent for survival is shown by his housing arrangement: He lived in a modest private apartment in a Buda suburb in order to remain independent from government perks.

From him I heard a fascinating analysis of Tito's break-away from Russian communism and his establishment of the Yugoslav cooperative type of communism: Tito had to devise his particular system because productivity differences between the various parts of Yugoslavia were of the order of one to seven! (To give the reader an idea of what that means it may be mentioned that productivity differences within the regions of Austria are about 1 : 1,66. Admittedly Austria is a particularly homogenous country.) Under state communism equal wages have to be paid to equal types of workers everywhere: But in the heterogeneous economic environment of Yugoslavia with the concomitant differentials in labour productivity paying equal wages everywhere would have been ruinous. So under Tito's Cooperative Communism firms were given to the workers as – temporary – gift, and, lo and behold, a differentiated pay structure was achieved, with the workers as owners receiving incomes commensurate with their different productivity levels! And now for the forecast: Csikos-Nagy was convinced that such a differentiated system could only survive under the iron fist of Tito and predicted its break-up after his death. As we all know, it did not take long for the huge productivity differentials between the different parts of Yugoslavia to break up the unity of the country.

Thus correct forecasts need not rely on a elaborate theory: They just have to use one central theoretical notion, perhaps not obvious to most.

Erich W. Streissler

"i.i.d."? or: On So-called Precise Statements in Economics[1]

1. Confusing expectations and non-homogeneity of actors

1.1 Economics is a quantitative science in two dimensions: money and time. Only insofar as it is a quantitative science may it claim objectivity and some general validity. In other words, only as long as the economist makes basically quantitative statements in terms of money valuations and basically over time may s/he claim to be an expert; as soon as political or other value judgements enter s/he speaks only as one among millions of political decision takers *aka* voters. The analysis of the manifold consequences of political decisions, however, can indeed be part of economic science.

Economics is close to history. But while history typically analyses unique (though possibly recurring) events, economics tends to group events into classes of similarities, so that history becomes a borderline case for economic analysis, and only for that of monetary phenomena. We are now in the midst of the eighth great financial breakdown since 1720, each one historically unique but also – as viewed by economic analysis – sufficiently similar to those that went before.

Economics tends to think of itself as close to the natural sciences and as such widely uses mathematical and statistical methods. But in contrast to the natural sciences proper, economics studies group behaviour, the behaviour of groups of human beings, often of very large groups of humans, as in the case of international financial markets (my main field).[2]

Nonetheless, as a quantitative science of only money valuations over time economics has little in common with sociology.

1.2 On the face of it, economics with its only two dimensions should be much simpler than the four-dimensional physical sciences. But because of the behaviour of a multitude of human beings it is actually rather more complex. The relevant set of human beings may have sharply divergent ideas about money valuations, and the changeability of their ideas can make economic "time" flow at quite different speeds through objective time – differently in fact for every single human being. In other words, as long as we are not dealing with momentary, hand-to-mouth transactions, human expectations over time are the be-all and end-all of economic analysis; and those different expectations are held with varying, often high uncertainty on the part of all the different actors, to boot. And in the monetary field since 1973 we lack any currency which can serve as a notionally unique standard of value.

---

1 I owe a large debt to the invaluable critical comments by G. Tichy on the original version of this paper. The same holds for his comments on the essays on the Financial Market Crisis and on Financial Consolidation.

2 Non-homogeneous group behaviour makes for the intricacy and complexity of economic problems and by necessity entails much more tentative conclusions than those available in the natural sciences proper. As the Nobel Laureate and former member of the Austrian Academy of Sciences Friedrich A. Hayek put it: "Physics is everything which is easily explainable"!

Once put in this way, it is practically self-evident that different individual money valuations, diverse concepts of the time dimension and diverse and uncertain expectations about the (unknown) future have to be taken into account by the scientist as best s/he can. Expectations, often idiosyncratic expectations, become vitally important in a developed world of very complex and long-term financial transactions and with legally guaranteed free international capital movements.

1.3 This problem of economics can be both generalised and discussed on a more theoretical level: While in the natural sciences proper we deal with humanly controlled experiments or, at worst, with natural experiments due to one clear natural change[3], in economics we deal with uncontrolled quasi-experiments, which result from the analysis of many non-understood changes. To deal with that, highly complex econometric methods and econometric reasoning have been developed. Thus, as Leamer pointed out, empirical analysis has merely "transferred findings from one historical experience to a domain in which they no longer applied". Usually lacking is "the admission that the historical data are compatible with countless alternative data-generating models". Economists mix together "thought experiments ... data from non experiments, accidental experiments and designed experiments"[4]. Attempts at too precise predictions are apt to founder on layer after layer of complex preconditions. Therefore, as Hayek put it, economists have to content themselves with mere pattern prediction.[5] Or, as I would put it, economists have to content themselves with statements which are likely to be more or less correct under not very precisely defined "normal" circumstances. And, as Alan Greenspan put it,[6] in his forecasts for policy purposes he constantly had to be hovering somewhere between Knightian risk, where probabilities of correctness can be given, and Knightian uncertainty, where probabilities remain unknown. No clear falsification in the mood of Popper is possible in economics: The realm of uncertainty is huge.[7] Even the availability of an ever increasing volume of data and the ever increasing sophistication of their analysis have not necessarily been helpful: Analysts feel overpowered and uncertainty once more increases.

1.4 And that makes for the topic of this paper: The attempt to derive ever more precise statements about a very complex environment, the attempt at over-generalisation (occasionally attempted in the quest for a Nobel Memorial Prize). This results in conflicting theories, undetected serious mathematical mistakes, assumptions far off any empirical reality and undefined fields of applicability. But in contrast to the natural sciences proper, tests for economic theories cannot be constructed; one has to wait, sometimes for many years, for the (at least more or less) appropriate economic conditions to come about. Thus, economics brims with remarkable conclusions whose invalidity is discovered only much later.

In monetary and financial economics, and especially in the case of unhindered international capital movements, expectations about future developments figure large and there is no way to coordinate divergent expectations about future financial developments. He who sells a given financial asset typically believes that it will fall in value, and he who buys it typically assumes the contrary, viz. that it

---

3 As was the case in an example noted by Ch. Sturmbauer, where Lake Victoria received a huge inflow of water from a river system, which changed the fish population completely. See Ch. Sturmbauer, "Die Seen Ostafrikas und ihre Buntbarsche", Biologie in unserer Zeit, vol. 30 (6), 2000, pp. 353–364. Sturmbauer notes in his "study of adaptive radiation": "Speciation rates in cichlid radiations are stunningly rapid, possibly amounting to one new species every 50 years." (p. 362).

4 Edward E. Leamer, "Tantalus on the Road to Asymptopia", Journal of Economic Perspectives 24/2, Spring 2010, pp. 31–46, here in succession p. 36, p. 38 and p. 44.

5 F. A. Hayek, "The Theory of Complex Phenomena"; M. Bunge (ed.), *The Critical Approach to Science and Philosophy.* In Honor of Karl R. Popper, Glencoe Ill., pp 332–349.

6 A. Greenspan, "Risk and Uncertainty in Monetary Policy", American Economic Review, Papers and Proceedings, 94/2, May 2004, pp. 33–40, here p. 36f.

7 F. H. Knight, *Risk, Uncertainty and Profit,* New York, 1921.

will rise. In fact, the market for futures will function only if there is such a divergence of expectations. Keynes rightly stressed its importance: "It is interesting that the stability of the system and its sensitiveness to changes in the quantity of money should be so dependent on the existence of a variety of opinion about what is uncertain"[8]. Such a variety of expectations about the future is typical of a state of relatively high economic development. But it is difficult to model and results in conflicting theories.

1.5 The centrality of expectations distinguishes economics from all other life sciences. But even more: the analysis of human action may influence those actions. In certain branches of economics practical actors learn, often quickly, what theory has to say, and act accordingly. The early Nobel Laureate Milton Friedman was the first economist whose ability to change economic behaviour by his teaching was noted. In fact, R. Klump has pointed out[9] an instance where Friedman's analysis of a certain type of market behaviour had got the facts wrong, but changed behaviour in such a way that his analysis became correct: He explained interest rates above all in nominal terms by expectations of inflation, and that changed market behaviour for decades.

So far such learning processes activated by economic analysis have been noted only in financial markets and in monetary matters, which in a financially global world with free capital movements become rather intricate[10]. And it was the most fundamental consequence of the Crash of 2008 that behaviour in financial markets, which had been learned from a certain type of economic analysis, was suddenly perceived to be wrong, with actors switching to the opposite behaviour – although that, too, was notably influenced by an economist, viz. Lord Keynes: So far, actors had thought in terms of an economic "equilibrium" rapidly reached and had thought at best in terms of risk, i. e. cases where all possible "states of the world" and the probability of the occurrence of those various states are known. Suddenly one reverted to the never fully analysed world of Lord Keynes with the likelihood of long-run "disequilibria" and uncertainty (instead of risk, which, in contrast to uncertainty, is quantifiable). Keynes' analysis, however, is short-run and what it leaves out are the long-run consequences of actions.

2. Contradictions in exchange rate theory

2.1 My first example of fundamental economic confusions is one where the different aspects of the financial markets analysed just do not fit together, so that we are left with serious contradictions. Can there be anyone who would assume for international capital markets that millions of different actors in various countries and environments will see the future, and often the very distant future in quantitatively the same terms, especially as there are often no invariant future prices to guide them? Unfortunately, there is an influential strand in present-day – above all US-American – economic thinking that takes all economic outcomes to be the result of the decisions of one single all-understanding "rational" actor.

This makes for one of the major methodological puzzles in present-day economics. The puzzle is, in fact, a not untypical example of a teaching tradition prevailing over established facts: It is fairly easy to calculate and to teach what prices and quantities will result from bargaining in a small well-understood and isolated market with mostly traditional behaviour. Some of those "teachers" go on to

---

8 J. M. Keynes, *The General Theory of Employment Interest and Money*, London 1936, p. 172.

9 Remark of R. Klump during discussion of his paper "Geldzins, Güterpreise und das Gibson Paradoxon: Besonderheiten und Implikationen des Erklärungsansatzes von Kurt Wicksell"; in: *Studien zur Entwicklung der ökonomischen Theorie* XVIII, E. Streissler (ed.), Berlin 1998, pp. 39–62.

10 See St. F. Le Roy, "Efficient Markets and Martingales", Journal of Economic Literature, Dec. 1989, XXVII, pp. 1583–1621.

conclude that things must be more or less the same on more complex markets, e. g. on the hazy and huge financial market of Euros against US-dollars. As an instructive exercise I suggest you consider how the recent political difficulties and uncertainties in a tiny country, Greece, have affected the Euro-Dollar exchange rate: they have certainly done so out of all proportion. Does that impress you as an effect of one unitary rationality?

2.2 Let us look at present exchange rate modelling. On the one hand, an exchange rate can be explained as determined on the goods market, the market for exports and imports. This explanation is called the purchasing power parity theory. It states: If home and foreign have different rates of inflation, then one is indifferent over time between buying at home or in foreign only if and when the difference in inflation rates is just compensated by changes in the exchange rate. If, e. g., foreign has a higher rate of inflation than home, this difference has to be exactly compensated by a corresponding depreciation of the foreign currency. When one buys in foreign one sees that foreign prices have risen more over time because of the inflation, but one acquires the foreign currency correspondingly cheaper on the market. But at present, inflation differences within the developed world amount to at most one per cent a year, therefore exchange rates should be practically constant, changing just by that one per cent a year.

The exchange rate is also determined on the market for financial capital. Here, the equally plausible theory is called the uncovered interest parity theory. It says that in order for one to be indifferent between letting one's financial capital "work" at home or in foreign, any difference in interest rates between the two currency areas must be exactly compensated by changes in the exchange rate. E. g., if foreign offers 3 per cent higher interest rates than home, then the foreign currency must depreciate by just these 3 per cent in order for one to be indifferent between investing at home or in foreign. Lately, however, in most countries of the highly developed world, long-term interest rates (i. e. on ten year government bonds) have differed within a range of less than one per cent only, therefore exchange rates should not change, or again only by one per cent a year.

Thus, because of similar goods market inflation rates and similar interest rates within the developed world, in particular between the USA and core Euro-Europe, the exchange rate of the Euro against the dollar should not change. But since its introduction in 2002 the Euro has appreciated by some 80 per cent if we look at its peak value in the summer of 2008; or by some 40 per cent if we look at the low point of the Greek scare in May 2010. It has thus appreciated on average by at least 5 per cent a year or up to 10 per cent a year; thus it is certainly not nearly stationary, as both uncovered interest parity theory and purchasing power parity theory would have it. And its annual fluctuations are quite large: in a few months about the beginning of 2010 the Euro-Dollar exchange rate dropped by 15 per cent[11].

2.3 On the other hand, a counterfactual stationary climate for exchange rates is assumed in many long-term financial contracts, where forward exchange rates hardly differ from spot rates. For the most advanced economies, exchange rates pegged to the US-dollar ended in March 1973. Now, however, 38 years later, this past exchange rate regime still tacitly dominates much of long-term financial market reasoning! The dollar is considered by many, in particular financially unstable countries, e. g. Russia, Argentina etc., not only as a "safe" haven, but also as a currency with an in-the-long-run stable value. Because of this belief the dollar shows a long-term (10 year) interest rate on government

[11] Actually purchasing power parity and uncovered interest parity theory would contradict each other, unless real interest rates, i. e. inflation corrected interest rates, do not differ between currency areas. For "PPP" says that the difference in the change of real exchange rates should be zero, while "UIP" says that this difference should equal the difference in real interest rates. Amusingly, at present when real interest rate differences hardly exist and thus the condition for conformity of the two theories is more or less fulfilled, both theories are, as pointed out, empirically overthrown particularly often.

bonds only one fifth of one per cent higher than that of Germany – notwithstanding the fact that its relative annual depreciation against the Euro of at least 5 per cent (or up to 10 per cent) should have resulted in an interest rate at least 5 per cent or even 10 per cent higher – according to the theory of uncovered interest parity.

Analysts are faced with a basic contradiction: Prevalent theories, e. g. uncovered interest parity, visualize a long-established stationary probability system from which an unchanging mean value, the long-run unchanging average exchange rate, is well-known to all economic actors. This assumed unchanging and commonly understood mean value provides the informational basis for assumed "equilibria". Actually, however, because of relatively rapid changes in markets we have to deal with constantly shifting economic constellations, which have not yet settled into any kind of equilibrium and are not fully understood by economic actors; and this is typically so for all macroeconomic constellations and, in particular, for international financial markets. Furthermore, the more – heterogeneous – actors there are in the world's markets, the less likely is it that all of them hold the same theories.

2.4 This becomes glaringly obvious when one has to explain fundamental economic theories like the above exchange rate theories to students and feels obliged at the same time to relate those theories to present-day empirical facts and figures. Right away, one stumbles on crass inconsistencies. It is a big challenge for a teacher plausibly to reconcile established theory and rapidly changing facts. In attempting such a reconciliation, not only students learn, teachers do, too. My experience in over half a century of university teaching is: *Docendo discimus.* We learn by teaching. Unchecked by facts, economic theory is insufficient. It is fascinating to see how many facts assumed for decades are by now outdated, e. g. the implicit assumption that all international capital movements just provide short-run finance for exports and imports. Examples of theories or theorems abound that are hailed and applauded for a long time before being put to the test of reality – and dismally failing.

Thus we arrive at the central topic of this paper: economics tries to be a quantitative science and a quantitatively correct science. But in times of fairly rapidly changing environments it tends to become a quarry of relics of quite different past circumstances. The attempt at precision in theory often leads to notions that are historically explainable and were correct once, but do not apply to the present.

3. Even Nobel Laureates in economics are fallible

3.1 Among the first cases of such conflict between theory and empirical facts was Milton Friedman's central notion that profitable speculation in markets for durable goods or for assets would reduce intertemporal price variation and would thus be price-stabilizing, a notion Friedman developed in 1950 and published in 1953[12]. His highly plausible argument for price stabilization by speculation ran as follows: If buying a commodity, holding it for a time and then selling it is to be profitable, purchase has to be made at a lower price than the eventual selling price. Therefore the experienced speculator will buy an asset when the price is temporarily lower than the average price. But by buying when the price is below average and thereby creating additional demand the speculator drives the price towards the average, thus reducing intertemporal price variations; i. e. he acts in a price-stabilizing way. On the other hand, the experienced speculator will sell when the price is above average, pushing the price down towards the average, once more reducing intertemporal price variation. Ergo: Profitable speculation is price-stabilizing by reducing intertemporal price fluctuations.

[12] M. Friedman, "The Case for Flexible Exchange Rates"; in: M. Friedman, *Essays in Positive Economics,* Chicago and London 1953, pp. 157–203. Especially in II A 3, "Speculation in foreign exchange markets will be destabilizing", Friedman argues exactly to the contrary of that caption.

But actually this plausible model, a favourite of many economists, is wrong and extremely misleading – for a number of reasons:

(1) It is true only for a stationary probability system with an unchanging mean value well-known to the actors. (Note the tacit assumption of a well-known average price in the above argument.) In fact, postulating an equilibrium in any model with a time dimension assumes a long-run, well understood stationary climate of the generating system. Friedman was soon advised that his model had actually been advanced already by John Stuart Mill in 1848 for the special case of the British wheat market[13] – for which the model was correct, because then supply changes were only caused by variations of the weather, a fact generally known. Demand was also stationary over time, or rather: In the long run, because of technical progress, supply increased in step with demand increase due to population growth. But a stationary probability system is not enough.

(2) The pricing function relative to the quantity must also be linear[14]. Otherwise, with a monotonically convex or concave price function relative to quantity the reduction of the remaining quantities on the market over time would change the average price, which had been assumed to be constant.

(3) Even worse, there has to exist a well-known average price. But there is none in the case of a random walk of prices, the random walk being highly relevant for the exchange rate of the dollar, for which Friedman used his argument in particular: With a random walk an average price does not "exist" in the sense that the variance of the average goes to infinity over time or, to put it differently, the best estimate of the average keeps changing with every new price, this best estimate being just the value of each past price quotation.

(4) Perhaps of least importance: If the volume of speculation becomes very large, it would nearly or even completely eliminate all price variation so that speculation would become unprofitable. So we arrive at a contradiction: If the volume of speculations becomes very large, there is no longer any reason for speculating, and speculation has to cease. The price would always be pushed to the average price or nearly so, and there would be no profit left in speculating. There would be no stationary average towards which speculation could move. But the lack of speculation would once more increase the need for it and we would arrive at a perpetual creation and then self-destruction of speculative behaviour.

3.2 The biggest problem of all is the first one in conjunction with the third: Does there exist a stationary probability system with an unchanging mean value, well known to the actors? Friedman's argument about stabilizing speculation was only subsidiary to his plea for flexible exchange rates[15] (rates determined freely on the markets – in contrast to fixed exchange rates, which are set by political agencies). So when in March 1973 the US-dollar left its former fixed value and was allowed to float, the majority of US academic economists joined Friedman in expecting the resulting exchange rate to be highly stable. Actually, in March 1973, everyone knew that the US dollar was overvalued but no one knew by how much. Thus, the appropriate mean value was not known, and due to the rapid large changes in basic economic parameters it has never been found out in the 38 years since. How do you learn in a rapidly changing system? Actually, as already pointed out, markets still expect (contrary to the facts) that in the very long run the dollar value relative to the Deutsche Mark, later – since 1999 – renamed the Euro, would remain at the value it had had before 1973. In the short run, however, they expect a constantly changing real dollar value. Short-run and long-run expectations are in conflict!

[13] J. St. Mill, *Principles of Political Economy* with Some of their Applications to Social Philosophy, London 1848, book IV, ch. II, § 4,5.

[14] This has been shown by G. Orosel, "Profitable Speculation and Price Stability", Jahrb. Nationalökon. Statist., 1999 (6), November 1984, pp. 485–501.

[15] See the title of his essay given in FN 12: "The Case for Flexible Exchange Rates"!

Anyhow, contrary to Friedman's expectations the average exchange rate variations of the various currencies did not decrease with floating rates, but rather, as Mussa (1986)[16] showed, increased by three to eight times. Speculation which, with a known mean value, might be stabilizing, tends much rather to be destabilizing when the mean is unknown. And furthermore, the type of monetary policy then matters especially in the long run. In 1953, Friedman had explicitly assumed that the economic world shows stationary probabilities, while at least in monetary matters little-understood frequent changes are evident, largely due to international capital movements.

Markets still have not realized that the type of monetary policy does matter for the long-run real value of an exchange rate. E. g., with the D-Mark and the Euro the sole legally fixed long-run policy aim is the prevention of inflation. Since Alan Greenspan (governor of the Federal Reserve from 1987 to 2006), the policy pursued for the US dollar has been aiming at the prevention of unemployment (without success since 2008) and the stimulation of economic growth. With fundamentally different policies in the respective currency areas, the assumption that the relative prices are everywhere stationary (i. e. a stationary exchange rate) is highly unlikely.

3.3 While Friedman would never admit his mistake about the (non-)existence of a stable mean value, the mistake of another Nobel Laureate, Edward C. Prescott, was quite primitive and was furthermore corrected by himself – although 18 years later, when his Nobel Prize, partly due to the resonant acclaim of the original methodologically incorrect article, was already assured. Typically, US-American theory looks at market prices unadulterated by government action. In other words: Effects of taxation are simply ignored. Also, for the sake of mathematical convenience, preferably only costs proportional to the quantity bought and sold are considered, while costs that are independent of those quantities – so-called "fixed costs" – are ignored: They would lead to considerable non-linearity in models. But actually the prevalence of such fixed costs increases over time.

Let me sketch that mistake: The "equity premium puzzle", presumably uncovered by Mehra and Prescott (1985)[17], was that "the average return on 'U.S. common' stock has far exceeded the average return on short-term U.S. government debt ... the average difference was 6.2 per cent per year in the 1889–1978 period". "They tried to account for this difference by construing it as a premium for bearing non diversifiable aggregate risk, but found that risk accounts for only a tiny fraction of the difference"[18]. The first problem is that Mehra and Prescott took as their measuring rod not the long-term but the short-term interest rate on US government debt, which is a rate relevant only for banks and similar institutions, while practically irrelevant for investors in stocks and shares, i. e. "equities". But Mehra and Prescott had also forgotten about taxation and the fixed costs of holding equity capital: "Taking into account some factors ignored by Mehra and Prescott (taxes, regulatory constraints, and diversification cases) and focussing on long-term rather than short-term savings instruments", the puzzle is gone, "the average real debt return [is] almost 4 per cent and the average real equity return somewhat under 5 per cent", the difference very modestly being "less than 1 per cent", easily accountable for by the higher risk of equity capital.

---

[16] M. Mussa, "Nominal Exchange Rate Regimes and the Behavior of Real Exchange Rates: Evidence and Implications", Carnegie- Rochester Conference Series on Public Policy, vol. 25 (1986), pp. 117–213. See also already M. Mussa, "Empirical Regularities in the Behavior of Exchange Rates and Theories of Foreign Exchange Markets", Carnegie-Rochester Conf. Ser. on Publ. Pol., vol.11 (1979), pp. 9–57.

[17] R. Mehra & E. C. Prescott, "The Equity Premium: A Puzzle", Journal of Monetary Economics, 15 (2), March 1985, pp. 145–161.

[18] This quotation and all the quotations following in this paragraph are taken from E. R. McGrattan & E. C. Prescott, "Average Debt and Equity Returns: Puzzling?", American Economic Review PP 93/2, May 2003, pp. 392–397, here p. 392.

Thus, Prescott had corrected his own mistake just before receiving the Nobel Prize one and a half years later, in October 2004. But actually some other puzzles remain: Equity returns were much lower than average in the 1970s: Evidently, referring back to the discussion of Friedman, average investors take very long to learn in how far averages in returns change.

And the average returns of stocks went up quickly from the later 1980s until 2000: Average investors thus tended to overestimate the effect of booms as well. "The high volatility of stock market returns is puzzling". There is an "excessive stock price volatility puzzle"[19]. Thus, it is not only mean values that are misjudged for long periods by market actors, but also variances. "Low volatility of productive capital returns" and "high volatility of stock-market returns" show that (information-wise) similar markets are not well coordinated. We are forced to use different theories for very similar economic phenomena.

3.4 While it is well-known that, as above, stock market prices and their changes are closely linked with what might be called the business cycle, be it as to its effect or its cause or both, the next Nobel Prize winner to be discussed, Robert E. Lucas, Jr., views the business cycle quite differently – and extremely narrowly so: He presents[20] "a simple [?] example of ... the central feature of the [?] modern [?] business cycle: a systematic relation between the rate of change in nominal prices and the level of real output"[21]. Typically, Lucas considers an extreme version of his and his Chicago colleagues' theorizing as "the" sole possible theory and, of course, the only one that is "modern". Reading on, we find that he thinks he "provides an explicit elaborate example ... of the characteristics attributed to the U.S. economy by Friedman"[22]. Maybe so. Looking closer into his model, we realize that Lucas assumes a given and unchanging demand for money and that, actually, by only one single person (for, what Lucas considers as "rational" action is only one unique possibility of action). The only thing that varies is money supply, in a stochastic way. That basically presupposes a dictatorial central bank and is at variance with any democratic regime controlling it. Lucas also assumes a goods market with a given aggregate supply function with only stochastic variations of output. Traditionally, this would have been assumed as the effect of harvest variations, but with Lucas it is due to the chance variation of the number of inhabitants – in its turn due to something (by assumption) close to immigration or maybe to variations in the labour supply of each individual depending on the expected "harvest". Apart from these stochastic variations aggregate supply – of only one single commodity, the "consumption good" – is stationary over time: There is only one factor of production: labour; and workers do not learn any new skills over time. In fact, after the beginning of the period individuals do not learn anything, while living in two different states: first as workers and income earners (in the real world perhaps for about 40 years) and then as old-age spenders of their savings and in addition of anything the government (whose sole activity is the creation of additional money) might add in proportion to those savings (in the real world for about 20 years). During those 20 or 40 years individuals learn nothing of economic relevance (for which reason I call Lucas' economy a "fruit fly" economy – fruit flies being organisms that live for a few days only, during which they learn virtually nothing).

What about money demand? Here Lucas presents us with a remarkable sleight of hand. He says[23]: "In the next section we show [!] that" Lucas' central equation (4.2) "has a unique [!] solution". Actually at the bottom of that p.lll he says: "It is a plausible conjecture [?] that solutions to (4.2) assume the form ..." and then writes down one version of the quantity theory of money. His equation would have an <u>infinite</u> number of solutions, but Lucas <u>assumes</u> only <u>one</u> "unique" solution, because that is

[19] McGrattan-Prescott (2003), loc.cit. p. 396.

[20] R. E. Lucas Jr., "Expectations and the Neutrality of Money", J. Eco. Theory, 4 (2), April 1972, pp. 103–124.

[21] Lucas (1972), loc. cit. p. 103.

[22] Lucas (1972), loc. cit. p. 104

[23] Lucas (1972), loc. cit. p. 111.

"a plausible conjecture", a mathematical hocus-pocus that has one shuddering: There is one unique money demand function assumed, and that is the money demand of the by now more than 300 years old quantity theory of money.

But that equation is only a statement of a final equilibrium under special circumstances and an equilibrium which David Hume in his extensive treatment in 1752[24] – Lucas quotes him copiously in his Nobel Lecture of 1995[25] – had called (not quoted by Lucas) a state "not easily to be accounted for"[26]. The question is whether there are equilibrating tendencies at all and how and when an equilibrium is reached. Thus, Lucas assumes (a) a certain form of money demand as "a plausible conjecture", (b) production of the "consumption" good with labour only, therefore (c) no capital which would be the link between past and future decisions in a capitalist economy. The not-considered capital would embody information most relevant to economic change, i. e. innovation in the production process. Thus, Lucas once more uses an essentially stationary model (and a rather primitive one, at that) to describe development!

Finally, the very essence of his model, the money side of it, is at least as primitive as the production side without capital or innovation: Lucas knows only cash, thus leaving out the money multiplier, which would show how banks change the money supply and, in addition, how individuals vary their demand over the business cycle between different types of money. Thus, even the money supply is wrongly specified. And the production process – quite lengthy in reality – remains non-financed with Lucas: The consumption sector, the sole production sector with him, is paid only at the moment of the eventual sale of the consumption good.

Lucas' main point, that individuals will have difficulties in deciding what actually happens when there is a mixture of "real" and monetary changes is not relevant when monetary changes per time period are so evidently much larger, become effective more rapidly, and are measured more precisely. Or would anybody suggest that Greece's problems of 2010 were mainly due to Greek workers suddenly asking for more leisure time?

Could the Lucas model perhaps be employed for an elucidation of the secular US boom of 1995–1999? Hardly, as that boom was due above all to a sectoral shift in production to computer hardware and software, a "new" sector in a double sense: an innovative sector that increased greatly in volume and was so profitable because it needed very little capital (a highly "capital saving" innovative sector). Could the Lucas model explain the US crash of the year 2008? Not at all: Lucas ignored all relevant real-world problems. In his model there is nothing like a "bankruptcy", there is no faulty investment due to an overestimation of expected future price increases, as in the housing sector, and there are no banks that have completely miscalculated their financing decisions. There is no over-stimulation by monetary policy, as in the USA in the autumn 2008,because with Lucas there is no monetary policy. And above all, in Lucas there is no other money than the US-dollar, there cannot be a huge current account deficit, there is no effect of foreign finance, there are no international capital movements: "Forget the 75 years between 1914 and 1989", was the advice of Robert Mundell;[27] so perhaps Lucas 1972 should best be forgotten, too. But was he not forgettable even before 1989, since he did not at all present, as he claimed, "the central feature of the modern business cycle"?

[24] D. Hume, *Political Discourses,* Edinburgh 1752.

[25] R. E. Lucas Jr. "Nobel Lecture: Monetary Neutrality", Journal of Political Economy 104 (Aug. 1996), pp. 661–682.

[26] Hume (1752), loc. cit, Discourse III, "Of Money", p.47.

[27] R. A. Mundell, "A Reconsideration of the Twentieth Century", American Economic Review 90/3, June 2000, pp. 327–340, here p. 327.

3.5 The fundamental methodological problem is this: The question of the empirical relevance of a model is normally not raised at all in present-day US economics. Its exponents are immune against criticism: Any critic would simply be told to improve his own knowledge of economics by coming to study in the USA! American economic theory is above all propaganda for one of the country's largest industries: university studies – not least in Lucas' Chicago.

While the problem with the ideas reviewed so far is that they assume precisely defined equilibrium situations with precisely defined, but wrongly specified complete or near-complete information, there has also existed – for nearly half a century now – a path-breaking literature on various types of incomplete information situations. That literature also depends on very fine differences in its assumptions, differences that make for considerable differences in their results. This strand of thought started already with the first pertinent model by the 1981 Nobel Laureate, George Stigler, "The Economics of Information" (1961)[28]. Stigler raised the question of the search for the best price for a given product. He assumed, e. g., constant marginal search cost for price, but falling marginal gains in terms of ever smaller price reductions the longer one searches. The optimum is reached when (in the last search step undertaken) marginal search cost just equals marginal lowering of the price. Thus Stigler determines the optimal quantity of search or the optimal number of search steps to undertake.

By the time he was awarded the Nobel Prize, standard opinion actually considered Stigler's solution wrong. For if, e. g., one happens to be offered a very good (=low) price for the intended purchase, why should one search on and not accept that first offer? Soon, standard opinion had changed again and took Stigler to be correct – although for one special problem: When (those were pre-Internet-times!) one searched by mail for the best price offer, then one searched in Stigler fashion with the need for determining the optimum number of letters to be mailed. If, however, one searches by actually visiting one shop after another in order to ask for the price of the desired good one will optimally determine the acceptance price, and the quantity of search, the number of shops one visits, will become a random variable. The question thus is whether one receives additional information in each search step or not.

3.6 In this case two correct optimum solutions for two slightly different problems were found. Quite otherwise in the case of the Nobel Prize winning article of Joseph E. Stiglitz (Nobel Laureate of 2000), "Credit Rationing in Markets with Imperfect Information" (co-authored by A. Weiss)[29]: 28 years after its publication it was shown that the solution suggested for the optimal credit policy of banks was actually non-existent! Stiglitz is famous for his exceptional inventiveness, but just as famous for never fully working out his ideas and depending on varying co-authors for that. In this case we find at the very beginning of the article in Figure 1 the picture of a nicely domed = "hump-shaped" curve with a unique maximum with the caption: "There Exists an Interest Rate which Maximizes the Expected Return to the Bank"[30], the existence of such a maximizing interest rate being again and again assumed, but never proved. In the meantime, it has been shown that the assumed unique maximum does not exist.

This proof was given in a paper by Arnold and Riley[31]. Note that Arnold teaches in Regensburg, Germany: He is not a US-American insider. Arnold and Riley show that there will be a "nonmonotonic [!] expected lender revenue function"[32]. They conclude: "For the central model analyzed by

[28] G. J. Stigler, "The Economics of Information", Journal of Political Economy 69, June 1961, pp. 213–225.

[29] J. E. Stiglitz & A. Weiss, "Credit Rationing in Markets with Imperfect Information", American Economic Review 71 (3), June 1981, pp. 393–410.

[30] Stiglitz & Weiss (1981), loc. cit. p. 394.

[31] L. G. Arnold & J. G. Riley, "On the Possibility of Credit Rationing in the Stiglitz-Weiss Model", American Economic Review 99 (5), Dec. 2009, pp. 2012–2021.

[32] Arnold & Riley, (2009), loc. cit., p. 2014.

[Stiglitz and Weiss] there can never [!] be a hump-shaped expected profit function for borrowers, and so rationing with a single [!] equilibrium loan rate is impossible. Instead, either the expected profit function increases with the borrowing rate and there is no rationing, or there must be at least two [!] turning points. High-risk borrowers demand loans at high interest rates, so any equilibrium with rationing will involve market clearing at a high loan rate and rationing at a second lower rate"[33]. Thus, potential customers not served at the low interest rate (when there is rationing at that rate) will indeed be offered credit, but at a much higher interest rate, while no credit will be given at the in-between interest rates. What Arnold and Riley show contradicts the very definition of credit rationing by Stiglitz and Weiss[34]. The latter defined an economic situation that can <u>never exist</u>: "We reserve the term rationing for circumstances in which either (a) among loan applicants who appear to be identical some receive a loan and others do not, and the rejected applicants would not receive a loan even if they offered to pay a higher interest rate; or (b) there are identifiable groups of individuals ... who ... are unable to obtain loans at any interest rate, even though with a larger supply of credit, they would". The former case was shown by Arnold and Riley not to exist, and the latter case remains unanalysed.

3.7 There is also a deeper methodological problem buried in the Stiglitz-Weiss model of credit rationing. We had long been familiar with the phenomenon that certain <u>well-distinguishable types</u> of potential bank customers do not get credit, particularly after a financial crash and in an economic depression. It is a commonplace that among applicants known to be different not everyone is necessarily served. For the market for used cars the Nobel Laureate Akerlof (1970)[35] had shown that under specified conditions, without legal safeguards and with asymmetric information of the two sides of the market (= prospective customers being less informed than suppliers), the market would break down while with equal information of both sellers and prospective buyers it would function satisfactorily. Stiglitz tried to show (without success, as it turned out) that in the case of credit rationing – this time the "suppliers", the banks, being less well informed how their customers are going to use their credits – there would be a <u>partial market breakdown</u>, some applicants receiving loans, but otherwise undistinguishable others getting nothing. The fascination of the model sprang from the idea of only a partial satisfaction of demand.

Actually, it is less important that theoretically this case, as modelled, could not exist, than that in practice this case is most unlikely anyway: Is it not weird to assume that a bank so far has had no experience of giving credit and that all the customers showing up are essentially first time customers without a credit history?

As Dell'Ariccia et al., 2008, have shown that was only plausible for <u>investment</u> banks which entered the housing market only late and then got the worst, mostly first time applicants.[36] But then it was highly incautious to charge into an unknown market, and for established banks to finance newcomer banks.

Even about new customers established banks will have some easily available information, above all whether the applicant's firm is big or small. Small firms are more likely to be rationed than large firms. For the present US crisis a recent empirical study[37] has shown that out of the 75 per cent of small firms in a sample 22 per cent said they were "very affected" by credit constraints, while only 16

---

33 Arnold & Riley, (2009), loc. cit., p. 2019.

34 Stiglitz & Weiss, (1981), loc. cit. 394 f.

35 G. A. Akerlof, "The Market for 'Lemons': Quality Uncertainty and the Market Mechanism", Quarterly Journal of Economics 84 (3), Aug. 1970, pp. 488–500.

36 I owe the reference to Dell'Ariccia to G. Tichy: Dell'Arricia et al, 2008, Credit booms and lending standards: Evidence from the subprime mortgage market, Centre for Economic Policy Research Discussion Paper No. 6683.

37 Nber Digest April 2010, "The Real Effects of Financial Constraints".

per cent of (the 25 per cent) large firms said so. As I know from practical experience with large firms that were turned down, a number of them were actually already bankrupt, some without being aware of it (or at least pretending to know nothing about it).[38]

The other criterion would be that firms that have a well-established longer-term business connection with a bank (and are therefore known to the bank) will get credit while unknown new applicants will be turned down. It is for this reason that well-established firms will hold a credit account or at least provide themselves with a credit line with one bank – if not with several banks at the same time. But the typical disapppointment is that in a recession when firms sorely need credit or more credit, credit is cut. The most important case of credit rationing, neither analysed by Stiglitz-Weiss nor in the critical article by Arnold-Riley, is that firms do receive bank credit but often much less credit than would be optimal for them, with the macroeconomic consequence that recovery from a recession is considerably postponed. And in the recent US "subprime" credit crisis the problem was actually just the opposite: too many credits were granted, not too few.

3.8 Finally let us have a look at the influential article by Nobuhiro Kiyotaki and Randall Wright, "Money as a Medium of Exchange"[39]. The authors look at a non-centralized economy, where trades are achieved only occasionally. By assumption there are at least three individuals, each producing one of three goods but consuming one of the other two. In addition to useful goods there is intrinsically worthless money on the market. Goods are distinguished by the amount of storage cost per period and by their likelihood of being accepted ("acceptability") by trading partners. Money has zero (or at least the lowest) storage cost and the highest acceptability, so that, though by itself useless, it is accepted in order to get the desired good more quickly, i. e. at less search cost. The set-up is thus very close to that of C. Menger (1871)[40], who had modelled money as the commodity with the highest marketability or saleability, as is mentioned by Kiyotaki-Wright[41]. Menger had used the term "Marktgängigkeit". It is interesting how old ideas sometimes crop up again and again.

In the model it is assumed that individuals are always fully provided with only one commodity at a time or that only money is held. Thus the possible states of the world are finite and countable, which makes analysis (comparatively) easy. Furthermore, it is assumed that the economy has already reached and remains in "a steady state Nash equilibrium"[42]. The analysis only of equilibria without considering whether they can actually be reached is not untypical and the above 0/1 analysis of storage appears a legitimate simplification. But unfortunately neither one nor the other assumption was critically investigated.

Fifteen years later Shevchenko and Wright[43] – one of the original authors plus a new collaborator – showed that using up all one's assets that were held in the form of one single commodity (or as money) would make for an unstable equilibrium that could never be reached. To establish this the authors used a deeper mathematical analysis: topological fixed point analysis. Happily, they also found an alternative solution to the one to be rejected: In order to save the basic idea of the model,

---

[38] How can one estimate a minimum credit worthiness? G. Tichy names as such an estimate the FICO scores, a mechanical projection of the credit risk based on customers' previous records, named after the designing firm, the Fair Isaac Corporation, FICO for short.

[39] N. Kiyotaki & R. Wright, "On Money as a Medium of Exchange", Journ. of Political Economy 97 (4) Aug. 1989, pp. 927–954.

[40] C. Menger, *Grundsätze der Volkswirthschaftslehre,* Vienna, 1871, ch. 8, ed. 1968, pp. 249, 252. The same, *Principles of Economics,* New York, London, 1976, pp. 256, 259.

[41] Kiyotaki & Wright (1989), loc. cit., p. 935.

[42] Kiyotaki & Wright (1989), loc. cit., p. 932.

[43] A. Shevchenko & R. Wright, "A simple search model of money with heterogeneous agents and partial acceptability", Economic Theory 24, Nov. 2004, pp. 877–885.

one has to assume that individuals differ not only in their final commodity demands, but also in other basic respects. Such additional distinctions are highly plausible in practice, and then several interesting equilibria result. So the basic idea of the model can be retained.

3.9 Thus, the problem of many recent US-American models is that they seek theoretically "interesting" and very specific conclusions without ever asking whether the assumptions to be made bear any relation to the world of facts. Stigler's original model had the methodologically interesting conclusion that one should not only look at averages but rather at extreme value distributions (the cheapest price!); but the model is applicable in only one special case. Friedman's model happened to contain a serious mathematical mistake. Lucas' model is so extreme in its assumptions that one cannot say when and where it may be applicable. Prescott had originally just forgotten about taxes; Stiglitz had made an impossible assumption and looked at an empirically virtually irrelevant case; and Kiyotaki-Wright (the only non-Nobel-Prize article reviewed here) employed an illicit simplification. Dominant macroeconomic models are hard to test. To quite an extent, economics has been turned into dogmatic reflection. Macroeconomics, in particular, has become in its most highly esteemed models a subject taught, but not tested. More and more one gets the impression of l'art pour l'art exercises divorced from practically useful elucidations of real life. Or, to put it differently, can these models serve as foundations for policy advice?

4. Probabilistic model specifications

4.1 We have seen that people at the very top of the profession tend to offer economic models that are too highly specialized, using assumptions that invalidate their conclusions. We now turn to the probabilistic specification of models for estimation purposes: And here once more we find that far too simple assumptions are used, which, if generalised, mean that there are no precise conclusions to be arrived at. We remain in limbo.

Their central modelling assumption provided the title for this paper: It is assumed, usually without reasons being given, that the error term of the model to be estimated is "i.i.d.", i. e. the error term is "independently and identically distributed". Actually, even more is usually assumed: that the error term is normally and therefore symmetrically distributed with mean zero and a given variance σ^2, which then is also independently and identically distributed (e. g. over time), to be abbreviated as $N(0,\sigma^2)$. This assumption is not unrealistic in sampling of economic data at a given moment, but highly problematic in macroeconomic models over time: Why should the errors in a model of a very typical slow adjustment process be independent of what has happened in earlier periods? And why should the distribution not change over time, sometimes being very regular with small fluctuations, in other cases with hectic and large changes?

The assumption of the symmetric normal distribution is a standard one. So one can quote many instances of its completely unthinking application even for samples at a given moment. It is e. g. well known that the distribution of the population size of towns is heavily skewed to the left, there being many small towns and only a few big ones. Assuming a symmetric distribution in this case would generate nonsense. I well remember a thesis where the assumption of a symmetric size distribution of towns led to the conclusion that there existed a large number of towns with a negative population!

4.2 The first case to be discussed here is of an article distinguished by the invention of five "P"s where normally only three would be used: the "purchasing power parity persistence paradigm" by Christian J. Murray and David H. Papell[44]. The authors take it as agreed upon that real exchange rates

[44] C. J. Murray & D. H. Papell, "The Purchasing Power Parity Persistence Paradigm", Journ. of International Economics 56 (2002), pp. 1–19.

show "high short term volatility ... with extremely slow convergence to purchasing power parity"[45]. In fact, the question is whether there is any such convergence at all or whether real exchange rates do not rather show random walk behaviour. Many authors reject the random walk, but then their "techniques are not appropriate for measuring persistence for three reasons. First, virtually all existent studies ... are biased downwards ... Second ... the methods chosen tend to be unreliable or even invalid. Third, most of the studies ... do not account for serial correlation" (p. 17)[46]. "Most important, the least squares estimates of the half-lives are biased downward in small samples. This imparts a 'double' bias ... they are constructed using biased estimates from a biased parametrization" (p.3)[47]. This is typical for slow economic processes: One would need a very large number of data, which one does not have and can never get, due to changes over time, particularly with major changes in political systems. Due to historical change one can hardly ever draw sufficiently large, but still sufficiently homogeneous samples.

The authors find: "Once the bias in least squares estimates is corrected ... the confidence intervals of half-lives of PPP deviations are too wide to place any credence in the point estimates ... all the upper bounds are infinite"[48][!]. An infinite upper bound of confidence intervals implies that the random walk model cannot be rejected for exchange rates. Careful assumptions thus permit the conclusion that exchange rate forecasts are in general impossible. This is shown by the authors for 20 countries, but in all cases for the exchange rates against the US-dollar. It is exactly the dollar whose value is unpredictable, because in that currency the largest amount of international capital transactions takes place and thus the dollar is so far "the" major reserve currency. Careful estimation proves that the exchange rates against the dollar cannot be forecast.

Murray-Papell rely on the fact that it is wrong to assume a normal distribution in case of a small sample of values, when the parameters of the normal distribution are not yet known and therefore have still to be estimated from the small sample at hand. In this case, as Weitzman[49] pointed out, it ought to be remembered that one has to assume a Student t-distribution, which converges to the Normal Distribution for large (actually: infinite) samples, but has much larger variance for small samples, and which converges to infinite variance for very small samples. Thus, the wide confidence intervals required make precise distinctions impossible.

4.3 So far, I have been concerned with the appropriateness of the assumption of the normal distribution of the error terms without yet turning to the question whether these will be independently and identically distributed ("i.i.d."), as is often assumed. (In the cases analyzed by Murray-Papell the error term also had time structures that did not show independent errors over time.) The first problem here is that with all types of assets the variance of asset prices is not at all constant over time: In the case of US common stock prices, incorporated in the Dow-Jones-Index, stock price variance made three big jumps upwards within the last 110 years: in 1931–33, in 1987 and in 2008. The three jumps were of about equal size: to a level of an app. 15 times higher variance than normal, i. e. larger changes were about 4 per cent in one day instead of about 1 per cent; and on a few days even 10 per cent price changes occurred (see the essay on "Rare Events" as well as the next essay). Such large price changes require large reserves; typically, they caught many banks unprepared. As these upward jumps in variance occur only rarely and with long time intervals in between, they require much caution on the part of financial investors, caution as recommended by historical experience.

---

[45] Loc. cit. p. 1.

[46] Loc. cit. p. 40.

[47] Loc. cit. p. 3.

[48] Loc. cit. p. 15.

[49] M. L. Weitzman, "Subjective Expectations and Asset-Return Puzzles", American Economic Review 97/4, Sept 2007, pp. 1102–1130.

Actually, large price changes and thus increases in their variance are rare, but still much more frequent than a normal distribution of price changes would imply: Contrary to simple models the distribution of relative price changes exhibits what is graphically called "fat tails", as compared with the normal distribution. In particular, large upward movements of prices are much too frequent. These large price increases show, as I demonstrate, a Pareto distribution, and not a Normal Distribution, causing a significant deviation from "i.i.d.".

While price changes are thus not identically distributed over time the fact that often they are also not at all independently distributed either, particularly on financial markets, creates even greater problems. Also it is well-nigh impossible to distinguish empirically between two quite different phenomena: on the one hand, variable (1) causing variable (2) and, on the other hand, an involved lag structure of variable (1) determining that same variable over time.

4.4 An important article by Engel and West, "Exchange Rates and Fundamentals"[50] demonstrates that nicely: The authors argue "an asset price manifests near-random walk behaviour if fundamentals are I (1) and the factor for discounting future fundamentals is near one ... this ... helps explain ... [why] fundamental variables such as money supplies, outputs, inflation and interest rates provide little help in predicting changes in floating exchange rates ... [but] that the exchange rate helps predict these fundamentals"[51]. To put it crassly in quasi-theological terms: the exchange rate is the uncaused cause of other macroeconomic variables while the exact opposite had been argued for a long time, viz. exchange rate movements being caused by changes within the internal economy.

Engel-West show this empirically for the period 1974:1–2001:3 for the US exchange rate vs. Canada, France, Germany, Italy, Japan and the United Kingdom. They find "there is almost no evidence of causality from the fundamentals to the exchange rate"[52], while quite a bit of evidence exists for causation the other way round. It has to be admitted, however, that "a vast part of the movements in exchange rates [is] not tied to fundamentals"[53] at all! In addition, "all our empirical results are consistent with at least one other explanation, namely that exchange rate movements are dominated by unobserved shocks that follow a random walk"[54]. In a word: At least for international financial markets, time structure and causal interrelationship of variables are so intricately intertwined that we can conclude practically nothing for sure.

And, after all, why should a complicated world be easy to explain just to suit simple-minded economists? Independent error distributions over time simply cannot be assumed once models become just the least bit complicated.

4.5 The result is not really surprising. Why, it has to be asked, should the factors determining exchange rates not change considerably over time, and the lag structure as well? What happens e. g. if vast amounts of additional international reserves are created and bought up by previously unsupplied agents, and these then start to speculate with their holdings? But changing structures cannot be derived from models that assume unchanging structures. Furthermore, in a financially integrated world, exchange rates are greatly influenced by third world repercussions as well. And are the variables usually embodied in exchange rate analyses still the most relevant ones? One thing at least seems clear: For internationally integrated financial markets, the "i.i.d." assumption is by now illicit! Quite apart from the fact that appropriate models would by now probably be non-linear. Non-linear models have

[50] C. E. Engel & K. D. West, "Exchange Rates and Fundamentals", Journ. of Political Economy 113/3, (June 2005), pp. 487–517.

[51] Loc. cit, p. 485.

[52] Loc. cit., p. 506.

[53] Loc. cit, p. 512.

[54] Loc. cit, p. 488.

often been suggested, but were seldom tried out. There is only one single linearity, but an infinite number of non-linear models to choose from!

The structure of world-wide integrated economic systems is far too complicated to be known in precise detail by any one agent. At best we can hope for partial understanding, which proves often, but by no means always, correct. Economic systems change over time and human learning is too slow to catch up with changing reality, especially as actors on financial markets are not at all interested in encountering well-informed trading partners. The less knowledgeable provide more opportunities for profit.

We have witnessed the development of ever more explicit economic models that have not been (or: are not being) tested against reality, because once-and-for-all testing is nearly impossible in economics since the basic probability systems keep changing over time – possibly in a circular way, too (as we see right now when the Crash experience of the 1930s has become relevant once more). Instead of being tested, some of those models have rather been turned into dogmas.

The question of the empirical relevance has more and more receded into the background of American economics, which is a profitable teaching discipline, but no longer policy-oriented. So what to do then, after 2008? Should one discard nearly all one knows and just continue with policies of the late 1930s and 1940s? That would mean forgetting completely that those policies were fiercely argued over and considered theoretically invalid from the late 1960s to the 1980s – quite apart from the fact that the framework of economic policy has changed fundamentally since the 1930s, with highly open economies and free capital movements now.

In this last part, we looked into the empirically testable structure of economic models – and discovered that models for testing purposes, too, had often been careless. The stochastic structure of a testable model is often just stuck on, like an afterthought: One finds an abundance of small sample problems, error terms that are neither identically nor independently distributed over time, and structures that cannot be identified but allow for various explanations. Therefore, it is perhaps best to end with the standard assertion of economic articles, although in a more pessimistic vein than usual: Further research is needed, but not necessarily along the routes taken so far. Advanced theoretical models and the search for higher precision have resulted in less objectivity, a decline in validity and greater uncertainty about practically relevant conclusions.

Erich W. Streissler

The Financial Market Crisis

1. Historical and methodological background to the analysis of the present crisis

1.1 Economics is a quantitative science in only two dimensions: money and time. During financial crises, however, time and money valuations become warped as the perspectives of the observers and of the actors in the fray diverge ever more, and "before" and "after" appear quite different.

1.2 Every financial crisis is unique, says the historian. But all crises that have occurred since 1720 have also had some typical features, says the economist. In this essay I shall try to combine the two approaches of the historian and the economic theorist. First, I shall sketch some of the background problems of the present crisis, using, as seems appropriate, alternately an historical approach and an approach of economic theory or of probability theory, or pointing to the serious difficulties of measurement. In the second part I shall offer an integrated historical and economic analysis of the present crisis.

1.3 In 1772, Hester Thrale, the noble wife of a great British beer brewer – and close friend of Dr. Johnson of dictionary fame –, characterized the serious difficulties of her husband in these words: "Thrale has overbrewed".[1] What can one do with an excess of beer, "overbrewed"? And what can one do nowadays, when a lot of people in a lot of nations have "overbuilt" houses and even more people have "overfinanced", using the most sophisticated financial instruments?

Actually, Thrale's "overbrewing" in 1772 was in no way different from what we see today: 1772 was the year of the second great financial crash in Britain during the 18th century. Thrale had actually "overinvested" in building a huge new brewery plant without considering the demand for his product, and his financier, an important big bank, crashed.[2] What has changed since then? May I remind you that Western Europe recently witnessed the bank-run on Northern Rock – the first bank-run in more than half a century, a type of panic by now well-nigh forgotten. Even that beer brewers, representatives of a highly capital-intensive industry, should figure as central entrepreneurs[3] and as important politicians, as the Member of Parliament[4] Thrale was, is a phenomenon not so long past in Austria, where Qualtinger once characterized a festive occasion as "die Bundesregierung, wie s' der Mautner

---

1 In June 1772.

2 See W.J. Bate, *Samuel Johnson*, London 1978, p.437. The banking house was Ned, Fordyce & Co.

3 See Edmund Fuller, *Boswell's Life of Samuel Johnson* (Selected and Abridged), New York 1960. Boswell writes already for late 18th century England: "Mr. Thrale, one of the most eminent brewers in England, and a Member of Parliament for the borough of Southwark. Foreigners are not a little amazed, when they hear of brewers, distillers, and men in similar departments of trade, held forth as persons of considerable consequence. In this great commercial country it is natural that a situation which produces much wealth should be considered as very respectable, and, no doubt, honest industry is entitled to esteem" (p.131f.).

4 John Wain, *Samuel Johnson*, London 1974, pp. 261, 274.

Markhof bei der Hand führt".[5] Time marches on, yet it seems to stay the same, and especially so in high finance.

1.4 The year 1720 witnessed the first major financial crash, nearly simultaneously in France and in Britain and in both cases quite typically engineered by the respective governments, which were struggling to get out of huge government debts accumulated during the War of the Spanish Succession. England then had a great Master of the Mint, who only three years earlier had created the first gold currency in Europe, when he advised parliament how to set the relative price of gold to silver in such a way that expensive silver would simply drop out of circulation.[6] No wonder, some would say, that this Master of the Mint should esteem gold above everything, for he was also a renowned alchemist![7]

The year 1720 saw the greatest stock market booms ever: Before the crash the respective stock prices had increased in France by about 55 times within only two and a half years and in Britain by seven and a half times within six months[8]. Compare that with the already milder stock market boom in the USA of 1924–1929, when stock prices increased by about four times and with the still milder one of 1995–2000, when stock prices increased threefold.

In 1720 the said English Master of the Mint speculated and finally lost very heavily. He summarized his experience: "I can calculate the movement of the heavenly bodies but not the madness of people". To Sir Isaac Newton – for that was the name of the Master of the Mint, monetary politician and alchemist –, to Sir Isaac Newton the "movement of the heavenly bodies" was regular and therefore well calculable, but not so "the madness of people".[9] And I consider it not the least of Newton's theorems – this time a theorem learned by painful experience – that the "madness of people" is nearly incalculable: Financial crashes – and also wars – are manifestations of the "madness of people", aberrant human behaviour very difficult to analyse, even ex post.

1.5 Let us turn from historical anecdotes to the solid facts of probability theory underlying economic analysis. We look at financial assets, meaning local currencies and their exchange rates, stocks and shares and bonds, independent of the underlying real economic goods. How do prices of financial assets develop? Percentage changes of their prices are well approximated by a normal probability distribution. To be precise, such percentage changes actually have to be represented by <u>two different</u> normal probability distributions: one – for ordinary times – is a distribution with a small variance, but in rare cases or events, like financial crashes, one needs a different probability distribution, one with a vastly larger variance. (Technically speaking, this latter distribution is also a "normal" or Gaussian distribution.[10])

---

[5] In "Travnicek und die Ballsaison", in *Qualtingers beste Satiren – Vom Travnicek zum Herrn Karl,* Munich-Vienna 1973, pp. 106–110, here p. 107.

[6] T.S. Ashton, *An Economic History of England,* London 1955, reprint 1966, ch. 6, "Money, Banking and Foreign Exchange", p. 171: "On the advice of Sir Isaac Newton, in December 1717, a proclamation was issued reducing the value of the guinea from 21s.6d. to 21s. ... This measure, however, proved inadequate: The drain of silver could have been checked only by a reduction that would have brought the rate close to that in the Far East". Gold coin soon replaced silver.

[7] Soon after 1717 Sir Isaac Newton expressed the opinion that "gold is now become our standard money, and silver is a commodity": Ashton 1955/1966, loc.cit. in FN6, p. 176.

[8] For the South Sea Company see P.G.M. Dickson, *The Financial Revolution in England* – A Study in the Development of Public Credit 1688–1756, London 1967, Table 17, p. 139. For the Compagnie des Indes see Antoin E. Murphy, *John Law: Economic Theorist and Policy Maker,* Oxford 1997, passim.

[9] Charles T. Kindleberger, *Manias, Panics, and Crashes – A History of Financial Crises,* New York 1978, Ch. 3, "Speculative Manias", p.34.

[10] Following Sylvia Kaufmann's analysis of variance switching in exchange rates between normal distributions I make this statement. The following essay unifies the analysis of varying larger switches into one Pareto distribution.

To illustrate: In so-called ordinary times it happens very rarely that the Dow-Jones-Index of stock prices on Wall Street changes by a full one per cent from one day to the next. But in 2008, extreme values of four per cent changes, particularly in the downward direction, occurred where formerly there were one or two per cent changes. In other words: on average, the variance had increased about fifteen-fold![11]

The great mathematician Newton was confused by a "rare" event in 1720. Nowadays we see hundreds of confused mathematicians, engaged in estimating the so-called "value at risk" of financial assets. They had wanted to collect the necessary data for estimating financial risk, but they simply had not gone back far enough in time, namely to the 1920s and 1930s, the time of the last major crash, and thus had not taken account of those rare events.[12] Thus, they did not work out the appropriate "normal distribution", and without that they did not estimate the risk correctly.

1.6. The front cover of *The Economist* of December 6–12, 2008 depicted a big black hole and the question: *Where have all your savings gone?* That, indeed, is a mystery to many. The answer is that savings that individuals thought they had made did not materialize in the end. They had simply disappeared:

Internationally binding conventions on national income accounting rules (they go back to John Maynard Keynes) define that, in a closed economy, total savings are identically equal to net investments, i. e. investments after deducting depreciation. Our whole world is one such closed economy – at least as long as there is no trading with the moon or with Mars. Therefore, world savings are *by definition* equal to world net investment. And it had been Keynes' vision that in developed economies it is investments which limit the savings equal to them: So if people try to save more than what the level of investment is, they delude themselves. In the end they find out that their incomes are smaller than expected. Their realized savings have dwindled to the level of realized investments. There is, indeed, a big black hole between intended savings and their realization.

1.7 For an individual country, in particular among the East Asian countries, China being the foremost, but also for Germany and Austria, savings actually can be higher than investments. But in that case there have to be other countries at hand willing to take up such excess savings and either to consume them or invest them. The sum of local excess savings has to be reduced to world investment levels by way of international financial transactions. There are three possible ways to do this:

(1) Excess savings by one country might be used by another country as armament and other military expenditure, which, by definition, would be conversion to a type of consumption: consumption by the government.

(2) Excess savings by one country might just lead to private consumption in another country, thus again disappearing.

---

11 Three times within the last century the variance of mean U.S. stock market prices, as measured by the Dow Jones index jumped up to a figure about 15 times higher than normal: in 1931–1933, briefly in October 1987, and then in the autumn of 2008.

12 The Nobel Laureate Myron S. Scholes, one of the men responsible for the near-crash of Long Term Capital Management, which went into "a form of negotiated bankruptcy" (p. 17), noted in "Crisis and Risk Management", *American Economic Review* 90/2 (2000), pp. 17–21: "To be consistent with market expectations, the realised quarterly volatility on an annualized basis on the S&P 500 would have to average 30 percent over the next five years ... In my view this is extremely unlikely ... [It] has averaged well below 15 percent over the last 10 years" (p.17f.). No other figures than for the 1990s are given in the whole article (!) and even 1987 is not discussed. Much larger volatilities of around 100 percent were then reached in 2008, as had been the case in the 1930s. In effect, Scholes, as many other U.S. authors, considered 2008 "impossible" under the new (?) financial circumstances.

(3) Excess savings in one country might be invested in another country in such a way that the end product of investment is worth little or even nothing, so that, in a sense, saving just evaporates into "thin air".

All three of these paths have been taken. And in 60–75 out of 100 cases the "other country" discussed have been the USA: Since 2000, the USA have frittered away those excess world savings by way of military expenditure, by way of unusually large private consumption and by way of a lot of practically worthless mis-investment. The relative lack of savings in the USA makes its appearance as a huge current account deficit, in other words: In 2006 to 2008, the USA had a surplus of imports over exports to the tune of around three quarters of a trillion dollars each year, or in terms of percentages: The USA had run a deficit of up to 6.5 per cent of gross domestic product; at the turn of 2010 to 2011 it was still 3.4 per cent (460 billion). For the current account deficit is once more identically equal to the excess of consumption-plus-investment over income. Above all, the USA are that big black hole down which the world's savings disappear![13]

1.8 Recently we learned – to our surprise and much too late – from the official arbiter of American business cycles, the National Bureau of Economic Research, that the USA had actually been in recession since December 2007! "In recession" means that their national product had not only not grown, but declined![14] But the full extent of the American decline cannot be read off from national accounts. For due to Keynes, who had famously quipped "in the long run we are all dead", national accounts are extremely short-run calculations and highly misleading in case of long-run financial crises. Due to Keynes, national income statistics only look at financially remunerated production and equivalently the billing of sales, assumed by definition to be equal to production values. But – a big BUT: National accounting does not care a hoot whether sold goods and services are <u>ever paid for</u> or whether produced goods are sold at all.

Thus, by assumption, the vast number of newly produced, but unsold cars that stood around in the USA in late 2008 and rusted but would never be sold or sold only for a pittance, had been added to national income at their too high production costs. And, even worse, all those US houses built and sold at a considerable price, whose value had plummeted by 2008 and whose original purchase price would never be paid, had increased national income at their evidently fictitious original sales prices. Mis-pricing of commodities and commodities sold on credits which are now unrecoverable, are said to add up to considerably more than ten per cent of present US national income, which means that the announced growth rate of the USA for the years 2003 to 2007 should actually be reduced by at least one half, perhaps up to two thirds, being more like an annual growth rate of 1 or 1.5 per cent rather than 3 per cent and more, as officially estimated. And even more: At the turn of 2010 to 2011 the total of by now probably unrecoverable private debt in the USA is estimated at 8 trillion dollars and for the whole developed world at 15 trillion dollars.

Or, to make the point drastically clear: If some nation should set its mind on sowing wheat on the ice sheet of Antarctica, diligently plowing and tilling the ice, that would increase its national income to the tune of the full cost of sowing, ploughing and tilling, in spite of the fact that the wheat will

[13] Carmen M. Reinhart and Kenneth S. Rogoff, *This Time is Different: Eight Centuries of Financial Folly,* Princeton 2009, showed that the effect of the U.S. crash of 2007–2009 was very similar to the five largest crashes in the developed world since 1960; in "Growth in a Time of Debt", *American Economic Review* 100/2 (2010), pp. 573–578, the same authors strike the warning note that "across both advanced countries and emerging markets, high debt/GDP levels (90 percent and above) are associated with notably lower growth outcomes ... Seldom do countries 'grow' their way out of debt" (p.577). The USA are now rapidly approaching this 90 percent threshold! (By now, two years after completion of this article, the USA are approaching 105 percent indebtness).

[14] According to official calculations the recession – i. e. the income decline – ended 19 months later, in mid-2009.

never germinate and there will be no harvest whatsoever. And to put it bluntly: Lately, the USA have done little else but fruitlessly trying to cultivate such a huge ice shield.

2. The specifics of the recent crisis: Dearth of investment opportunities and surfeit of savings

2.1 Reviewing the economy worldwide during the first decade of the 21st century, we face a lack or dearth of real investment opportunities and, on the other hand, a surfeit of world savings. When real investment opportunities are lacking, all that remains is speculation in the sense of a mere redistribution from one financier to another. This is difficult to understand and also a highly inconvenient truth for financiers and actors in financial markets: In the hope of profit opportunities they try to convince the investing public and even themselves that there are such opportunities. It is a most painful process to learn that there are no such opportunities, that profitable investment opportunities have been overestimated, that initially saved funds are not needed, that the whole presumed boom had just been "the madness of people". In the end, however, such learning changes common perceptions. Many years ago, a former member of this Academy, in a farewell speech to American summer school students at an inviting Austrian lakeside misconstructed an adverb and told those kids to their great surprise: "I congratulate you, you have hardly studied". In recent years, financiers the world over have very pleasantly hardly worked, but will now have to work very hard – if they happen to find any work at all.

2.2 In order to understand present investment opportunities we turn now to Joseph A. Schumpeter and his analysis of business cycles published, for him unfortunately, in the year 1939 when potential readers had other priorities.[15] Schumpeter saw investment opportunities materialising during waves of technical innovations.[16] He found out that such waves of massive innovations occur only every 45 to 50 years and called those long waves of innovations in memory of a Russian analyst the Kondratieff waves or cycles. Schumpeter was a perceptive forecaster, because at his time there had only been completed three Kondratieff waves, while we lately witnessed the fifth Kondratieff boom: the first boom of industrial innovations, centred on England, and there on cotton and iron, took place in the 1790s, the second, the railway building boom, around 1855, the third from 1895–1905, manifold and particularly well described by Schumpeter; the fourth one took shape around 1955 and was centred on the USA, and finally the fifth, our last one, appeared in 1995–2000, to which we shall turn in a moment. Besides these large booms there are less significant, non-innovatory – or rather less innovatory – investment booms, especially in housing.

Great financial booms and busts can arise in the course of financing the waves of industrial innovations. But they are actually older than the Kondratieff cycles and not necessarily synchronous with them[17]. The busts are especially due to financial break-downs after wars, the first one, already mentioned, in 1720, six years after the end of the War of the Spanish Succession, the second in Britain in 1772–73, not directly war-related, then one, variously dated to 1819 or 1825, four to ten years after the end of the Napoleonic wars, furthermore the crash of 1873, starting in Vienna at the World Exhibi-

[15] Joseph A. Schumpeter, *Business Cycles,* 2 volumes, London 1939.

[16] Such waves of innovations need not cause waves of markedly different rates of economic growth. They might just keep rates of growth from going into long-run decline, i. e. stabilize growth in the long run. For an historical example from the paper industry see D.C. Coleman, "Industrial Growth and Industrial Revolutions", in E.M. Carus-Wilson (ed.), *Essays in Economic History,* vol.III, London 1962, pp. 334–352. He writes p.341: "The 'second industrial' revolution in the [paper] industry offers nothing more, in quantitative terms, than a continuation of the rate of growth initiated during the classical industrial revolution period".

[17] The dating between booms may be a little artificial. The dating between the corresponding deep busts, or depressions, in particular shows even more strongly varying interval periods.

tion and occurring seven years after the war of 1866 against Prussia and the milder simultaneous downturn in Germany three years after its war against France. 1873 was actually the nadir of a Kondratieff depression between the boom years 1856 and 1895. We have already mentioned the depression of 1929–1933, the so-called "Great Contraction" – neither related directly to war nor to a Kondratieff boom. Just as the American financial crash of 1907 followed the preceding third Kondratieff boom, the financial crash of 2001–2002 followed the fifth Kondratieff boom of 1995–2000 – but: That crash was deferred by political action to 2007, 2008 and later. And a deferred crash must eventually turn out to be much worse than it would have been originally.

2.3 Now we will examine the fifth, "our" Kondratieff boom of 1995–2000 in detail: The thing that strikes one right away is its comparatively narrow base. It was mostly based on innovations just in computer hardware and computer software. Great innovations in the pharmaceutical industry and medical innovations, which had been hoped for, mostly did not materialize; and as far as they did they were only partly commercially viable, for they happened largely in the fully or partly state-run sector of universities and academies.

The computer industry had a further unusual feature, which was marvellous for consumers, but correspondingly ominous for further business development: The computer industry needed very little capital investment. Unusually, the growth industry generated so-called "capital-saving" innovations; in earlier times, that had happened only once, in the case of the cotton industry in Britain around 1800. Finally, the high degree of competition in the computer sector caused the advantages swiftly to be passed on to the consumer. There was no lasting profit surge and thus no lasting series of further innovations. Thus, the rapid decline of computer prices entailed a dearth of further investment opportunities.

2.4 In the dearth of profitable industrial investment opportunities after the year 2000 many countries, above all the USA, but also Spain and to a lesser extent Britain and Ireland, had turned to housebuilding – instead of short-term to long-term investment. But long-term investment, as in the construction of houses, tends to yield lower rates of return than good investments in manufacturing; and if you overdo it, producing houses that don't sell, there will be no return at all. Curiously, it was especially socialist governments in Spain or Britain that became interested in highly unprofitable housing projects, because while being built they offer good employment opportunities for unskilled workers, while the inevitable losses will be made by rich, but foolhardy investment projectors – not exactly the clients of socialist parties.

All over the world we have a backlog of so-called infrastructural investments, road building for example. But for many different reasons in most countries infrastructural investment did not materialize; and in Japan, where it was undertaken, it was of little use and brought little profit.

Product development in the pharmaceutical industry and biological and medical research require very long investment periods with high levels of risk; and then the respective governments want to get the final products at not much more than their marginal cost of production – which, of course, would not cover the fixed cost of lengthy development. So research in those fields is not profitable, and government funds prove insufficient. Thus since the year 2000 there has been an overall lack of privately profitable investment opportunities

2.5 While there is a world wide dearth of investment opportunities, we also have a surfeit of savings. Let us first look at the USA:

At the end of the 1980s President Ronald Reagan fought the most successful world war ever, "star wars", as he called it, a world war without a single shot fired, simply by stepping up rearmament: The Soviet Union tried to draw even with US rearmament, was financially unable to do so and could not but break up. Since then the USA, the sole remaining military Super Power, have no longer had to spend (= to consume) so much on "defence". Reduced armament expenditure increased world savings by reducing government dissaving. Positive saving, on the other hand, was increased very much since 2000 by the newly flourishing South Asian and South East Asian countries, China in particular, even India, and since 1990 by Japan. During the recent oil boom, oil producing countries on the Arabian Peninsula, but also Russia, have added further to world savings.

2.6 While government savings boomed especially in South Asian, South East Asian and oil producing countries, US private consumers drastically reduced their already low personal savings during the stock market boom of 1995–2000: Because of rising share prices they assumed they were getting richer even without saving part of their current incomes; and in the USA one half of the households holds stocks and shares (so at least one half thought they were getting richer). Then they believed the same as to their private homes: the prices of houses went up; so they were becoming richer without currently saving – they thought. In the meantime house prices began to fall rapidly, and in 2008 US stock market prices were about 30 per cent below their peak in 2000 and more than 40 per cent below the peak in early 2007. American personal saving had even turned negative in 2006 and 2007, while it stands at present at around 10 per cent in Austria and 11 per cent in Germany. US personal saving will have to increase, because many citizens have very little left for retirement. But such saving might once more lead to a recession in the USA, and such a recession will carry the world with it into an even more general recession.

2.7 Both the USA and with them the entire developed world and parts of the developing world were already going into recession after the end of the Kondratieff boom in 2000. But that recession was, as I said, deferred by American political action and understandably so from the point of view of the respective politicians. President Bush II took office in January 2001 and two months later, in March 2001, the USA found themselves in a recession not of his making. Bush immediately cut taxes for the rich and then rapidly started one relatively small war after another, first in Afghanistan, then in Iraq. He was actively supported by the central bank president, Alan Greenspan, who cut the short-term bank interest rate as drastically as never before: from 6.5 p.c. to 1.75 p.c. already in 2001, and a little later to a mere 1 per cent. These rates were and still are actually less than nothing in real terms as the rate of inflation was well above that 1 per cent. Thus, it is a fact that many people in the USA recently got credit for free, and some were even paid to take it. Temptingly, this created a mass of borrowers unable ever to repay. Above all, and still, it is the banks, which are in fact abundantly subsidized by the Federal Reserve: They get credit nearly for free and then lend it back to the government in long-term loans at around 3.5 p.c. interest.

When the terrorist attack of September 11, 2001 occurred, Bush grasped the opportunity and made it a patriotic duty for Americans to consume. They were only too happy to comply. Bush's acceptance quota shot up to 85 p.c. of voters and a brief boom ensued largely engineered by the monetary policy of Alan Greenspan, which carried Bush successfully into re-election in 2004. Both the USA and the rest of the world are now suffering from that stop-go policy of hectic stimulation and outright unsound low interest rates.

2.8 What must we expect now? Since the year 2000, the USA have been – what irony! – financially a virtual satellite of Communist China. Of course, everything in economics always necessarily has two sides: We might also say that China has become highly dependent on the USA, its main debtor. China had up to recently steadily financed about one third of the US current account deficit, amounting at its peak in 2008/09 to some 800 billion dollars a year. In the recession from 2009 onward, the US current account deficit has shrunk to 460 billion (3rd quarter 2010), but the trade deficit still stands at 640 billion dollars (October 2010). In 2007, China was appreciating its currency relative to the US-dollar by 10 p.c. a year, then stopped doing so at the depth of the recession and is now once more appreciating mildly at 3 p.c. a year. In 2007, it lost an amount equal to 100 dollars per capita of the

1.3 billion Chinese, or more than 5 per cent of their incomes! Figures for the 3rd quarter of 2010 say that the current account balance of China amounts to 316 billion dollars and China now frantically tries to disentangle itself from financing the deficit of the USA. But where else should China invest its surplus, if not in the USA? So far, the Euro area as a whole has had little need for outside finance, although China is now trying to step in here a bit. Gold is fluctuating in price mildly relative to the dollar, at present slightly appreciating. And the oil price, which stood at 147 dollars in early 2008 and then dropped to some 40 dollars at the depth of the crisis, now (February 2012) stands at about 100 dollars. So it is very hard for China's enormous sums to find alternative assets to the dollar both available and at a stable value. Commodity prices fluctuate strongly.

After 1933, some European countries stimulated their economies by building "Autobahnen" and "Höhenstrassen" as well as by rearmament, while Franklin D. Roosevelt in the USA tried to boost the economy by huge public works projects (although these did not increase national income above the level of 1929 before the war came). Today, Central Europe seems above all keen on refinancing the (w)ailing banks, which will, however, have hardly any employment effect. It would be infinitely better to invest into the environment – e. g. into solar energy projects, hydrogen cars etc. But for such projects governments are not likely to find any money, too much of which goes into pensions, unemployment relief and other social services – expenditures without lasting benefits. And in the longer run budget deficits anyway run up against debt limits imposed by sceptical international financial markets, quite apart from deficits seeming to become less and less effective as they are accumulated.

2.9 Let us now summarize the global perspectives and consequences of the recent crisis for the shorter run. Such a summary has to refer to economic policy, above all the economic policy of the USA. Just as in 1720 the – speculating – people did not realize the policy background of governments trying to get out of huge war debts, so now the global problem of financial interactions of many different economic policies and many different private financiers is not clear to the "players". A little light was shed on this by the Nobel Lecture (in 1999) of a Canadian economist, highly critical of the USA, Robert Mundell. In his lecture titled "A Reconsideration of the Twentieth Century" Mundell[18] offered three propositions:

(1) The 20th century was the century of the financial dominance of the USA. I should like to add: The recent crisis is the end of this dominance, somewhat delayed because neither the money holders in unstable economies, like Russia and Argentina, can yet think of any other "safe haven" than the US dollar, nor have many central banks, particularly that of China, found any other easy way to hold reserves as yet.

(2) The entire 20th century was one series of costly monetary policy mistakes centered on the USA. To this diagnosis of Mundell's of 1999 nothing need be added but that the first decade of the 21st century suffers once more from tremendous mistakes of US monetary authorities.

(3) Already in the 18th century and then in the 19th century the most highly developed economies were financially fully integrated thanks to the gold currency, established at the advice of Newton. This financial globalization based on capital market integration lasted until 1914 and re-emerged, according to Mundell, in 1989, and Mundell states explicitly: "Forget the 75 years between 1914 and 1989!"[19] But the USA have not done so: US economic policy still runs along closed economy lines, ignoring its consequences for other nations as well as the repercussions that those international consequences

---

18 Robert A. Mundell, "A Reconsideration of the Twentieth Century", *American Economic Review* 90/3 (2000), pp. 327–340, Erratum *AER* December 2000, p. 1535.

19 Mundell 2000, loc.cit., p.327.

must eventually have on the USA themselves. So far, the other nations have permitted this self-centred closed economy attitude, but they seem no longer willing to do so.

Alan Greenspan, the most effective monetary politician of the 20th century, was president of the US central bank, the Federal Reserve, from August 1987 to February 2006. His well-documented policy stance[20] was to do next to nothing when times were good: He did not check the boom of 1995–1999, thus permitting its eventual excesses. When times were bad, however, he switched to hyperactivity, lowering bank interest rates far too much and for far too long. Greenspan ignored the US balance of payments problems, he ignored the fact that finance external to an economy is much riskier and massively affects the exchange rate of one's currency. Thus, the current account deficit of the USA, which exploded from 2001 onwards, was to a considerable extent of Greenspan's making. Running a bank interest rate which is negative in real terms must lead to a financial crisis: and it surely did. And now US fiscal policy leads to the highly dangerous government deficit levels of more than 90 percent of GDP.

After the year 2000, the world had an unusual surfeit of savings. And above all Greenspan thought it all right that the then still per capita richest nation, the USA, should just gobble up about two thirds of excess world savings and spend them on excess consumption. This is simply the story of Raimund's *Verschwender:* Everybody is happy as long as overspending by the spendthrift keeps the world running at full swing. But eventually doubts must accumulate and the end will inevitably be a gigantic financial crash – of which we have just seen the beginning, so far.

[20] See especially Alan Greenspan, "Risk and Uncertainty in Monetary Policy", *American Economic Review* PP 94/2 (2004), pp.33–40. Also Alan Greenspan, *The Age of Turbulence* – Adventures in a New World, London etc. 2007. Note that Greenspan thinks monetary policy is an adventure (!) and is a main proponent of the now disproved notion that we live in a "new" world.

Erich W. Streissler and Christoph Streissler

Rare Events: Varying Asset Price Variances

In *Portfolio Selection – Efficient Diversification of Investments* (1959) Harry M. Markowitz (Nobel Laureate 1990) "proposed that investors select portfolios on the basis of mean and variance"[1] of the rates of return of financial assets. In characterizing probability distributions of rates of return Markowitz was content with only these two parameters and plumped for a symmetric and unimodal distribution (p. 52). It was soon pointed out that he had assumed either a quadratic distribution for rates of return or a normal distribution for their error term. While the quadratic distribution of the rates of return appeared unappealing, the normal distribution of error terms was at first thought to be very acceptable.

By now it is well known that returns for many assets, i. e. the first derivative of their logarithm for given time spans, are not exactly normally distributed. At the least they have "fat tails", i. e. large positive as well as negative deviations of rates of return are much more likely than for the normal distribution.[2] Not so well known is that regularly large positive deviations of return rates are somewhat more likely than large negative deviations. In periods of downright financial market crises this becomes much more marked and the distribution of logarithmic return rates is markedly skewed towards the right.

Sylvia Kaufmann has repeatedly suggested one should postulate two normal distributions of rates of asset returns – in her case for exchange rates: one with a small and – much rarer – one with a large variance, with transition probabilities between these two states.[3] As there is a strong positive autocorrelation of rates of return over a relatively short range of consecutive periods there is evidence for periods in which certain variance levels predominate.

But such switches between only two distinct variance levels of rates of return are persuasive only for relatively short and relatively homogenous periods, but not for very long ones, when the magnitudes of relatively large return variances differ significantly over time. Since markets for financial capital are for most developed nations internationally integrated (originally for Britain and France, with Holland added, since about 1720) we have experienced about eight major financial asset return declines ("crashes") with minor ones in between. In order to capture these rare but still in their magnitude different events in one single probability distribution we thought at first of a Poisson distribution of the logarithm of variances of returns as the most appropriate model.

1 Preface to the second edition 1991, p. vii.

2 The 1997 Nobel Laureate Myron Scholes said in American Ec. Rev. PP May 2000, p. 19: After Russian default in Aug. 1988 swap spreads "shot up from 60 basis points to 80 basis points in one day .... a move of 10 standard deviations in the swap spread....the volatility.... increased from 0.8 of a basis point per day to 8 basis points."

3 Sylvia Kaufmann and Sylvia Frühwirth-Schnatter, "Bayesian analysis of switching ARCH models" Journal of Time Series Analysis 23 (4), 2002, 425–458; Sylvia Kaufmann and Martin Scheicher, "A Switching ARCH Model for the German DAX Index", Studies in Nonlinear Dynamics and Econometrics, 10 (4), 2006, Article 3. Both these analyses depend on James D. Hamilton and Raul Susmel, "Autoregressive conditional heteroskedasticity and changes in regime", Journal of Econometrics 64 (1–2), 1994, 307–333.

If x is the logarithm of the rate of return variance for a time period, the Poisson distribution assumes as probability Pr:

$$Pr[x = k] = e^{-\theta} \theta^k / k!, \theta > 0.$$

θ will be small. Thus it would follow that the rare events of large percentage asset price changes per day or, equivalently, large daily return variances arise randomly and independently in time and, as the time between one unusually large return variance and the next would be distributed exponentially, independent of the time that had already passed since the occurrence of the last variance peak.

Empirically, it was, however, found that very large return variances, though rare, were still substantially more frequent than postulated by a Poisson distribution. Christoph Streissler therefore suggested as a still more appropriate size distribution of return variances a type of Pareto distribution, i. e. a power law.

If X is some value of interest of the return variance, x a value to which it is to be compared, and x_0 some lowest possible value of the variance, then the probability function $P(x) = Pr[X \geq x]$ will for the Pareto distribution be:

$$P(x) = Pr[X \geq x] = \left(\frac{x_0}{x}\right)^a, x \geq x_0; \ a > 0$$

With a below 2 this probability function will have no finite variance. The corresponding discrete distribution function will be the so-called Zeta distribution or "Zipf-Estoup-Law", which, however, we do not write out explicitly. Decades ago, a Pareto distribution was suggested for one of our cases, i. e. for stock prices, though latterly the log normal distribution has been preferred; this, however, does not fit well for extreme values, in which we are interested[4] (cf. fig. 3 for a graphical representation for the goodness of fit of the Pareto distribution compared to the log normal distribution).

Cases of variance bunching of relative asset price changes can easily be found and we exemplify them from indices of stock prices, from exchange rates, gold prices and wheat prices.[5] All these asset price changes depend to a relatively small extent upon quantitative supply, as stocks held tend to be large, while future demand is uncertain and discounted in value to the present at times of highly variable interest rates. In our graphical presentation we use the logarithm of variances.

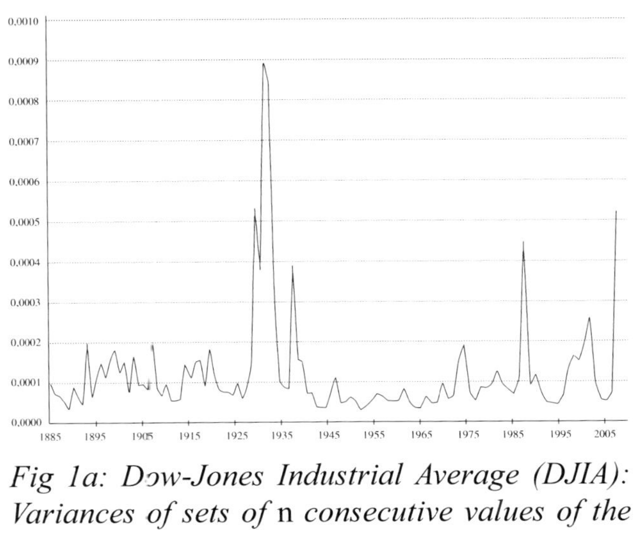

Fig 1a: Dow-Jones Industrial Average (DJIA): Variances of sets of n *consecutive values of the relative change of daily closing values,* n *=300*

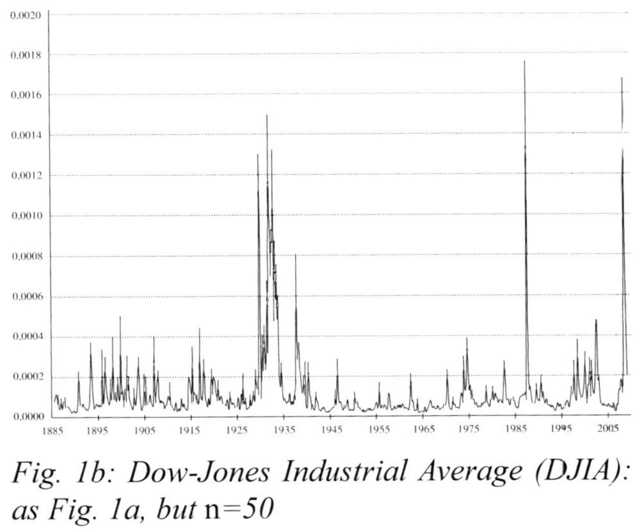

Fig. 1b: Dow-Jones Industrial Average (DJIA): as Fig. 1a, but n*=50*

[4] See N.L. Johnson, S. Katz, *Continuous Univariate Distributions* 1, New York 1970, pp, 234 and 242.

[5] An elaborate analysis of such rare events, due to the illiquidity of the market, in asset pricing of financial assets, has recently been published: Francis A. Longstaff, "Portfolio Claustrophobia: Asset Pricing in Markets with Illiquid Assets", American Ec. Rev. 99 (4), Sept. 2009, pp. 1119–1144.

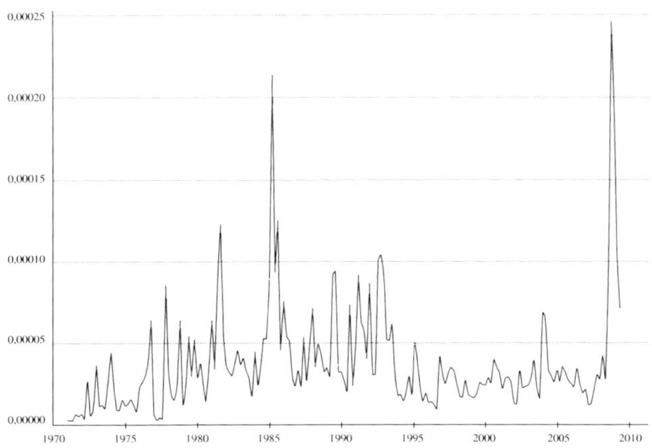

Fig 2a: Exchange rate of the British pound to the US dollar: Variances of sets of n *consecutive values of the relative change of daily values,* n=*50*

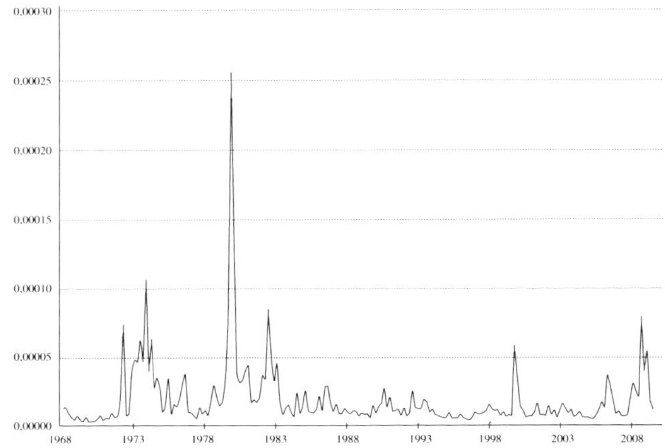

Fig 2b: London gold price fixing (noon): Variances of sets of n *consecutive values of the relative change of daily values,* n=*50*

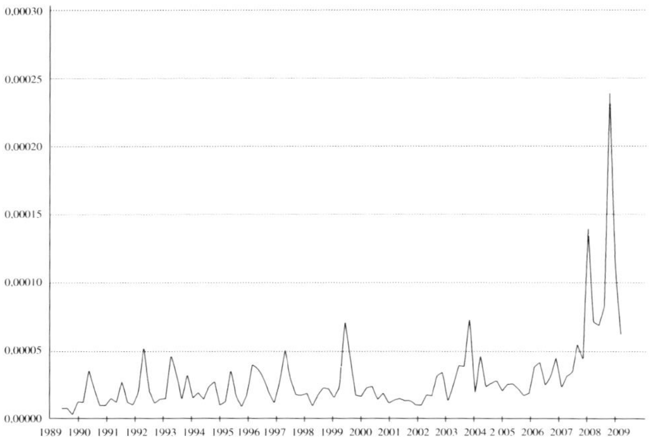

Fig 2c: Wheat spot market (Kansas): Variances of sets of n *consecutive values of the relative change of daily values,* n=*50*

The indices of stock prices are particularly variable and also particularly well documented. Figs. 1 a,b give variances of daily closing value prices for the Dow-Jones Industrial Average for nearly the last 125 years, from Feb. 16, 1885 to Aug. 14, 2009, averaged over 300 (Fig. la) and 50 days (Fig. lb) (precisely: consecutive data points). In the first case there are about 6 variance peaks of different size, in the second the three variance peaks in the early 1930s, in 1987 and in 2008 stick out as of approximately the same magnitude.[6] Figs. 2a–c show the corresponding distributions for the exchange rate of the British pound to the US dollar from Jan. 4, 1971 to Aug. 14, 2009, for the London gold price fixing from Jan. 2, 1969 to Aug. 17, 2009, and finally for the wheat spot market (Kansas) for the shortest period of these three, from June 9, 1989, to June 11, 2009, in each case averaging variance over 50 days. Ordering the variances and estimating the probability that variances are larger than the given value gives an estimate of their probability distribution function. Because of many chance effects small variances seem to be log-normally distributed, while large variances are distributed as in a Pareto distribution, our cut off point between the two distributions being the median variance, which can be seen to give a good fit (Fig. 4a–e). The plot of these data for the Dow Jones Index (fig. 3) shows near linearity for the large variances on double logarithmic scales, indicating a good approximation by a Pareto distribution[7]. Therefore, for those

[6] While in 1987 and in 2008 the monetary authority – i. e. the Federal Reserve – immediately stepped in to calm the market, in 1931 to early 1933 there was notoriously too little political counteraction, which caused the much longer turbulences. See M. Friedman, A. Schwartz, *Monetary Statistics of the United States* – Estimates, Sources, Methods, New York etc. 1970.

[7] In fact, a Pareto distribution of the second kind, $Pr[X>x]=(x_0/(x+c))^a$ gives a reasonably good fit over the whole range of variances. However we do not investigate this distribution as we are mainly interested in the distribution of very high variances and as the Pareto distribution of the second kind and the basic one converge for x>>c and finally as estimating three parameters instead of two becomes too speculative on the basis of rather sparse data sets.

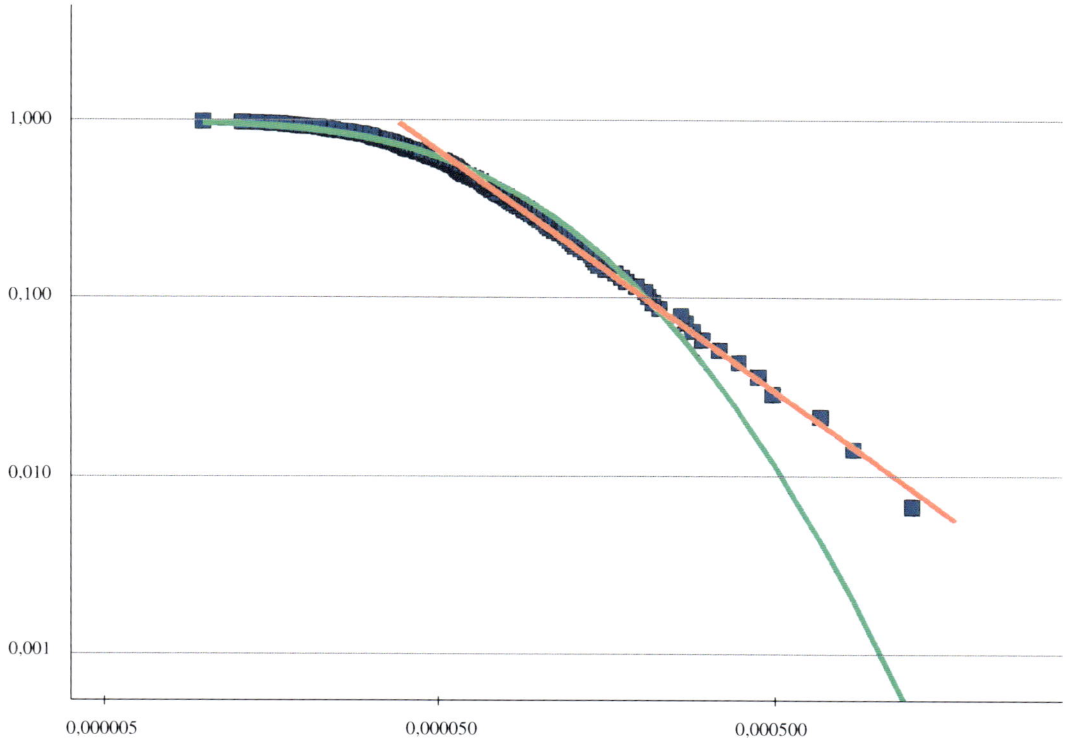

Fig 3: Dow-Jones Industrial Average: Pr[X>x] versus x on a double logarithmic scale for the variances shown in fig. lb (variances of sets of 50 consecutive values of the relative change of daily closing values). Notice that variances span more than two orders of magnitude. The near linearity for larger values of x indicates that for large x a Pareto distribution would give a good fit of the data. Pr[X>x] was estimated using the rank order of the respective values, binning five values together at a time. The red curve shows the best fit for a Pareto distribution based on the data exceeding the median. The green curve shows the best fit for a log-normal distribution. It can be seen that the log-normal distribution underestimates the probabilities of large variances.

variances exceeding the median, the parameter *a* of the Pareto distribution was estimated (figs. 4 a–e), yielding for the Dow-Jones Industrial Average a=1.35 (R^2=0.998) in the case of n=50 and a=1.46 (R^2=0.977) in the case n=300. For the exchange rate of the US dollar versus the British pound we find an estimate a=1.84 (R^2=0.971), for the London gold price fixing a=1.25 (R^2=0.953) and for the wheat spot market price a=1.86 (R^2=0.987).

Thus the estimated parameter *a* of the Pareto distribution is 1.35 for the short run averages and 1.46 for the long run averages of stock prices, 1.86 for wheat prices, 1.26 for gold prices and 1.84 for the US dollar – British pound exchange rate, wheat prices and exchange rates being closest to a log normal distribution.

As to the strength of the variation in variances, J.M. Keynes had already most perceptively remarked: "It is interesting that the stability of the system and its sensitiveness to change in the quantity of money should be so dependent on the existence of a *variety* of opinion about what is uncertain".[8] And the duration of a "variety of opinion" depends in part upon credible political action.

[8] J.M. Keynes, *The General Theory of Employment Interest and Money,* 1936, p. 172.

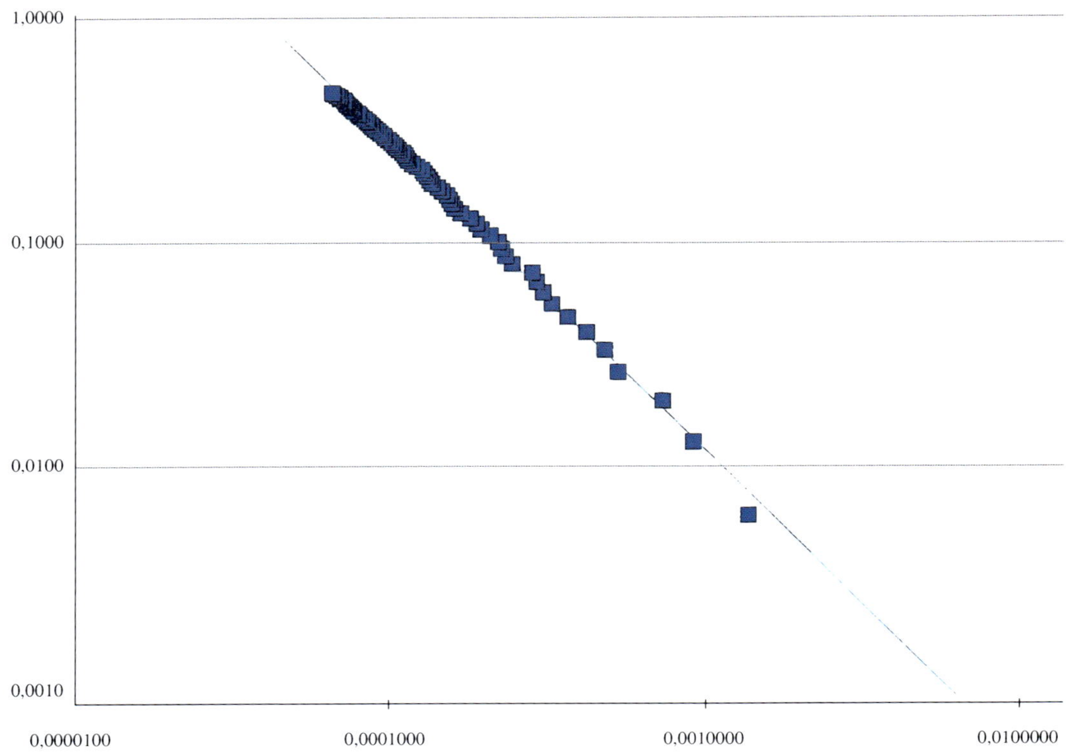

*Fig 4a: Dow-Jones Industrial Average: Estimating the Pareto exponent for variances (*n*=50) exceeding the median: a=1.35 (R^2=0.998)*

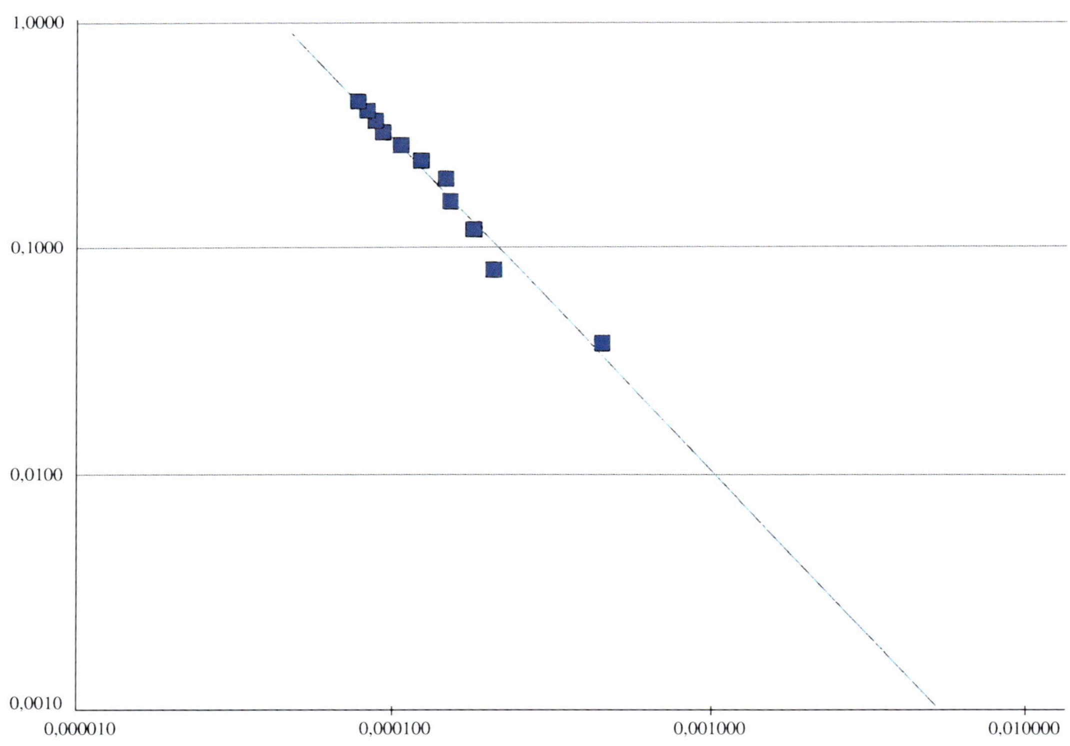

*Fig 4b: Dow-Jones Industrial Average: Estimating the Pareto exponent for variances (*n*=300) exceeding the median: a=1.46 (R^2=0.977)*

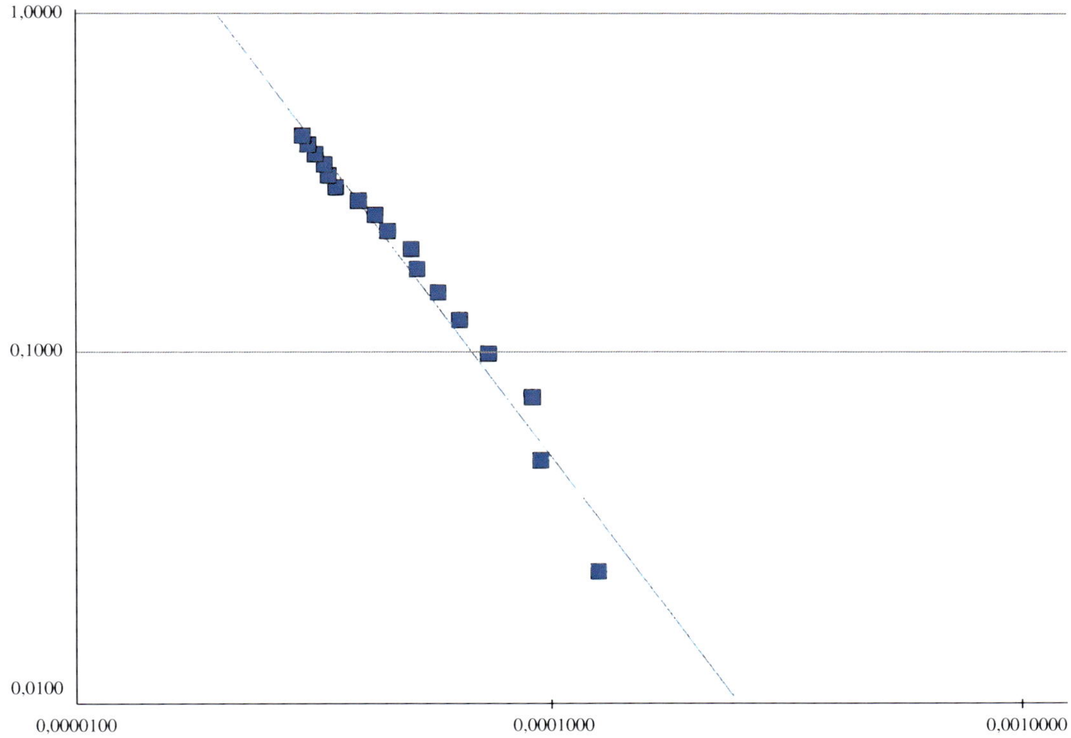

*Fig 4c: Exchange rate of the US dollar versus the British pound: Estimating the Pareto exponent for variances (*n*=50) exceeding the median: a=1.84 (R^2=0.971)*

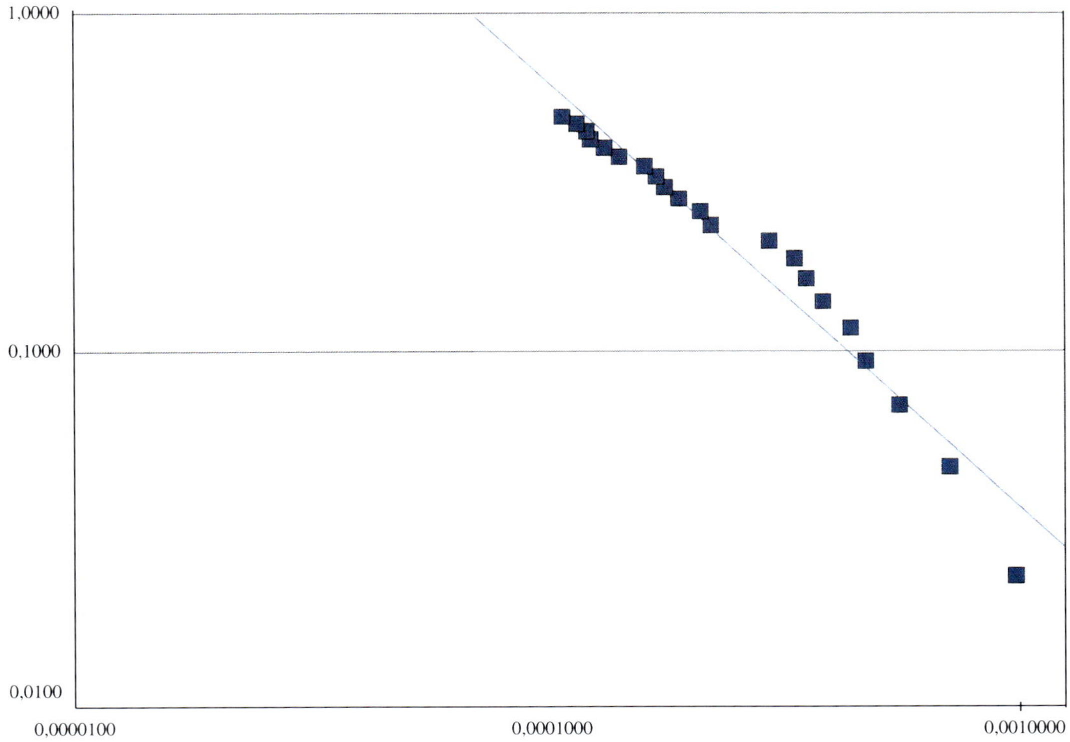

*Fig 4d: London gold price fixing: Estimating the Pareto exponent for variances (*n*=50) exceeding the median:* a=*1.25 (*R^2*=0.953)*

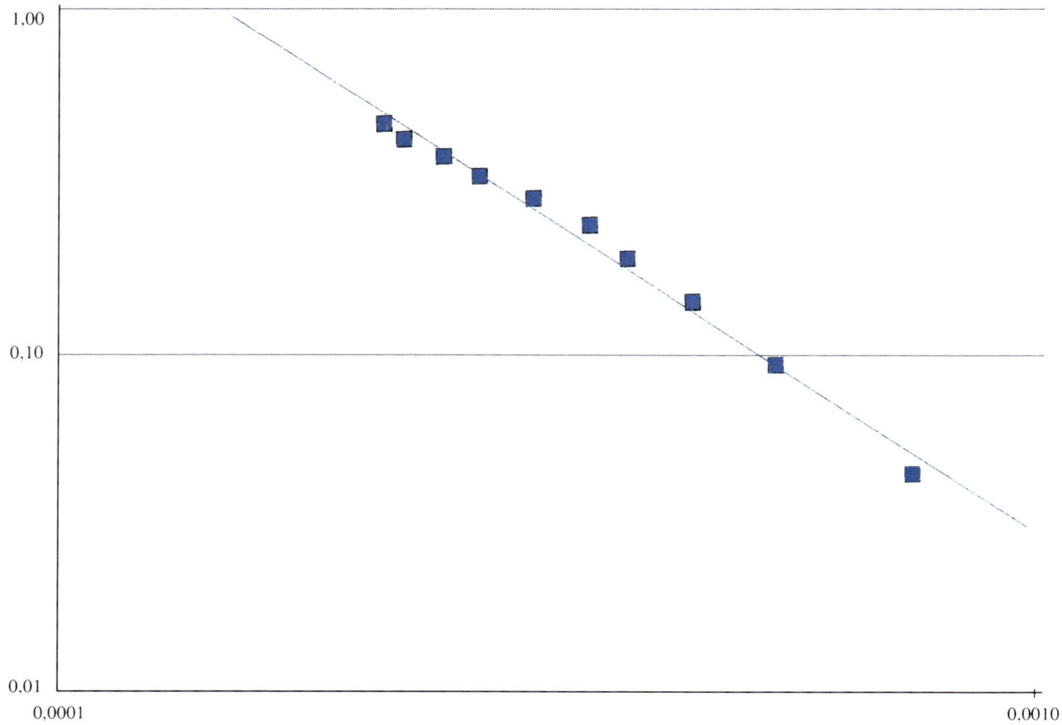

Fig 4e: Wheat, spot market (Kansas): Estimating the Pareto exponent for variances (n=50) exceeding the median: a=1.86 (R^2=0.987)

The variance peaks of the prices of different kinds of assets are temporally correlated, particularly in the years after 2000. This is easily understood as due to futile attempts to find, in spite of a dearth of real investment opportunities for businesses, other opportunities to use savings profitably. For the world as a whole total world investment is by definition of national accounts necessarily equal to total world savings; and, with relatively low total world investment after the boom years, investment limited realized savings and frustrated many attempts to find profitable uses of savings in financial markets.

When investment opportunities shrivel and investment price variations explode this poses a particular problem for banks: Even if they do not go under for having bought too many loss-making assets, they have rapidly to increase their reserves because the variance of the prices of their financial assets suddenly increases steeply. But as the rate of return on financial assets held as reserves is, practically by definition, relatively low if not even zero, bank profitability tends to drop and new loans made in order to finance even slightly risky activities tend to dry up. On the other hand, in a business recession (and even long after) it is difficult to find businesses able to offer higher interest rates on loans that are relatively safe still.[9] Thus bank profits are on average high before a variance peak of asset prices but low thereafter. Or, as a top banker put it: We shall not again attain recent profit levels "for another 50 or 100 years" (more exactly, according to our data on stock prices, for another 40 to 80 years; the interval of variance peaks in stock prices between 1932 and 2008 was 76 years.)

[9] J.E. Stiglitz and A. Weiss, "Credit Rationing in Markets With Imperfect Information", American Ec. Rev., June 1981, 71(3), pp. 393–410.

Erich W. Streissler

Waiting for Financial Consolidation

1. The international monetary disequilibrium

1.1 Let us start out with basics. What is the reason for a war? A lack of understanding on the part of at least one of the parties to the conflict as to the likely outcome of that war. What is the cause of a financial crisis? Just the same, only more so: a lack of understanding on the part of at least some of the numerous participants in financial markets as to the eventual consequences of what they are doing.

At any moment of time, economic actors understand only small segments of all the relevant markets. Long-term financial asset markets are hardly ever – I repeat, hardly ever – fully understood. This is so because they relate to specific prices in the future, and there is no way to find out what all the relevant actors expect. In fact, there is no need for the main actors, as long as they are trading, to make sure of more than one basically correct central notion or precaution.

1.2 There is a study about the strategy of a still existing British private bank and its dealings during the first great financial boom and crash in England in 1720: It was C. Hoare & Co, founded in 1672.[1] That bank foresaw correctly that rising stock prices of the South Sea Company were excessive. So it made a long series of purchases followed by rapid sales of this stock, putting all the running profits from those transactions into safe loans or into cash, and timing its final exit more or less perfectly. When the crash came, this bank lost a little on the last batch of transactions, while all the former profits remained. The important point was that it had not increased its engagement in the risky asset over time. This is exactly what loss-making US banks or the Swiss UBS did: In a financial market that was getting riskier all the time (and that was exactly what those banks did not see!), they put ever more money into the riskiest part of the market. In fact, many US banks felt safe because they had staved off to a subsidiary the risky business of financing house purchases. But then they financed that subsidiary by large loans. Eventually – only too late – they discovered that because of those loans they actually had not shifted the risk off their own balance sheets.

A second case would be the discounting of a bill of exchange in terms of foreign currency of an exporting firm. Payment would typically be due in half a year's time. What price should the bank charge when discounting such a bill, denominated in foreign currency? It is very difficult to forecast movements of exchange rates even over half a year. Typically the bank assumes a random walk without drift of the exchange rate. That is to say: by forgetting about the value of the exchange rate it will sometimes lose substantially and sometimes gain, but in the long-run average its estimation of an unchanging exchange rate is correct. However, it shoulders a high exchange rate risk over time. In

[1] See the inhouse article by Stuart Fieldhouse: "C. Hoare & Co. Conservatism Where it Counts – Business as usual for the last of UK's privately-held banks."

order to compensate for that the bank charges a substantial fee (fixed cost) for purchasing such a foreign exchange bill – assuming that this fee will cover the risk.

1.3 The problem is that – relative to the Euro – the US-dollar performs more or less a random walk, but with substantial downward drift. Since the introduction of the Euro at the beginning of 2002, when the dollar stood at a price of 0.87 dollars per Euro and now, eight years later, when it is 1.30 dollars per Euro the dollar has depreciated by about 4 percent annually. But things became even more complicated: Since the middle of 2008, the very time when the full extent of the crisis became known to all and sundry, the dollar has appreciated by close to 20 percent with very large price fluctuations around that: For because of the crisis many citizens of crisis-struck countries purchased dollars as a "safe" haven for their financial wealth, regardless of the fact that relative to the Euro, the second most important world currency, the dollar is an utterly unsafe haven!

Thus we have arrived at the first great worldwide problem behind the current financial and economic crisis: International financial markets are in a chaotic state, a problem that the actors on those markets do not even realize, but that will be with us for many years to come – though real economy optimists think otherwise: All over the developed world, we are headed towards the dilemma that I would like to dub the "Japanese dilemma": For nearly 20 years now, Japan has been in financial chaos with an average annual growth rate of less than one half of one per cent; and all over the world we are headed in the same direction.

1.4 According to the purchasing power parity theory of exchange rates, equilibrium exchange rates should change concordant with the difference in the respective rates of inflation. But in EU-Europe and in the USA there is practically no inflation, if not a mild deflation; and the difference between such, actually non-existent inflation rates of the USA and of core EU-Europe (Germany or France or Belgium, the Netherlands, Austria, or even Italy) is 0.5 to 1 per cent. So according to this goods market exchange rate theory, the exchange rate should not change; in fact, the dollar should appreciate by a tiny amount, at the moment 1 per cent a year. (As an aside let me mention: The general public in Austria actually expects inflation, and inflation is also the hope of many indebted governments. Except for imported raw materials and of imported grain, these counterfactual expectations are not likely to be fulfilled, apart from possible tax changes – and those should not count as market movements.)

According to uncovered interest parity theory, i. e. the capital market explanation, the exchange rate should change according to the respective differences of interest rates. But the differences in interest rates on 10-year government bonds between the USA and EU-Europe are no larger than the differences in inflation rates; e. g., the USA now have 10-year interest rates on government bonds of 3.48 percent and Austria of 3.35 percent! Within EU-Europe and leaving out Greece, Spain, and Italy, but adding Britain, the interest rate differences are just 1.0 percent, nearly symmetrically bracketing the US rate. So once more, on average the exchange rate between the Euro and the US-dollar should not change at all – which, as I argued, is also exactly the expectation of Austrian banks in discounting bills of exchange. But the dollar actually depreciates, by about 4 percent a year. Equilibrium would only be reached if the US long-term interest rate were a full 4 percent higher than in Europe, at 7 percent instead of 3 percent. The pivotal prices of international financial markets are in fundamental disequilibrium.

1.5 In response to this economic and financial pricing crisis the central banks, urged by their governments, have only increased the monetary chaos: In the USA the bank rate was lowered to 0.25 percent or even less. In EU-Europe the European Central Bank has lowered it to 1 percent. Here, by the way, is the next fundamental disequilibrium: Over the last ten years, the European Central Bank varied its interest rates more or less in step with the US Federal Reserve, but only by half as much, its bank rate thus showing only one quarter of the variance of that of the USA. This has not been grasped by the general public because – as Alan Greenspan noted six years ago[2] – central banks have lost their influence over the long-term rate, i. e. the 10-year government bond interest rate.

So what actually happens is this: The central banks spoon-feed their commercial banks at an interest rate of 1 percent or less. The commercial banks then lend the money to their governments – apart from those sums of the near costless money that they stack onto their own reserves. The governments run huge budget deficits and pay a mere 3 or 4 percent interest. Thus the commercial banks make a tidy profit (4 percent minus 1 percent); they are not even, as normally happens, rationed as to the amount of money they can take from the central bank! And indirectly, via the commercial banks, the central bank finances the government budget deficit, which it is legally forbidden to finance directly. This makes for a new type of merry-go-round.

By the autumn of 2008, the Federal Reserve had increased its monetary base by two and a half times, from 900 billions to 2.3 trillions. Has this unprecedented monetary expansion turned out to be inflationary? Not at all! Part of it remained inside the banking sector, boosting insufficient bank reserves – at very little cost. Another part financed, as shown above, governmental budget deficits, which, in a depression, are non-inflationary. Still another part increased cash holdings among the general public: At near zero interest rates people have near-unlimited cash demand: They might, after all, need the money some time later; and in between it costs next to nothing.

1.6 Bank balance sheets thus show cheap government loans bought at little cost. On the other hand, up to very recently their loans to producing firms were going down and down. Here they do charge high interest rates because small and/or new businesses are highly risky at present. But then the firms willing to invest do not wish to take out credits at those high interest rates because at such rates investments might not be profitable. And the safer large firms do not need credit because they can self-finance.

Can this go on? It can, as long as there is no economic growth. Thus we actually have to hope for a decade of stagnation – and such stagnation, many think, must be kept from turning into a deep depression by constant monetary stimuli. In fact, both in the USA and in Europe we have to hope for the Japanese scenario! Stagnation occurs because there is not yet a speck of hope for new investment in new types of production, in new industries. The old industries, on the other hand, do not need investments because they are overinvested due to the hopes of growing demand that those industries had before national incomes declined.

Thus financial markets are stuck in various types of disequilibria and will be stuck there probably for a long time to come, with little hope of rebalancing soon.

2. Keynes' ideas for the present?

2.1 American and even British mainstream economists have very little to say about financial markets because, as I showed, those markets cannot be analyzed without explicit recognition of their obvious disequilibria.

Chicago economists proclaim – in what is actually a sales talk for students to come and study at Chicago at high fees – they proclaim that you always have to have a general economic equilibrium model of some type or other: dynamic general economic equilibrium, stochastic economic equilibrium and what not, all of them fascinating as strictly mathematical exercises. (Let me point out, though,

---

[2] Keeping bank interest in the USA very low both from 2002–2004 and even more so from 2008 onwards had no lowering effect on the long run (10 year bond) government interest rate at all. Towards the end of 2010 the latter had even increased markedly, i. e. by more than one percentage point, without any change in the bank rate.

that the originator of modern general equilibrium analysis and the first Nobel Laureate for it – the youngest Nobel Laureate ever in economics –, i. e. Kenneth Arrow, thought his model showed that people could hardly ever behave that way; and his three further main ideas were all concerned with disequilibria.)

2.2 What you cannot fit into a general equilibrium analysis, however, are bankruptcies, the central feature of financial crashes, because in continuously foreseen market equilibria situations bankruptcies simply cannot occur. In an equilibrium framework you would also have the greatest difficulty to fit in current account deficits, particularly very long lasting ones in the richest nations of the world. But the USA have had a constant deficit since 1982, i. e. for 30 years now (!!), with just one year of a very slight surplus in 1991, and an all-time high of 6.5 percent deficits in the two years 2006 and 2007 – just before the crash. The current account deficits are evidently the result of the action of very different types of actors all over the world: The up to recently per capita richest nation of the world gobbled up fully two thirds (!!) of world excess savings over investments, with 70 percent of US net borrowing financed up to recently by China, which grows so rapidly that it does not know what to do with all its savings. Chinese savings run constantly at around 50 percent of GDP: Usually only 43 percent can be invested at home, while 7 percent have to find some outside use. And the other half of world savings comes from oil exporting countries, for whom the oil price has recently jumped up, increasing first about five times to 147 US-dollars the barrel, then nearly dropping back, then more than doubling again, and now (the turn of 2010 to 2011) being well above 90 dollars. Finally, the difficulty is that in an equilibrium framework unemployment can only be voluntary, meaning that at current wages people prefer to take more leisure. But let us face the facts: Within one and a half years US unemployment jumped from 4.7 percent of the work force to 10.1 per cent, and still stands now, hardly moving, at 9.0 p.c. Can anyone seriously believe that all those unemployed merely wanted to enjoy more leisure?!

2.3 It is amusing to see how American economists are treating Keynes to whom they think they have to look now: A chief economist at the IMF (basically a monetary authority), W. White, refers explicitly to Keynes' "interesting equilibrium theory".[3] But Keynes' *General Theory of Employment Interest and Money* is called "general" because it treats "equilibrium" as only one case, implicitly a rare case, too. Keynes' foremost and central idea is the likelihood of involuntary unemployment which, as it is not desired, makes exactly for a disequilibrium situation. It is defined as people being willing to work at the current wage (or even a little less!), but not being able to find work.[4] So in the case of involuntary unemployment there may not even be any "unique equilibrium value" of wages, but "an infinite range of values".[5] Keynes after all had studied mathematics, so an infinite number of solutions to an equation was nothing odd for him.

The second basic idea of Keynes was the importance of uncertainty: one's not having any clear idea of what the future would bring, not even being able to spell out what mainstream economists define as risk, where all possible "states of nature" and their exact probabilities have to be known.

So we have three ideas most useful for analyzing crises and their aftermaths: (1) the likelihood of long periods lacking general economic equilibrium, in other words many markets not "clearing" for long periods of time, (2) the idea of involuntary unemployment, which is an important subcase of non-clearing markets, and (3) the prevalence of basic uncertainty. Such a general Keynesian framework of thought is vital at present.

---

3 William White, "Modern Macroeconomics on the Wrong Track", Finance and Development, Dec. 2009.

4 J. M. Keynes, *The General Theory of Employment Interest and Money,* London 1936. Keynes' precise definition of involuntary unemployment on p. 15 is somewhat more complex.

5 Keynes 1936, loc.cit, p. 26.

But while we can learn much for the present from looking at the experiences of the 1930s, the last period of a large and drawn-out general depression in the sense of a substantial fall of national income, it is important to stress that Keynes' experience was also quite different from our own. First of all there is nothing in Keynes about the relevance of bankruptcies, evidently because Keynes thought their effect obvious, and he had no general equilibrium framework anyway. There is nothing in Keynes on current account deficits, and in fact there could not be: For Keynes analyzed only a closed economy, in which there cannot be an imbalance of foreign account because there is no such thing. Keynes has only consumption and investment, but neither exports nor imports! That was most appropriate for his own times because by 1936, when the *General Theory* was published, most countries had closed their borders to exports and imports.

Actually in the 1930s most countries found it a marvelous idea to close their borders to imports and thus to keep all their local demand at home, only to find themselves in the ditch, however, when all other countries retaliated. This mistake seems to have had salutary effects on present politics, and within the EU closing borders to trade is – happily – even forbidden nowadays. And, of course, Keynes, because of his closed economy model, said nothing about international capital movements. They did not exist within his framework. But today our great problems are open economies: We must import in order to export, and above all we have free international capital movements.

2.4 In fact, the differences between the 1930s and now go even deeper: In the 1930s no government did anything to alleviate the crisis until its end in 1933, when both Hitler in Germany and Roosevelt stepped in decisively: Roosevelt with actually not very successful measures, Hitler successfully by re-armament, which is not the fashion nowadays (although the USA are actually fighting several small wars). In the 1930s there were many bank crashes, the USA losing one half of the number of its banks by default; lately we have had only one large bank crash in Britain and one in the USA, Northern Rock and Lehman Brothers respectively. Then, within three and a half years – from late 1929 to early 1933 –, the USA witnessed a fall in real GDP by a full 22 percent;[6] now the decline which in the USA lasted officially for 19 months has been between 4 and perhaps 5 percent, leaving out the worst cases (Iceland, Ireland and furthermore Europe's "Far East"). This was due to governments massively stepping in right away. Not so massively in EU-Europe, as governments are restrained by the European Central Bank.

Our problem now is that everywhere a group of highly statist economists have rediscovered Keynesian "deficit spending" with a vengeance. Such deficit spending is only suggested in Keynes and not at all analyzed by him on the longer-run basis of sustained deficits. (Remember Keynes presents only a short-run analysis! Just think of his much-quoted "In the long run we are all dead".) The question now is whether short-run stop and go measures – and in particular, as e. g. in Austria, only consumption stimulation and forgetting about any and all measures to boost investment – whether such short-run orientation is not only keeping us at a stagnating level of income, but is not also deferring a long-run and sustained GDP upswing. Deficit spending also means completely forgetting about the fact that one has to pay substantial amounts of interest on government debt, of at present around 3.5 percent long run per annum – interest payments which constantly mount with further deficits and entail a heavy monetary burden for the future! Will we not end up with government budgets that have to carry a huge interest load, interest payments that are not used by recipients in employment creating ways? The experience with such budgets, heavy in interest payments, in Italy and Greece is not encouraging.

6 See Robert A. Mundell, "A Reconsideration of the Twentieth Century", Amer. Econ. Rev. 90/3 (June 2000), pp. 327–340, here p. 330.

3. The surfeit of savings

3.1 We have seen that Keynes' notions of economies remaining at underemployment levels for long periods of time, with frequently involuntary unemployment and with basic uncertainty on the part of economic actors, are most appropriate after the 2007–2008 economic crash. But Keynes contributed still another important idea, which is much neglected at present but provides the key to understanding what happened in the first decade of the 21st century and will be central for the next decade as well: In a closed economy savings necessarily equal investments. In poor but developing economies relatively low savings limit investment; already Adam Smith had pointed that out. In rich countries, on the contrary, there is the danger, as Keynes pointed out, that for long periods relatively low investments limit the possibilities of savings. Thus investment opportunities tending to outrun savings make for flourishing economies, and the attempt to save more than investment opportunities allow leads to inevitable losses on capital markets and stagnating if not declining economies.

3.2 But is this Keynesian analysis – or in other words the official United Nations national income analysis, which builds on Keynes – not one for a closed economy? True, but we have to deal with one very important closed economy, of necessity a closed one: the world as a whole, as long as there is no trade with little men from Mars or Moon. So world savings cannot exceed world investment. For each and every open economy another national income identity holds: An excess of investments over savings has to be equal to its current account deficit; vice versa: an excess of savings over investments will be equal to its current account surplus. Running a current account deficit, as the USA do all the time, is only possible if you find willing foreign lenders to the tune of your deficit. And running a surplus is only possible if you find willing foreign borrowers. When calculated correctly,[7] all current account deficits world-wide have to equal all current account surpluses world-wide, as the world as a whole can have neither a deficit nor a surplus. So they have to balance out by complicated interactions.

3.3 The first decade of the 21st century showed an attempt world-wide to save more than could be invested. Before then, there had been a huge investment boom, as shown by the rise in stock markets. From 1995 to 1999 Wall Street stock prices trebled; and in Europe it was much the same. This was, above all, a boom due to new developments in computer hardware and software. As to computers, however, it was an extremely capital saving boom. When it ended computer prices had fallen steeply and there was no need of much further investment in the years following. So from 2000 or at least from 2001 onwards there were very few investment opportunities while (attempted) savings abounded. A worldwide decline in economic growth, if not a world depression, had to come sooner or later.

It came at a rather unfortunate moment for the newly elected President Bush II: He took office in January 2001, and the recession, not of his making, the drop in national income started only two months later, in March 2001. But then he had what – politically speaking – was a piece of extraordinary good luck: "9/11", the terrorist attack on New York and Washington. Bush then proclaimed that it was the patriotic duty of every American to consume, a message gladly taken up by the US public. But consumption was the very opposite of what would have been the appropriate economic decision, both for the USA and the world: The USA should have invested more, not merely consumed more. Greenspan, head of the US Federal Reserve, the monetary authority, contributed his unhealthy mite: He drastically reduced the bank rate from 6.5 percent to 1.75 percent during 2001 and a little later to only 1 percent.

[7] Actually for that purpose current accounts are not calculated correctly internationally: Imports are calculated "CIF", i. e. including transport cost etc., while exports are calculated at their border value, i. e. excluding freight, so that the sums of the two necessarily differ.

These excessively low interest rates were maintained for quite some time[8] and caused a big housing boom in the USA – and soon after the same thing happened in Britain and in Spain. But, relative to the ability to pay for houses, far too many houses were built, and far too many people were eventually overburdened by debt, having been lured into the market by far too low interest rates. (It is typical that after a boom in real industrial investments economies turn to investments in housing.)

Short-run political economic stimulation first achieved its political purpose: Bush II was reelected in 2004. American economic growth apparently mounted to 3.5 percent a year. That was a mere miscalculation, however, as national accounts only add up bills of sale, but never ask whether those bills are ever actually paid. The un-payable housing debt probably amounts to 1.5 trillion dollars, or about 10 percent of the annual national product. Spread over the five years 2002–2006 this means that calculated US national income (more precisely GDP) was overestimated by some 10 percent altogether, or 2 percent for each of those five years, implying that GDP growth was not the booming 3.5 percent a year, but a mere 1.5 percent. In 2008 the crash came, and it was a crash especially of banks. It came as a great surprise for US banks and even for many US economists. It was a bigger crash than it would have been in 2001–2002, because deferring a crash by political manipulation makes it only bigger in the end. With all due modesty, I should like to point out that I had forecast the crash in the summer of 2002, saying that eventually it would have to come.

3.4 The basic problem, as pointed out, is that the world tries to save more than investors are willing to invest. After 2000, the savers hailed mainly from China, then after 2005 also from oil producing countries and in Europe from Germany, Norway, Switzerland, the Netherlands and a little bit from Austria, which also has a modest surplus of savings. The USA took up two thirds of the world's excess savings and China used to finance one third of that and lately even nearly one half. In recent years, though, China has only put about one half of its excess savings (and now even less) into the US current account deficit so that roughly speaking, China's savings surplus comes close to the present US savings deficit. At present China is trying to terminate additional financial investment in the USA.

The USA have, in fact, provided the world's foremost machinery for destroying intended excess savings: At first funds flow into the USA via their current account deficit. Some funds are then taken up by the US government and spent in such a way as to increase US consumption, which destroys savings. Others are taken up by US private citizens and once more used for their consumption purposes. Actually, in 2006 and 2007 private personal savings in the USA had stood at –2.5 percent of income; in other words: private citizens consumed two and a half per cent more than their incomes, while in Germany or Austria personal savings amount to +10 or 11 percent a year. And finally firms took up savings and tried to invest them by financing the building of houses; but the attempted investment turned out to be zero, when house prices fell: Investment is only achieved when investment placements are worth something.

US banks made huge losses, which were only the reverse side of this destruction of savings. But to quite an extent, US banks also involved British banks, Swiss banks, EU-European banks and even Iceland's banks in their savings destruction processes. And thus large chunks of eventual US capital losses were shifted to Europe, to Iceland, to Ireland. While the British – ironically: above all the Scots – and the Spaniards set up their own machinery of savings destruction via quite unprofitable house building. Accordingly, it was exactly in those countries that government deficits were largest in 2009: as a percentage of GDP about 14 percent in Britain, about 12 percent in Spain and about 10 percent

[8] That a low short run bank rate was kept in the USA for much too long was criticized by Taylor: See John B. Taylor, "Lessons Learned from the Greenspan Era", paper presented at the 2005 Jackson Hole Conference, Federal Reserve Bank of Kansas City.

in the USA. Interestingly enough, Britain with its huge banking sector actually figures as the worst-off among the larger countries.

3.5 Has the Financial Crisis been taken care of, is it over? To put it bluntly: no, not at all; it has merely shifted. While private savings stood at –2.5 percent in 2006 and 2007 in the USA they have now gone up to + 3 percent. Fine, that is a movement in the right direction. But, on the other hand, the government budget deficit has increased to about 10 percent. The net effect is that the current account deficit has decreased from –6.5 percent to a little above –3 percent.

The recession, in fact, has to go on, so that the overspending USA can no longer afford to import that much and, with low demand at home, should export more. The alternative would be a really drastic dollar crash, a drastic fall in the value of the dollar. That would make imports unaffordable to many people in the USA and US exports quite cheap the world over.

For the short run we might simplify: the world's problem is that the USA consume too much or, what amounts to the same thing, save too little; alternatively we could say that China saves too much and does not find sufficient investment opportunities at home for her hugely growing national income. Private people in Austria and Germany put their money into the banks and do not understand why eventually no savings result because of the complicated interactions between millions of people all over the world. Because of all those interactions world-wide most of the people concerned cannot understand the consequences of their actions. They have to act under uncertainty. Well understood rational action and therefore constant economic equilibrium are impossible on a global level.

Actually we now live in the Hayek scenario of *Prices and Production* (1931):[9] only with the small difference that it is not only banks that provide loans for not very profitable investments but now also governments; and that the resulting disequilibrium process continues much longer before the eventual crash occurs. Crashes are likely to repeat themselves.

3.6 In the long run the problems are even worse: As the main creditor of the USA, China tends to lose constantly from the value of its 2.9 trillion dollars' financial investments, about two thirds held in the USA. She would like to shift away from the dollar as the main world currency; so would Russia and under Strauss-Kahn the IMF. They would prefer a bundle of currencies as the international monetary standard, a bundle made up of the US-dollar, the Euro, the British pound and probably the Chinese Yuan. But if the dollar lost its near monopoly position as world currency, it would crash and lose some 40 to 50 percent of its value. Furthermore, huge holdings of cash dollars are kept outside the USA, estimated formerly at 70 percent of all dollars and now perhaps at between 40 and 50 percent, as the amount of base money dollars has been increased so much. They are held largely by financially little educated nonprofessional investors for their own private account: in countries like Turkey, Russia, the Argentine, etc. as "safe" stores of value against their own instable currencies. What if these people realize that the dollar is falling in value, i. e. against the Euro, and if they decide to shift out of the dollar into Euros or Yuans? If they attempted a rapid shift, the USA would be unable to pay them in gold or foreign currency and would have to make the dollar inconvertible! If they shifted slowly they could be paid by the sale of vast amounts of US real estate or US firms. Those would truly be financial crises, some of which might easily come about in the near future.

4. Environmental investments

4.1 I have analyzed the consequences of the attempts to save more than the low amounts of present world investment. The most appealing alternative would be to increase investments. This would re-

[9] Friedrich A. Hayek, *Prices and Production,* London 1931. (Simultaneously also in German.)

quire governments in the rich parts of the world not to spend haphazardly and mostly on consumption, but instead to stimulate investments. It would require less developed countries, Brazil e. g., and above all China, to invest more themselves. But as those countries are already investing much that seems difficult. Above all, it would mean developing new investment industries, developing new types of products, as the computer boom did in 1995 to 1999. What will be the new type of leading industry, needing investment?

One hope is for medical research and the pharma industry. But much of possible pharmaceutical research is not undertaken because of the very high R&D costs often not being refunded: Public health authorities are not willing to bear them once a new medicine with low production costs has been found; and advances in genetics may have salutary effects for patients, but the research must be funded out of public money. In other words, investments are often not private, while private research has quite uncertain returns.

4.2 The great hope for the future should be investments in environmental improvement and in such provision of energy as would retard and reduce climate change. What is needed are more and more sources of renewable energy. Locomotion has to be switched away from petrol burning motor cars. Solar energy can be used in many ways more directly. Biofuels can be substituted for fuels using prehistoric energy accumulations. Even substituting natural gas, which as fuel damages the environment much less than the burning of coal, reduces the heating up of the atmosphere. And the fuel efficiency of vehicles shows promise of substantial improvement over time and particularly so if not only the mere improvement in the course of use is considered but if major investments in their improvement are made. Altogether the use of agricultural techniques to provide fuel is, however, likely to make food more scarce and thus will raise food prices. As the possibilities of environmental improvement are so vast, the likelihood is also substantial that the industry of any country, which first finds a promising road of improvement, will also achieve a semipermanent lead in the provision of that type of technique world wide. Thus strict standards in any one direction in a given country will create in that country industrial leaders providing alternative techniques and products. That had been the experience of Austria in the early 1990s. Thus the clamor of industry that no restrictive environmental standards must be set, which damage given employments, is actually extremely short-sighted: These employment opportunities will in general be in rapid decline anyhow and strict standards actually create promising new employment opportunities.

Eventually no techniques which increase the temperature of the world's atmosphere must be used – and that eventuality has to be reached relatively rapidly: "Our analysis of risks and targets points to the need for aggregate green house gas stabilization targets of below 550 parts per million carbon dioxide equivalent, arguably substantially below", writes Nicholas Lord Stern in a major survey.[10] He adds:[11] "The scale of markets for new technologies will be very large." And furthermore: "incentives to discovery could generate a Schumpeterian burst of growth". Finally he concludes: A key lesson "is that the costs of stabilizing below 550ppm CO_2 are generally far lower than the costs of the damages from climate change that would thereby be avoided."[12] The investment opportunities are huge, but environment improving investment is very costly. It could not take place without public subsidies for developing new environment-friendly techniques, while levying high taxes on the damaging techniques employed at present.

Unfortunately, the world-wide recession is delaying such new techniques instead of advancing them. Unemployment relief and additional public pension schemes are becoming more urgent. And

[10] Nicholas Stern, "The Economics of Climate Change", Amer. Econ Rev. 98/2 (May 2008), pp.1–37, here p. 3.
[11] Nicholas Stern (2008) p. 11.
[12] Nicholas Stern (2008) p. 19.

lately, both in Germany and in Austria we have witnessed subsidies (a scrap bonus) on cars in order to safeguard jobs in the car industry. It is to be feared that the concerns about present jobs and the high cost of future new jobs will rather reduce fruitful long-term investment instead of advancing it. Thus, the crisis is going to be prolonged, not alleviated.

Erich W. Streissler

Forecasting World Trends During the 2010s[1]

1. Preliminary remarks

1.1 This essay is devoted to the daunting task of a long-run forecast of the economic development of the developed and the rapidly developing part of the world for the next ten or fifteen years. Forecasting is highly hazardous work. After giving my students a number of instances of my successful forecasts I tell them my actual forecasting experience is rather good: I have been correct in about 52–55 out of 100 cases! Certainly, the reader will have to think through critically each one of my seven forecasts and to pass judgement whether they are likely to be among the 52–55 percent correct cases or rather among the 45–48 percent likely failures.

I divide my forecasting scenario into two parts: I shall deal first with a real macroeconomic forecast and then with the monetary developments. Behind that is a central premise: the idea that the real and the monetary side of development are only loosely connected.

In other words, that the real and the monetary side of the economy are relatively independent from each other. In this, I follow the notions propounded by Robert Mundell in his Nobel Lecture, "A Reconsideration of the Twentieth Century", which showed that the 20th century history of the USA had been one long series of monetary policy mistakes with relatively small effects on real growth rates (at least those effects were not felt till several decades later, which would imply that if there is any connection between the real and the monetary side of development it is only one with very long lags).

1.2 Once more[2], I also follow Karl Marx, who in *Capital* presented one of the first analyses of long-term monetary effects, but still thought the real effects more important: He gave us the first economic theory of innovations, thus providing a foundation for theories of long-run real economic development and indirectly for its forecasts. As my forecast concerns the medium long-term, ten to fifteen years, I follow Marx's investment and innovation centred view and not the secular long-term view, where saving becomes decisive. The question whether technical advances are more endogenous or more exogenous I leave aside.

1.3 Marx is above all the first theoretician of the so-called "bias" in technological development. That is the question whether technological progress is likely to be either relatively capital-saving or relatively labour-saving. This, in its turn, depends upon whether the extent of technical progress is likely to be larger in the production of capital goods or in the use of capital goods for the production of consumer goods.

In the huge 13th chapter of *Capital,* "Machinery and Great Industry", a chapter which makes up one fifth of the total first book of *Capital,* the only one published during his lifetime and therefore actually

---

[1] I am highly indebted to Karl Hardach for meticulous textual corrections.

[2] See "Saving and Investment in the Long Run", section 2, p. 66 of this volume.

by him, Marx argues: "Die Produktion der Maschinerie durch Maschinerie verringert ... ihren Wert, verhältnismaßig zu ihrer Wirkung"[3] and: "Die ... zur Produktion der Arbeitsmittel selbst, der Maschinerie, Kohle usw. erheischte Arbeitszunahme muss kleiner sein als die durch Anwendung der Maschinerie bewirkte Arbeitsabnahme"[4]. Chapter 13 is innovative, highly complex, and full of arguments as well as counterarguments. But reduced to its essence the argument quoted above says that the rate of technological progress is greater in the production of capital goods than in their use in the production of consumption goods. Thus capital becomes relatively cheap in production and this would make on balance for labour-saving technical progress and for relatively falling prices of capital goods, as was typical for the whole 20th century. (Labour-saving in contrast to labour-using production of capital is also at the back of Marx's idea of a depressed state of labour demand in the long run: Relatively less and less labour is needed.)[5]

Actually, Marx was not correct for his own mid-19th century: Railway building was extremely costly and was therefore in fact very much capital-using; but by lowering transport costs it made consumption much cheaper. The same was true for steam ships from the USA bringing cheap American wheat to Europe. Thus quite a bit of capital saving occurred actually in the consumption sector then. On the other hand, Marx's theory is well suited to the most recent Kondratieff boom of 1995–1999, the computer hard- and software boom: Computer production was cheap and brought huge capital-saving technical advances. The question is: Is the capital-saving technical advance, as typical of most of the 20th century, going to continue?

2. The likely future bias in innovation and real economic development

A) The direction of attempted innovations

2.1 By now we tend to be faced with exactly the opposite development to that of the late 20th century: The environmental problems now facing us and the difficulties of mitigating climate change are going to entail highly labour-using technical changes. Most environmental improvements are costly and not to the direct and short run advantage of the consumer. Strongly labour-using technological developments in the production of environmental investment goods are the central feature of my first basic forecasting proposition (to be elaborated below): Small investments required to generate growth are turning into costly investment for growth purposes or even large investment just to keep the social product from declining. We are entering a period where highly labour-using advances will predominate, replacing labour-saving advances.

Labour-using technological development is in particular due to the costly research efforts required to find environmentally friendly techniques: highly qualified research effort is needed, which, as being very expensive labour, is in a sense very "much" labour. *The Economist,* Oct 30th 2010 reports in a special feature "The future of biofuels", pp. 80–82, numerous attempts to find substitutes for oil from prehistoric reserves, in each case partly financed by one of the large oil firms: Synthetic diesel fuels as "drop-in" into present motorcar fuel tanks derived from (Brazilian) sugar via the use of en-

---

[3] K. Marx, *Das Kapital.* Kritik der politischen Oekonomie, vol. I ("Der Produktionsprozess des Kapitals"), Hamburg 1867, cited from MEG, vol. 23, Berlin 1969, p. 411. As always I quote sources in the original language and translation of Marx is particularly hazardous. Approximately: "The production of machines by machines reduces their value relative to their effectiveness."

[4] Marx 1867/1969, p. 466: "The increase of labour required for the production of the supports of labour, of machinery, coal etc., must be smaller than the reduction of labour due to the use of machinery."

[5] G. Tichy, however, rightly pointed out that as environmental investments are likely to require much public finance, finding the means for such public finance might easily cause the reduction of the supply of labour-intensive services and thus in total result in an indeterminate direction of the bias in production.

zymes and bacteria to produce ethanol, other techniques which produce butanol or techniques to have algae generate oil. All these techniques are in the first stages of trial production and still are far too costly.

Actually mitigating climate change and safeguarding and/or improving the environment is like railway building in Marx's time, only more so. Then the railways were at first only little used and were replacing other means of transport, in particular costly horses. Now we have to replace gasoline-guzzling cars or their present fuel consumption and have to re-design thousands of technological devices that have proved to be not sufficiently environment-friendly. There will be hundreds of possibilities of reducing the waste or deterioration of environmental facilities and just as many ways of reducing CO_2 emissions. As many of those new techniques will be highly specific there will be few possibilities of capital-saving economies of scale; highly individualized labour inputs will be necessary. High prices of the pertinent labour – which may equally well be expressed as a proportionately larger quantity of labour, prices and quantities being alternative analytical devices – and thus much labour input will result in labour-using technological change. Therefore, as stated, my first proposition is this: In contrast to 1995–1999 we are now heading towards a period of in the aggregate highly labour-using technological developments.

2.2. Improving environmental conditions and mitigating climate change is, however, only one possible direction of innovation. Various kinds of other scientific developments also improve welfare and sometimes very much so. How to evaluate them? For the economist the answer is clear: as much as people – call them consumers – are willing to pay for the end product of scientific production, e. g. how sizable the willingness to pay for the resulting publications is. In the humanities both the amount of input cost and the amount of output of economically relevant innovation is frequently very low. But cost effectiveness can be even worse in certain long established fields of research in the natural sciences, where the stage of highly diminished if not to say already near vanishing returns has already been reached.

Because of their huge scale such scientific projects should be left, if at all, to the very largest economies.[6]

2.3 Environmental and scientific development is very good for stimulating employment, but of course only of highly skilled workers. On the other hand, many of the now existing public or private administrative workers will become redundant. And a further problem, already touched upon: Large-scale development of new technologies requires the financial support of the government, in other words: public investments, just as building railroads once did: Very long-run and highly risky investments (hazardous because their outcome with respect to our environment is uncertain) are usually too risky for private investors. Which governments will give such support? Of course only those that have not frittered away their scarce means in (backward looking) pension funds or in unproductive unemployment relief. Those countries that are the first to develop new scientific and/or environment-friendly technologies will profit relative to the technological late-comers. Those who concentrate in eco-

---

[6] There is, however, a promising field of scientific research best suited for a small country like Austria, the field of innovative directions in medical research, and this for two reasons. On the one hand Austria has a long established tradition of medical innovation, which can be reanimated; and, on the other, medical research can make advances already in case of relatively modest financial inputs.
The Austrian Academy of Science is a major actor in the forefront of economic innovation and is intensifying this effort. The reason this type of development has to be publicly financed – or would at least be a private/public venture – is due to the length of the investment period of some 10 years till practical results can be hoped for and to the extreme riskiness of these final results. The institutes IMBA and CEMM of the Austrian Academy of Sciences are starting to become hopeful beacons in such new lines of research and show with three to five publications a year in *Cell, Nature* and *Science* already high promise.

nomically shoring up the past will be environmental latecomers. About fifteen years ago Austria was rather successful in creating new environmental solutions[7]. Will it be so in the near future? The position of the world's new environmental leaders is up for grabs; so far it is impossible to forecast who that will be.

B) The likely volume of future growth effects

2.4 My second proposition is that the rate of growth of output will be substantially below what it was recently estimated to be and that this output growth will be determined by investment into environmental improvement and the mitigation of climate change. In 2000, Paul Krugman[8] estimated: "Whereas in 1995 a conventional view would have put the rate of growth of U.S. potential output at slightly more than 2 percent ... it now seems plausible that the rate of potential output is around 3 [percent]". This was a then fashionable overestimation. As I shall soon argue, three percent of real growth, widely quoted for the USA, was true only for the Kondratieff boom of 1995–1999 and rested afterwards on much inflated measurements for the decade of the 2000s. Actually for the USA, as A. Sinai pointed out: "Between 2008:1 and 2009:1, real household net worth declined from $ 16 to $ 10 trillion"[9]. This gigantic decline of wealth to the tune of close to 40 percent of one year's American GDP implies that US growth was actually already close to zero over the entire decade of the 2000s.

For the whole of the old-established industrial world, on the other hand, it has been estimated that the total losses in capital values amounted altogether to 15 trillion dollars, i. e. together to one year of GDP of the USA. (By the old-established industrial nations I mean the core nations, i. e. central and western nations of Europe as well as the USA, Canada, Australia and New Zealand).

Therefore I estimate that even a 2 percent total annual growth rate for the industrialized leader countries is now a thing of the past: For the old-established industrial nations there is now a marked downward kink in the growth curve after 2000, because (a) for the future there are only environmental and climate improving innovations left and (b) those are unusually costly to bring about in terms of their necessary investments. Various kinds of miscalculations of GDP and misleading accounting conventions have merely clouded the issue.

Therefore I assume total average growth rates of 1 percent to at most 1.5 percent per year for the innovatory leaders and of zero to half a percent for the laggards, whose foremost characteristic is that they make do with little innovation. About 0.5 per cent or even less is the annual growth rate achieved by Japan in the decades of the 1990s and the 2000s. Most of us Europeans are heading towards the Japanese scenario.

There is one further argument for these unusually low estimates of GDP growth rates: Much of first-class genetic research in medicine improves health and prolongs life, but such improvements do not enter into the GDP statistics. They remain unmeasured.

2.5 How and why do I arrive at this estimate of at most only 1–1.5 percent of annual GDP growth for the industrialized leader countries and for many countries only one of 0.5–0.75 percent growth? (Total world growth may be larger as the South and the South East Asian countries are merely catching up with the industrialized leader countries.) This notion of a downward kink in long-term growth

---

7 Several articles and the doctoral thesis of K. W. Steininger suggested solutions. See K. W. Steininger, Trade and Environment, The Regulatory Controversy and a Theoretical and Empirical Assessment of Unilateral Environmental Action, Heidelberg 1995.

8 P. Krugman, "Can America Stay on Top?", in: Journal of Economic Perspectives, 14/1, Winter 2000, pp. 169–175, here 171.

9 A. Sinai, "The Business Cycle in a Changing Economy: Conceptualization, Measurement, Dating", American Economic Review, Papers and Proceedings, 100/2, May 2010, pp. 25–29, here p. 26.

is a "guesstimate" arrived at by historical analogies; and due to the nature of long-time forecasting it cannot be anything else: For, as has been aptly remarked, econometrics is an exercise in merely forecasting the past, and this is true of more general statistically based forecasting exercises as well.

For the post-war period of the 20th century, i. e. after 1945, the developed (industrialized) world showed substantially higher rates of economic growth, partly due to the back-log of development after two global wars, but also due to the fact that (a) innovations could go into many different directions and that (b) innovations tended to be more and more capital-saving, none more so than those of the last Kondratieff-boom of 1995–1999. This, to repeat[10], was the computer hard- and soft ware boom: Before that boom the general tendency had already been one of forecasting low growth rates, particularly in the USA around 1980 or still around 1990. After the computer boom, growth estimates went up to insupportably high levels, and, as argued, US economic policy made for overestimating growth because of miscalculations of the long-run profitability of both the housing and the financial sector. Now certain parts of the economic — or should I rather say the banking — profession tend to over-optimism and hope for growth, or at least for avoiding GDP decline by means of huge, but virtually unproductive government budget deficits. Budget deficits cause redistribution towards interest groups in the public sector. But with rapidly rising government debt levels large government deficits without any business investment cannot be maintained for long.

Greece, in particular, was the most recent warning example. Two American economists wrote: "It is evident that there is no obvious link between debt and growth until public debt reaches a threshold of 90 percent." The authors give a possibly rather problematic averaging estimate: "Observations with debt to GDP over 90 percent have median growth roughly 1 percent lower than the lower debt burden groups."[11] In 2009, public debt in the US stood already close to those 90 percent, namely, at 84 percent of GDP, is now (April 30th, 2011) 93 percent and is estimated soon to reach 110 percent; in the United Kingdom it stood at 72 percent, in Austria a little below 70 percent. Thus in the long run deficit spending is no way out of growth decline, as Japan has shown, by now (with a public debt around 230 percent of GDP) the most highly (publicly) indebted nation in the developed world. When government debt levels become too high, a financial crisis may ensue because of over-indebtedness.

Therefore, the only field where one can hope for growth by long-term innovation is environmental improvement and the mitigation of climate change which is capital-using and therefore yields little growth of consumption per unit of investment. That is exactly the scenario of the mid 19th century railway age: Then long-term economic growth rates of final social product were at best about 1 or 1.5 percent a year, which provides a main reason for my economic forecast. Furthermore more environmental investment and even medical innovation are very long run projects with uncertain outcomes, just as the investments of the railway age, and just as the railways they will require much governmental financial support.

Again, I add that the increases in health and life expectancy through medical advances do not figure in GDP data[12], which are in that sense underestimates. Furthermore, advances in the basic pharmaceu-

---

[10] Discussed in the preceding essay.

[11] C. M. Reinhart & K. S. Rogoff, "Growth in a Time of Debt", in: American Economic Review, Papers and Proceedings, 100/2, May 2010, pp. 573–578, here p. 575.

[12] There are so many conceptual difficulties with the GDP and national income concepts that I cannot start to discuss them all. (One difficulty is dealt with under C) below.) It has to be remembered that the whole national accounting framework reflects theoretical concepts typical for the 1930s, when it arose. As such it is geared above all to industrial production (see already the name "gross domestic product"). Services, which since have vastly increased (even as a share of the total), present the greatest conceptual problems, and medical services are only one case in question. GDP concepts are for comparability's sake fixed by what amounts to United Nations law, but that does not necessarily make for the highest degree of contemporary relevance.

tical industry are throttled by standard government policies, which in the health care sector are not willing to pay the huge capital expenditures of research, but only a little more than the recurring production and marketing costs of new medicines, thus stifling research. So only environmental and climate improvements remain. And those are slowed down by the motor-car manufacturers lobbying to get governments to subsidize their output in order to safeguard employment in this outdated industry.

C) Difficulties with the measuring rod of national income and GDP

2.6 Finally we might pose the question whether GDP actually is still the relevant measuring rod for future long-term economic development? The different parts of GDP are of quite distinct importance for our future survival: Man can live without motor-cars and even without computers, but certainly not without food.

The production of food has shown above-average productivity growth for the last three centuries. In fact, the rates of productivity increase of manufacturing or of GDP (including services!) were exceeded by agriculture: In the 18th century that productivity increase was due to new crops and more strongly individualized (rather than collective) production, in the 19th century due to mechanization and drainage, and in the 20th century due to genetic improvement of crops (with time-lags in different parts of the world). So let me risk a forecast, in spite of its smacking of Malthusianism with its repeated failures: Many types of improvements in agriculture are approaching their physical and biological limits; and climate change (storms, droughts, desertification due to increasing global temperatures) and environmental degradation are lowering the possibilities of agricultural productivity increases. Furthermore, in many ways the attempts to create renewable energy sources reduce the areas available for food production. The cultivation of rape seed, the oil of which is to be used for fuelling motor cars, may serve as an example.

The consequence is that food production will only increase by perhaps 0.5 to 0.75 percent a year, i. e. much less than GDP at its maximum growth rates, or, to put it differently: quite in contrast to the last quarter of the 19th century and the entire 20th century, when foodstuffs tended to become relatively cheaper than most other goods that make up GDP. They became cheaper exactly because the rate of productivity growth in agriculture was above average. In our days we have to look forward to food becoming on average more expensive because of below-average productivity growth in its production. This increase in the relative price of foodstuffs will continue even when world population will cease to grow after 2040 or 2050 or so.

3. Regional monetary developments

3.1 In the long run real economic development will depend on the realization of the potential for innovations; and this will have to take place globally, although as yet it is very difficult to make out in which parts of the world the necessary elements will be available. But where exactly marked development may happen, will depend on the monetary side of the story, in particular on financial market developments. It is my third proposition that financial market developments have only a small effect on global growth as a whole, but they will determine where possible developments could occur.

A note of warning: The amount of world savings relative to their use in the form of investments does have an aggregate and not only a distributive effect, but only in so far as high savings stimulate additional investment. Such stimulation of investment by higher savings is not at all usual, though it may occur in the future if very costly environmental investments increase investment opportunities for savings. Environmental investment might be stimulated most if one were to find means of linking private savings with public finance of environmental projects.[13]

I divide the world into three regions to be evaluated separately: First America and Australia with New Zealand, to be represented by the United States. Second continental Europe, i. e. the Euro zone, dominated by Germany. Third, rapidly developing East Asia, typically China and to a lesser extent India.

3.2 Starting with the USA and my fourth proposition: Due to the self-serving perspective of a large number of US economists, and the particular importance of large banks there, the positive development potential of the USA is vastly overestimated. Actually it is on the point of decline if not, quite possibly, on the point of the next financial crash. As Robert Mundell stressed:[14] "The Greatest Fact of Modern History ... was ... the rise of the United States, the 20th century becoming the 'American Century'". But the 21st century does not and (most probably) will not continue the 20th century experience.

After more than a century of monetary strength of the US dollar and of financial dominance of the USA it is extremely difficult to relearn long term trends and to change perspectives: In the 1920s the British citizen Keynes did not understand that the high equilibrium exchange rate of the British pound and the strong financial position of Britain was over after a century (if not two) – while the Swede Ohlin, later a Nobel Laureate, looking on from outside, understood that. In the same way, many present-day American economists overestimate the long-run "soundness" of the value of the dollar.

Since 1982, with one brief and slight intermission in 1991 (during the First Iraq War), the United States have had a constant current account deficit which reached the dangerously high level of 6.5 percent of GDP in 2006 and 2007 and has by now accumulated an international indebtedness, which – in absolute terms – is the largest in the world. In the depression of 2009 this deficit declined somewhat, as is typical for a serious recession, but only to some 3.3 percent or the still huge sum of about 470 billion dollars (according to The *Economist,* April 30, 2011). Nowadays, the sector that is overspending hugely is the government: to the tune of nearly 10 percent of GDP.

The scenario is quite similar to that of present-day Greece before its crash, though certainly the US government acts more adroitly than that of Greece.[15] What if the foreign creditors of the United States suddenly want their money back? China alone has a huge foreign exchange surplus of $ 2.9 trillion,[16] about two thirds of which have been lent to the USA. But as Sinai points out, "the United States ... has only $ 127 billion in foreign exchange reserves, or 0.9 percent of GDP"[17] in other words reserves of hardly more than one quarter of one (!) year's present current account deficit. (The current account is the balance of payments for visible and invisible trade plus private and official current transfers for an economy within a given period.) Gold holdings of the USA have also declined, so all the reserves can only cover at most one half of the Chinese loans to the Americans. Chinese holdings are US bonds, and the Chinese government is not likely to demand its loans back rapidly; but as these loans are relatively short-term loans the Chinese actually hold the USA financially captive. Being the largest creditors of the USA, they are not the only ones: Huge but unknown amounts of dollars are held in cash by private individuals in financially insecure countries and considered there as store of value.

---

13 The latter statements owe much to critical remarks by G. Tichy.

14 R. A. Mundell, "A Reconsideration of the Twentieth Century", American Economic Review 90/3, June 2000, pp. 327–340, here p. 327.

15 In contrast to their sizes the causes of government deficits are, however, as G. Tichy pointed out, quite different in Greece and the USA: In Greece governmental wages and other distributional problems are at the fore, in the USA on the other hand budgetary problems of the central government and an outdated industrial structure.

16 Using American and not European reckoning, because of the quotation below.

17 Sinai (2010), loc. cit, p. 28.

At present, parts of the world regard the dollar as "a safe haven". But what if it is decided to switch to Euros, or gold, or soon to Chinese Yuan, as even safer stores of wealth? Such flights into another currency happen rapidly and uncontrollably, the recent Greece-inducted flight out of the Euro providing a warning example.

3.3 But it is not only their extremely hazardous current account position that is endangering the USA. The huge budget deficit creates political conflict between Democrats, up to recently in power, but with their former dominance visibly shrinking, and the Republicans, and this, too, could easily frighten foreign investors away. Again Sinai: "Labor market and consumption data confirm that the United States is largely a 'services' economy"[18], depending for its exports basically on one sole sector, the computer industry. It would be difficult for the USA to right their current account deficit if the world no longer wished to increase its lending to them. In other words: The USA do not have much recovery potential.

Furthermore, unemployment has shot up in only one year, 2009, from some 4.7 percent in 2008 to more than 10 percent, high by European standards. It has been nearly stuck at that level, standing in late April 2011 at 8.8 percent. In a word: From whatever angle you look at them, the USA are in an extremely hazardous economic position. Victory hoots on the part of self-serving financial marketers cannot distract from the crass facts. It is one-sided to look only at GDP growth rates, biased as these are by social accounting conventions, as measuring rod of economic well-being, and not, as Keynes had done, at unemployment. And it is doubly biased if we only look at average GDP growth and not at the mounting inequality in GDP distribution. Youth unemployment, i. e. unemployment of ages 16–24, in particular stands at "almost 20 %" *(The Economist,* October 30th, 2010, p. 52): The hoots of triumph in the USA can only be, as is well known, those of the uppermost fifth of income groups, while the medium income earned in the USA has hardly risen at all within the last 25 years.

So the future scenario for the United States is either a slow decline in relative GDP or a precipitate crash. Already from 2002, when the Euro was born, to early 2008 the dollar declined from 0.87 to the Euro to 1.56, or by some 10 percent a year. Now, in late April 2011, after the much discussed and ever more troubling Greek scare, the dollar stands at about 1.45 per Euro and has thus declined by about 6 percent a year since early 2002. There is no getting around it: The USA have to be seen in a continuous decline in the world: on the one hand, in terms of their share in global GDP and, on the other hand, of their dollar exchange rate value.[19]

Looking at their production structure one cannot easily imagine the USA once more becoming a major exporter, as in the 1950s. Services are mainly local products apart from tourism and banking, in which the USA no longer excel either.[20] The computer sector is too narrow a base and suffers from increasing foreign competition. Economic recession relative to the outside world reduces, in the case of the USA, the current account deficit. The most likely scenario is that the USA will become an approximately self-sufficient nation, at most paying interest on its foreign debts. It will have low domestic prices but it will lack broad-based innovative exports. Neither will low long-term interest rates remain a competitive American asset for long: They are likely to shoot up as the USA are becoming a doubtful debtor. (Think of Italy at 4.8 percent and Spain at 5.5 percent interest rates at present. The USA, now at 3.4 percent, are likely to end up in an even higher bracket.) Higher future self-sufficiency of the USA will create problems for placing further investments there by the net-saving nations.

---

[18] Sinai (2010), loc. cit. in FN5, p 27.

[19] Since 2008 the per capita richest nation of the world (leaving out tiny tourist centers and oil producers) is Norway, and no longer the USA.

[20] It should, however, be pointed out that university teaching is a major industry in the USA and that teaching of foreign students provides a significant export sector.

Thus the USA may have to withdraw economically to more or less "splendid" (perhaps rather: tawdry) isolation rather soon, with however rather depressive effects world-wide. But that implies: International capital market movements are likely to decline as the USA can no longer afford to pile up more and more additional debts. Remember: Lately, the USA have been taking up about two thirds of all net savings of the world! In other words, the future world, due to USA difficulties, will show less financial integration and not more compared to now. What we are going to witness is an "old USA", as one formerly spoke of "old Europe". The reason: The USA have seriously overdone borrowing, are already no longer competitive in most economic sectors, and are financially attractive only to backward-looking minds.

3.4 Europe, on the other hand, is not as "old" as it is made out to be in American propaganda. But it is highly heterogeneous in its external financial position: Norway, Switzerland, Sweden and the Netherlands – in that order – are, relative to their size, massive creditor nations, followed by Denmark and Austria: Norway having as of the end of April 2011 a 13.1 percent of GDP current account surplus, Switzerland one of 10.6 percent, the Netherlands 6.2 percent, and Denmark 4.0 percent, while Austria has a much smaller one of 2.9 percent. But the absolutely most important international creditor is Germany, with a surplus of 5.3 percent.

Germany is in one sense very similar to the USA and in another their exact opposite: Germany has an even lower ratio of net investment to GDP than the USA, viz. 5.3 percent, while the USA managed 8.5 percent over the period 1995–2008. The head of the well-known Economic Research Institute (Ifo), Hans-Werner Sinn, has called Germany a Bazaar economy, due to its considerable merchandising trade, that is selling commodities but not producing them. At least its tiny investment rate looks indeed Bazaar-like. However, there the similarity to the USA ends and the contrasts begin: For Germany has a high net savings rate of 11–13 percent of net national product. But 60 percent of that saving are lent out to foreign countries, Germany achieving a current account surplus of 5.3 percent, while the USA had a current account deficit of about 6.5 percent in 2006 and 2007. (Austria, on the other hand, had high investments of 9.7 percent over 1995–2008 and, with a savings rate of about 9–11 percent, only a small current account surplus of 1.5–2.0 percent, now 2.9 percent).

In fact the international balances at present are hardly different from the late 1980s, before the former East Germany became part of the Federal Republic: Then Germany and Japan between them and in equal parts were financing the then US current account deficit. Today, simply in accounting terms it is once more nearly the same, the present US deficit of $ 470 billion being approximately equally financed by the surpluses of Germany ($ 188 billion) and Japan ($ 194 billion). Of course one could do these sums also differently: pointing to the fact that on the world stage China with a surplus of 331 billion dollars is financing two thirds of the US deficit.

But perhaps we should not think of Germany as largely financing the USA, though that particular view would correspond to President Obama's suggestion that Germany should not save so much because the USA are thereby forced to have a current account deficit. In contrast to the USA Europe is already now a basically self-sufficient area in terms of its current account: Only last year the small Euro area's current account deficit of $ 60 billion corresponded exactly to the Swiss surplus of $ 60 billions, Switzerland being European, but outside the Euro; and the British deficit of $ 33.7 billion was nearly equal to the Swedish surplus of $ 31.5 billion, both countries being outside the Euro. So we may conclude: Europe as a whole is already a nearly self-sufficient area in terms of international finance, a position which I have suggested the United States will have to achieve in the foreseeable future. Basically, therefore, Europe trades with itself and finances itself. There is integration within the block of Europe but very little outside of it. My fifth proposition is therefore: Both because the USA have to reduce their borrowing and because Europe is already nearly self-sufficient there is likely to be a decline of world financial integration, which will partly be replaced by block-wise integration. The adjustment need be, however, neither smooth nor necessarily painless.

3.5 One decisive point typically not recognized by Austrians is that (quite in contrast to the U.S. Federal Reserve) the European Central Bank (ECB) has as its main, or, in fact, only, policy-aim the avoidance of inflation. Therefore European programs for righting budget deficits generally permit only three years for the deficits to be reduced below 3 percent of GDP and only in exceptional cases five years. This means that the Euro area now has an average rate of GDP growth of only 1.7 percent, not much larger than the slightly-more-than 1 percent on average which I foresee if we make a determined move towards environmental improvement and climate care.

Thus because of its general currency policy Europe will be faced with low growth with small ups and down: 2011 with the start of mandated budget reductions all round is likely to see again zero or small negative growth rates, or as it is put popularly, a "double dip" recession, while the unchecked long-term deficits of the United States and Great Britain and their already very high indebtedness are heading towards another market crash and much lower, i. e. practically nil, growth rates afterwards. Remember: In a time of general decline of current account deficits each country tends to expect it will at least be able to export more – while actually exports become more difficult for everyone!

Exactly because of those relatively early restrictions on growth by the ECB the Euro stands a good chance of constant further appreciation against the US dollar. In periods of international capital market integration the exchange rate no longer depends on purchasing power parity, which holds only when the current account consists of exports and import transactions only. It should not be forgotten that Robert Mundell[21] already in the 1960s saw the exchange rate above all dependent on current account deficits (and surpluses), which have to be financed by the purchase (or sale) of foreign currency and therefore determine the relative prices of those currencies. As the current account of the Euro area is already in (near) equilibrium the Euro will appreciate against the US dollar at least until the USA will have set right their current account balance.

What about the longer run? I think it likely that Europe will be in the forefront of environmental improvement and climate mitigation, being on average more ideologically "green" than the rest of the world, and with Britain (and also the Netherlands and parts of Northern Germany) being threatened by rising sea levels! But that would mean slightly higher growth rates in Europe by capturing new technologies; or in other words other countries looking "old" relative to a rejuvenating Europe. And this I'll call my sixth proposition. Remember: monetary strictures may eventually stimulate long term technological investment!

Eastern Europe has still much potential to catch up in living standards with core-Europe. Thus within the block Europe is going to finance the catching up of the East and perhaps somewhat also of the South.

3.6 And when the USA have finally set right their unsustainable current account deficit and Europe remains with its present equilibrium, what does this mean for the rest of the world? The rest of the world, as far as it counts at all in terms of GDP levels, is Eastern Asia with India added on.

If and when both US and Europe are close to equilibrium in their balances of payments and, synonymously, in global financial terms, what does that mean for Eastern and Southern Asia? They have

[21] R. A. Mundell, "The Pure Theory of International Trade", in: American Economic Review 50/1, March 1960, pp. 67–110. Above all R. A. Mundell, "The Monetary Dynamics of International Adjustment under Fixed and Flexible Exchange Rates", in: Quarterly Journal of Economics, vol. LXXIV, May 1960, pp. 227–257, J. M. Fleming & R. A. Mundell, "Official Intervention on the Forward Exchange Market", in: International Monetary Fund Staff Papers, vol. XI, 1964, pp. 1–19.

to be in such an equilibrium as well! That would be a serious problem for China with its huge current account surplus of, at present, $ 331 billion dollars, or about 3.9 percent of its GDP (to say nothing of Taiwan with an 8.0 and Thailand with a 2.7 percent surplus at present). China is being punished for having turned the USA into its satellite – remember those $ 2.9 trillions of capital that China holds in other currencies, one fifth of the annual American GDP, and largely lent (short term) to the USA. China is punished for not having disciplined its debtor at an earlier stage! In fact, sooner or later a country becomes the prisoner of its debtor. If the dollar depreciates China will encounter devastating capital losses – that, of course, is why China at present is trying to shore up the dollar. But in the long run China will not be able to safeguard the value of the dollar and will manifest to the world the curious scenario of a communist country being exploited by a capitalist one. The short run scenario looks very favourable for China, less so the long run situation of its foreign capital values.

Or is it the other way round that China is by now actually the leader of a new type of capitalism?

But eventually a near-equilibrium in Europe and of necessity also in the USA will mean that South and East Asia will also have to become a more or less autarkic block. China will have to learn to invest more at home – still more, because even now it is already investing more than 40 percent of GDP there. This will probably result in major investments in China's own infrastructure, since investment in Africa, which China is already trying out, does not bring much. Japan is in a similar fixture as China: It too will have to find more investments at home or it will make huge losses by mere misinvestments abroad, particularly in the USA. Financially, the future is going to look quite different from the present, when everybody tends to forecast further developments which are unsupportable in the long run. And this brings me to my seventh and actually in conventional wisdom long established and last proposition: Long-term capital imbalances have to be set right eventually;[22] and so far no place in the world can be found which needs for investment purposes much foreign capital and yet is not too risky – especially not politically too risky for the foreign investor.

3.7 One more difference to the recent past is that with low and faltering economic growth and hardly any demand for investment we are going to be faced with a slightly deflationary general scenario all round. Some economists in the USA, e. g. Blanchard or Krugman, are hoping for the contrary: for mild inflation. The Americans reduced the real load of their federal debt by inflation: once drastically, from 1945 to 1953, and once more mildly so, in the 1970s. But both times, the rate of inflation came as a surprise; and debtors cannot be taken by surprise again: they will have learned. Furthermore, mild inflation presupposes willing spenders and in a stagnant economic climate those are rare. The experience of Japan has taught us that faltering growth, which we are going to face the world over after the Kondratieff boom of 1995–1999 for at least the next decade, makes for repeated bouts of mild deflation. The European Central Bank has as its central objective the prevention of inflation and therefore forces European nations to a speedy cure of their budget deficits. That will have deflationary effects, on the average. And the USA, whose government likes to overspend, have surpassed the 90 percent of GDP national debt threshold which, according to Reinhart and Rogoff, forces nations to retrench, if in the case of the USA the political backlash of the two thirds of the population who gain nothing from deficit spending does not come even earlier. Finally integrated world markets make inflationist economies suffer. Thus, the general economic climate for the next decade is going to be mildly deflationary everywhere. Mild deflation does not hurt economic growth, as long as real interest rates after adding deflation do not shoot up.

22 Interestingly one of the main authors of U.S. current account imbalances, Alan Greenspan, in his memoirs takes exactly the opposite position, considering constantly increasing current account imbalances as the modern trend. See A. Greenspan, *The Age of Turbulence* – Adventures in a New World, London etc. 2007, especially ch. XVIII.

3.8 To summarize the central ideas of my long-term global forecast: Historically, economic development has been driven by major innovations in the production of goods and services. But the leading sector in the future will (have to) be environmental development and the mitigation of climate change. This sector will be labour-using. Future economic growth will be very expensive and, in particular for the fully developed richest nations, much lower than what was until recently taken to be normal. It may amount to little more than 1 percent. Policies of investing in the protection of environment and climate are more likely to be at the fore in Europe, which could then hope for slightly more than the likely near-zero growth in the USA, which will be hampered by their over-indebtedness. The present scenario of large parts of the world financing the overspending USA will come to an end. In consequence thereof the world will become less integrated, financially, rather than more so.